P9-ARU-728

STAFF
INXS

Tour 9091
INXS

UPPORT
INXS
BEFORE
INXS
BEFORE

INXS

ATRIA BOOKS

New York London Toronto Sydney

INXS and ANTHONY BOZZA

ATRIA BOOKS
1230 Avenue of the Americas
New York, NY 10020

ISBN-13: 978-0-7432-8403-5
ISBN-10: 0-7432-8403-8

First Atria Books hardcover edition November 2005

10 9 8 7 6 5 4 3 2 1

ATRIA BOOKS is a trademark of Simon & Schuster, Inc.

Design by Joel Avirom and Jason Snyder

Manufactured in the United States of America

For information regarding special discounts for bulk purchases, please contact Simon & Schuster Special Sales at 1-800-456-6798 or business@simonandschuster.com.

This book is dedicated to the memory of Bill Beers, Jill Farriss, Jack Pengilly, Kell Hutchence, and Michael Hutchence. They are all deeply missed.

CONTENTS

FOREWORD

A Detailed Review of a Life Well Lived, Thankfully with Notes

THERE'S A HELL OF A LOT I CAN'T REMEMBER, but luckily I have diligently kept a daily diary since 1979. So much has happened during our career that the diaries became my memory or backup data and safeguarded me from losing the minutiae of my life's most precious memories. I enjoyed writing down the events of our lives as they unfolded, and from the first time I did so, it was my intention that one day there would be a book about the band. It *is* spooky when I think about how I knew even back then that we would achieve enough to warrant a book that chronicled our history. I had a strong premonition from the first time this band jammed together that one day we were going to "make it big." And we did. I can't put my finger on how I knew it would happen, but that premonition was strengthened even further when we changed the name of the band from the Farriss Brothers to INXS and were taken on by our first real manager, Gary Morris. It was our destiny.

That was mid-1979 and up until then, Tim and I were the band's official manager and treasurer, respectively, for the band's first three years. We came together, six schoolmates from the northern suburbs of Sydney—and the fact that we stayed together and remain close after so long is a feat in itself. Also the fact that we came from a place as far away from the rest of the world as you can get and have sold over 30 million records is something I still marvel at. We had no idea where it was going back then, but we knew it was going somewhere, because we knew one thing for sure—we had a sound that was different and a very special chemistry.

But we soon learned that talent and drive were not the only ingredients we needed. Behind every successful band there is sharp management, a committed record company, a clever producer, savvy agents, dedicated publicists, a relentless road crew, and a Herculean amount of hard work—and that's not all. You also need great songs, true belief in yourself, impeccable timing, and a giant chunk of luck. To get a bunch of Top 10 albums around the world, everyone and everything has to be on the same page, working together at exactly the right time.

Take it from me, when it *does* happen, it happens at the speed of light. All of a sudden, everyone wants a piece of you and everyone tells you how fantastic you are. We'd been together for over ten years by then and had earned our success in increments. We grew popular in steps, winning over listeners territory by territory, country by country, until we had a worldwide web of fans and peers. Then the demands on us skyrocketed higher than we'd ever dreamed of—and nothing could have prepared us for that. It was a head trip that I can't fully explain, and I don't think anyone else who has lived through it could either. We did our best to remain sane with our feet on the ground, and for the most part we did. We were aided by our down-to-earth Aussie upbringing, but there were times when we just looked at each other and said "*This is insane!!!*"

From the outside, hitting the big time looks pretty glamorous, and let me tell you, there were many moments of glamour, but they were truly earned and didn't happen overnight—it took us ten years, six albums, and over a million miles by road and air to get there. We were reared on travel from the start, from the days we piled ourselves into beat-up cars to traverse enormous distances in Australia, and often all six of us squeezed into the one car. Looking back, we're lucky we made it at all—our cars were old and worn out, and if we'd been stranded long enough on some of our country's desert highways, the heat and desolation would have killed us as it had so many Australian explorers on those paths a century or two before. When we hit the peak of our stride, we never forgot where we'd come from—the Aussie pub circuit where we'd learned to play.

The Australian pub scene in the first half of the eighties was a unique culture that will never be equaled—it was a phenomenal, organic meeting of talent, timing, and community. In Melbourne, Sydney, and all across the land we would perform every night, sometimes two or three times in different venues the same night. It was a renaissance of youth, a generational spirit and the birth of a native musical identity. There were venues galore—a band could play nearly every night for a month in Melbourne or Sydney and never play in the same place twice. There were no regulations, so the music went loud and late every night in smoky, sweaty, beer-soaked rooms that got so packed and hot, the condensation dripped from the ceiling like rain. In a scene like that, you very quickly worked out what an audience wanted to hear. If you couldn't cut it live, you soon knew it. Fire codes and occupancy limits did not exist in those days—people were admitted until the place could hold no more. Naturally, those conditions bred many a fight, even though there was little room to move, let alone throw a punch. It was rough and tough and crazy and loads of fun. How well you packed a pub meant more to a record company interested in signing you than what was on your demo tape.

Those times are done in Australia—in the late eighties and early nineties, the pub scene was slowly shut down. The government eventually crashed the party, passing new licensing laws and strict drunk-driving laws (a good thing), and began ticketing venues that exceeded their occupancy limit, making it virtually impossible for anyone to make a decent buck. At the same time, the DJ culture took hold and the raucous rooms that bred everyone from AC/DC to Midnight Oil to us—as well as other local legends who never fully "cracked it" internationally, like Cold Chisel, the Angels, the Divinyls, Richard Clapton, and countless more—were transformed into lounges and restaurants. Later on, to make matters worse, new regulations allowed pubs to make room for "entertainment" of the most mindless variety—slot machines or Pokies, as we call them.

History does repeat itself, however, and I'm happy to say that the times, they are changing—or returning, as it is. Live music in Australia is making a comeback, and the kids, once again, want to go out to see live bands and be entertained, not just watch DJs playing records. It will never again be as it was, but there's a great resurgence in the live scene, and a number of pubs are turning back into live band venues.

In 1983, we left our homeland to conquer America and the world. It took time and relentless toil, but we did it, and by the time we returned to Australia we were too popular to play the pubs. I remember that realization, more than any other, made the scope of our growing success hit home to me. I was proud, but I was also sad—it was a classic case of "careful what you wish for. . . ."

Friends always commented on how lucky we were, going to so many places and seeing so many things—and I can't disagree with them. I've always been grateful for all the things this career has brought me, including the travel. But the reality of being on tour nonstop came down to this: we saw airports, highways, hotels, stages, our instruments, the audience, the dressing room, and maybe, if we weren't driving overnight to the next town, a bar and a succession of nightcaps, then the backs of our eyelids. Then the next day, we would do it all again somewhere else. After we'd "made it," it remained the same, but with the dizzying addition of lavish record company dinners, a very cool private plane with INXS emblazoned on the tail, the awesome spectacle of sold-out stadiums around the globe, massive stage ramps to rock upon, endless crates of Dom Perignon backstage, a pile of awards and award shows to attend, a heap of accolades in print and otherwise, and more parties thrown in our honor than I'd thought humanly possible. Also, there was a continuous supply of strangers and "new best friends" offering us anything and everything (both chemical and natural), including their own bodies.

That's many a man's fantasy, but that, in truth, was our job. We made time for play, of course, but for the most part, it really was hard work. The toughest trial was how long we were away from our families and loved ones—that was the greatest sacrifice. We were on a mission to be the biggest band we could be and we weren't going to stop short of world domination; we were committed, no matter what the cost. We had our fun, each to our own limits, but none of us ever let the perks outshine the job. I'm proud to say that no one in this band, no matter how far he dove into self-indulgence, ever let the rest of us down. Even in the wildest of times, after the longest of nights, when we felt worse than that first time we'd ever got smashingly "teenage" drunk (and I think many of you know what I mean), we always found the strength to give it our all and keep our performances consistent and strong. I'm glad it took us so long to get to the top, because along the way we learned the most important lesson: the music, the show, and the performance come first. Without them, there would be no audience, and without an audience, a band has no reason to be.

The six of us grew up together. We were family, half of us through blood and the other half through shared spirit and vision. We changed, matured, and evolved together, finding ourselves and reinforcing our connections with one another over thousands of hours of living in tour buses that became more familiar than our homes. Together we watched endless movies on those bus trips, we listened to music, we invented our own language, and we had a lot of fun and laughs just hanging out together. We were a club, a gang, a unit, a brotherhood that stuck together through it all.

A number of books have been written about us over the years, most of them in the wake of Michael's death, but none of them has been authorized by us or is in any way reflective of our point of view. We've always been a tightly knit group, one that would rather say nothing than dignify false allegations with a response. Michael described our point of view perfectly in the chorus of "Dancing on the Jetty": "Watch the world argue, argue with itself." We have always chosen to hold our cards close to our chest because we've always known who we are. I'm sure it's hurt us at times, but so be it—we couldn't have done it any other way.

This book is the band's history whilst Michael was alive, and the only one we have ever endorsed and been personally involved in. It's our self-portrait, and to the best of our memories, a true and honest account of *our* lives as INXS. This book is all of us, united as we've always been. It's a shame that Hutch isn't here today to add his account of our story, his way. We all miss him greatly. We've done our best in these pages to speak for our fallen brother, baring our souls, which, up until now, weren't ready. We've also enlisted those who knew Michael and us best and were also ready and willing to help make our thread of history come alive.

There are so many stories to tell, far more than this collection, for the sake of coherence, can contain. It has been a daunting, revelatory process putting twenty whirlwind years in print. I am so grateful that we found Anthony to piece it all together. All of the many friends, family, and professionals that he interviewed spoke highly of his integrity and sensitivity during the process. It would have been impossible to find and include every single person who played a part in our lives and this band's history—

and, truth be told, some chose not to take part for their own personal reasons. Compiling this book and making sense of our story was a tall task for all of us, and I give thanks to everyone who contributed his or her memories, reflections, and personality to this work. We have done our utmost to do our story justice and I hope you enjoy reading it as much as we have living it, through the best and worst of times.

By my count, I estimate that, personally, I have met well over a million people in the last three decades. Some of them came into our lives and vanished in the blink of an eye. Others remained with us in one way or another, whether I see them every day or pick up where we left off no matter how long it's been. Every single one of them, in some way, contributed something to the history of INXS—and that is a monumental truth. From my heart, I thank all of you on behalf of all of us. An equally dear thanks goes out to each and every one of our fans—every one of you who bought our records and attended our shows. We've played well over three thousand concerts to date, and as I said earlier, what is a band without an audience? Again, all of us thank you.

It's been quite the life and quite the ride, and I know I speak for my bandmates and brothers when I say that I would change nothing at all—but would give everything to have our soulmate Michael here with us today. He left us too soon, too young, too fast, and it's too bad, because if there is one thing I've learned in the course of reliving our past for all to read, it is that Michael would have loved this. He loved words, he loved feelings, he loved love in all its complexity, he loved being human in all of its extremes—and most of all he loved finding the language to make the intangible universal.

Without further ado, herein lies our story.

—Kirk Pengilly

Sydney, Australia, April 2005

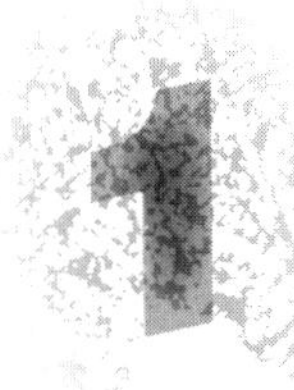

If Three Were Six: How the Brothers Farriss Doubled Their Numbers

BROTHERHOOD, WHETHER IT IS GENETIC, chemical, or ideological, has long been fuel for rock. There is of course the brotherhood of music, the one that sees no colors or borders; the one that inspired Chuck Berry to turn an old, white, hillbilly folk song called "Ida Red" into "Maybellene" in 1955—essentially the first rock-and-roll song ever recorded. The same color-blind bond drew Sam Phillips to begin recording the godfathers of rock and roll, from B. B. King to Howlin' Wolf to Carl Perkins and of course Elvis Presley.

There is also the blood brotherhood of familial jammers, a band situation that often yields as much blood as it does beautiful music—sometimes more. Ray and Dave Davies of the Kinks were as much of a concert draw for their onstage brawls as they were for their tunes. The Everly Brothers (Don and Phil) went years without speaking to each other, though every night they harmonized like parakeets in love. The three Wilson brothers in the Beach Boys—Brian, Dennis, and Carl—fought famously from the start over whether they were to be the sonic equivalent of saccharine surf wax or a complex acid-test beach party. In the end they did both, and it wasn't a smooth ride. More recently, Chris and Rich Robinson of the Black Crowes fought over life-changing topics such as who should put Sharpie to paper and write the night's set list. But Noel and Liam Gallagher of Oasis truly carried the rock-and-roll bro torch into the new millennium in a sea of name-calling, onstage sabotage, and critically acclaimed prattishness.

In its worst moments, genetic brotherhood has made for great rock drama because it is true life, with a sound track, unfolding before the audience. Regardless, bands with brothers also enjoy balance, an anchor, a constant, that others lack. This fraternal bond, even if it's blatantly dysfunctional, has helped many a band weather hard times. The brothers Young, Malcolm and Angus of AC/DC, kept the band on track when original singer Bon Scott died. The sisterhood of Ann and Nancy Wilson of Heart steered their band to its highest peaks just after the two brothers they were dating within their circle—Roger and Mike Fisher—left them and the group.

There are three brothers in INXS—keyboardist and guitar player Andrew Farriss, guitarist Tim Farriss, and drummer Jon Farriss—who fall within a niche subset of rock-and-roll brother units: like the Bee Gees, there are three of them and they grew up in Australia. The Farriss brothers weren't raised to be onstage brawlers, but they certainly have navigated stormy moments in the thirty-odd years they've made music together. They're all very different men whose musical differences became assets in the company of the compatriots they found in their youth: guitar and sax player Kirk Pengilly, bassist Garry Beers, and singer Michael Hutchence.

The Farriss brothers and their younger sister, Alison, were born in Perth, Australia, a conservative beach community on the western edge of the country. Their father, Dennis, was the West Australian manager for a global insurance company. An Englishman by birth and a former navy man, he was, unlike the continent's original Anglo settlers, sent there for good behavior. He met their mother, Jill (who passed away in 1995), fell in love, married, and set about raising a family. In 1971, Dennis was promoted to assistant manager of the company for all of Australia and relocated the family to Sydney, just as their eldest son, Tim, turned fourteen; the family settled in the leafy suburb of Belrose, a short drive from the inner city.

The story usually goes that parents who produce musicians—let alone three of them—are musicians themselves. Not so here. In this case, two avid music fans appear to have willed musical ability into the DNA of their children. "My wife and I were a sweet team," Dennis says. "We were huge pop music fans and I had a banjo and a ukulele and was always on to one thing or another, but I was never remarkable. I'd give them to the three

Tim Farriss (seven years old), Andrew Farriss (five years old), and Jon Farriss (three years old) in Perth, 1964.

boys to perform for us for half an hour before bed. It taught them to make a noise and it was a good way to tire them out." Dennis's love for an impromptu jam became a Farriss family institution over the years and continues to this day. "It happens every Christmas dinner," says Tim Farriss. "After everyone has had plenty of wine, my dad puts on some music, usually Sergio Mendes and Brasil '66, and insists that everyone pick up something and make a noise. People play bottles, spoons, the table, this wash-bucket bass made out of a broomstick and a string. It's quite hilarious. Last Christmas our sister, Alison, was very seriously playing a rake."

The Farriss parents were very supportive, allowing their sons to choose whatever instrument they liked, furnishing them with lessons, and exhibiting the saintly degree of patience required to cohabit with three tykes practicing three different instruments. "They were always behind us," Jon says. "I mean, they just let us play all the time. I was playing drums in my bedroom. We had a very typical, middle-class life, not wanting for anything, but our house was in no way big enough that you would not hear all of it. And for a long time there, I'm sure it was just an awful racket. Coming out of one room, you'd hear a guitar, another, drums, and in the other, piano. And none of them playing together." By the time he was twelve, Tim, the oldest, was an accomplished guitar player, who learned flamenco stylings under the guidance of his teacher Peter Federicci, who played with the Australian Symphony Orchestra. Middle brother Andrew took to the piano intuitively. At just five years old, Jon began drumming. "I bought him a tambourine drum and screwed it to a stool—that was his first one," recalls Dennis. "We got him professional lessons later, but he just took to it right away. When we'd go to his school to see him play in the drum-and-fife assembly, we could always pick him out easily—he was the kid drumming away as if his life depended on it."

Along with their parents' undying support, one childhood event should be considered when analyzing the Farriss brothers' musical evolution: the first rock-and-roll band they ever saw was the Beatles—though their memory of it is as hazy as marmalade skies. They were three (Jon), five (Andrew), and seven (Tim) and were in London visiting Dennis's family, when an old school friend of their mother's named Rolf Harris, who hosted a TV show on the BBC, gave them tickets to a taping featuring the Fab Four. "I vaguely remember meeting George Harrison backstage," Andrew says. "But I do remember people screaming their heads off when they played. I think we were too young to know exactly what a rock band was but we were just staring with open mouths—just look at *that!* And what we did learn is that whatever *that* was, we wanted to do it."

Soon enough, long before they developed the musical language to play together, they began to play in the same place. First it was the basement, and then it got serious—they moved into the kind of rock-and-roll womb where legends are born and dreams are made: their parents' garage. The house where the boys grew up is, from the outside, identical now to the way it was then: modest, two-story, brown with green trim, with a backyard swimming pool that was dug by the boys (under Dad's dictum) one summer when they were teens. The driveway slopes down to a wide two-car garage door behind which the Farriss boys played their instruments relentlessly. "We'd let it go as long as we could and as loud as they wanted," Dennis says. "But not always. Jill and I would be sitting in the lounge directly above them and whenever she thought it was coming to a killing crescendo, she'd grab her walking stick and flail the floor with it. That was their warning to turn it down."

The boys began to form bands on their own at an early age. Jon played drums for his older brother Tim, but as Tim's musical endeavors moved out of the garage and onto local stages, the fifteen- and sixteen-year-old members of Tim's early bands weren't exactly thrilled to have a ten-year-old drummer. "It wasn't a lot of fun for those guys having a ten-year-old brat hanging out," Jon says. "I mean, it's just not that cool to have to get your drummer home before his bedtime." Jon moved on to a more age-appropriate outlet when he turned eleven, playing drums for a Christian choral group who wanted to jazz up their image by adding drums to the choir. He also began to jam regularly with middle brother Andrew. "Andrew and I would practice and got into it really well. He had this little organ and we learned each other's style and sensibilities. Early on we learned to feel rhythm and tempo and how to play off each other when one of us would push forward or hold back."

In 1971, the eldest Farriss, Tim, made a friend at high school who became an honorary Farriss—Kirk Pengilly, with whom he pursued all of his musical endeavors. Kirk and Tim attended the Forest High School, and met one day in science class when Kirk, already an avid bedroom guitar player, noticed that Tim had drawn a guitar on his pencil case. Pengilly was born in Melbourne, Australia, the more urban, edgier, and darker—in both weather and attitude—sister city to Sydney. If Sydney is Australia's version of Los Angeles, Melbourne is certainly its New York—it is the scene that spawned the literary misanthropy of Nick Cave, and little more explanation should be necessary.

When Kirk, the youngest of three brothers, was eight years old, the Pengilly clan found their future home on the sunny side. During a family holiday spent sailing the Hawkesbury River on a hired thirty-six-foot cruiser, they eyed a unique house for sale in Cottage Point, an isolated weekend destination town nestled in the center of a national park twenty-three miles outside of Sydney. "The house was right on the water with its own mooring, pontoon, and a shark-fenced tidal swimming pool," Pengilly says. "It was 1966, and back then there were about fifty houses, a general store, a small yacht club, and a boat repair shop. There were only a dozen families living there on a regular basis, two-thirds of which were fishing and drinking their lives away." Kirk picked up his love of music from his oldest brother, Mark, a guitarist and songwriter in his own right, who eventually left home for London to follow his dream. Tim became Kirk's partner in music and the two were quickly as inseparable as Vegemite and butter (for the uninitiated, that is how you are supposed to eat Vegemite—with butter, on toast, with much more butter than the salty malt tar that has been a staple of Aussie nutrition for years). Tim and Kirk were so inseparable at school that their math teacher, Mr. Labalestier, seemed convinced that the young lads were what some call "special friends." "We thought it was hilarious and led him on whenever we could," Kirk says. "When we knew he could see us, we'd start holding hands and nearly piss ourselves as we watched him nervously look the other way."

Kirk's house was so far from school that he was soon spending weekends and school nights chez Farriss. "Jon had a bunk bed, so I'd sleep in the lower one," he says. "He was such a little kid then. But we'd sit in there and talk about music. Years later, on a few occasions, after a few drinks, Jon has told me how amazing that was for him to be taken seriously that way, to just hang out as an equal, because there's quite a big difference between a ten-year-old and a fourteen-year-old. That gap matters less the older you get, but when you're young, it's huge." Big brother Tim's room was downstairs, where, as a teen, he'd created a Greg Brady–style pad by building a wooden partition in what was formerly the brothers' rumpus room. "Tim had this kind of partitioned office where he slept, which was bizarre," Kirk says. "He'd play records down there and we spent lots of time there, but I also spent lots of time with Andrew in his room because he was quite private. I always liked to go and jam with Andrew or just chat about music. He and Tim didn't always get along, as brothers will, so he'd often be up there strumming a guitar and writing songs. He and I had some great times."

Tim and Kirk put a band together and they were called Guinness, named after their bass player's dog; in a later incarnation the group featured a thirty-two-year-old American pedal-steel guitar player named David Stewart. They were always something different, and had a very unique blend of influences: Tim's classical-style guitar and Latin conga playing; Kirk's Steely Dan rhythms, Hendrix-influenced leads, and Eagles'-style vocals; bass player Steve Spencer's Yes-meets-Pink-Floyd excursions; plus Malcolm Walker's jazzy, Buddy Rich–style drumming. By all accounts it was as out there as that last sentence sounds, even by mid-seventies standards.

During the same period, Tim and Kirk joined another group, one which, historically, has changed more lives and converted more souls than rock at its most Satanic—the Born Again Christians. "We were in public school and it's weird to think about it now, but we used to have a scripture lesson each week—and it was nothing but purely Christian scripture," Kirk says. "We were fourteen or fifteen and this guy came in for an hour a week. It wasn't very fair to any of the Muslims, Asians, or other cultures in our school." The head honcho of the Forest High School Bible sessions was John Kidson, whose task it was to make Christ cool. However he did it, he had a David Koresh–esque effect on Kirk and Tim. "We totally got sucked in to it like people in a cult," Kirk says. "A group of about a dozen of us would go down and have these in-depth Bible studies once a week after school. We'd go to someone's house and study a passage for three hours and really get into it." Kirk and Tim became full-bore Bible pushers who trolled the hallways of their high school, hell-bent on conversion. "Tim was amazing at it. He is the kind of man who goes all the way, all the time, with whatever pursuit he's chosen, which I've always admired him for," Kirk says. "And he's such a charmer that he got so many people into being Christies, as we'd call it. He even got this really tough guy, the head of this really tough bunch in school, to start coming down to our meetings. Actually, that guy went on to become a minister."

Kirk and Tim did what Mr. Kidson couldn't accomplish alone—they gave Christian scripture street cred. At Bible meetings they did guitar jams while Tim preached the word in their school's locker-lined trenches. But they also gigged as Guinness and prayed at the altar of rock and roll. And they did so for the same reasons that so many rockers before and since have done: to justify smoking pot and kiss many girls. Miscommunication was afoot and eventually Mr. Kidson held an intervention. "One day he took us aside and told us that we couldn't go around smoking pot and having sex with girls any more," Kirk says. "He said we had to decide whether we were going to be Christians, which would not allow for smoking pot and having sex of any kind before marriage, or whether we were going to live like young men who wanted to be rock stars." The two looked at each other, said, "Okay, then," and dropped Christianity quicker than a rabbi would a cheeseburger. "We felt bad about it because we'd really converted a lot of people and made the Christian thing in our parish really popular," Kirk says. "It had become a rather large group of kids who'd just get together and, well, be very Christian. But we left it as quickly as we took it on. It was very bipolar, really." Ironically, it wasn't the last time the pair was confronted with a Christian ultimatum—and perhaps if they'd been so inclined in their teens, Kirk and Tim might have led the world's funkiest Christian rock band.

Kirk and Tim chose to rock, smoke pot, listen to Pink Floyd, Steely Dan, Creedence Clearwater Revival, and gig wherever they could with Guinness. Perhaps their Christian affiliation had protected them before, but once they were openly devoted to being band dudes, their reputation at school took a turn for the worse. "The disciplinary officer at our school was Mr. Mullins and he was just the scariest guy," Kirk recalls. "I wouldn't be surprised if he'd been a narcotics officer because there was a period where he focused on ridding our school of anyone who smoked marijuana." Mr. Mullins led a Tokers' Inquisition, calling in suspected dealers, those who sat next to suspected dealers, those who might know suspected dealers, and those who were blatant lovers of Mary Jane. Kirk and Tim were no strangers to the mighty Cheeba, but though they might furnish their friends with pot for a fee, they were in no way doobie-dealing kingpins. Regardless, they came under the wily eye of Mr. Mullins. "We were like, 'Oh, fuck,'" Kirk says. "We were called into his office, sat down, and he just stared at us. He says, 'I believe you two have been selling marijuana in school. I have a list of names here of the people who have been supplying, and I want you to tell me what you know about them. There are going to be expulsions and much worse.'" Of course Kirk and Tim knew everyone on the list but, like true good fellas, they denied everything and implicated no one. And in the way that yin and yang, light and dark, and hypocrisy and truth do, this worked out against all odds. "He stared at us for a while and then he said, 'Okay, here's what we're going to do,'" Kirk recalls. "'My wife runs all these charity fetes for the schools and other organizations. If you play all of the dances she asks you to, I'll turn a blind eye to you guys and take you off this list.'" And so these members of Guinness passed Go and earned their Get Out of Jail Free card.

Unfortunately, when their thirty-two-year-old American pedal steel guitar player decided to return to his homeland to pursue other things, Guinness dissipated like head on a poorly poured lager. It was for the best, because while Tim and Kirk followed their muses—musical and otherwise—Andrew Farriss formed a creative kinship that became the stuff of legend.

Australian public schools are government regulated and each student is issued a uniform. In the fashion of British schools, said uniform generally consists of white shirts, both short and long pants to abide the change in seasons, a blazer emblazoned with the school's crest, and given the strength of the Australian sun, a hat.*

When Andrew Farriss was set to enter high school, he was, in the strange way that land zoning, taxation, voting electorates, parking regulations, and so many other bureaucratically controlled facts of life defy logic, enrolled not in the Forest High School, the one his older brother Tim attended, but in Davidson High School, an institution equidistant from the house in which they both lived. The only problem was that Davidson High School did not yet exist—it was under construction until Andrew's third year. In the interim, those future Davidson graduates were redistributed among several schools in the surrounding area. This system looks vaguely logical on paper until you consider the fact that said students were never issued new uniforms—instead, they wore their Davidson High School colors. High school isn't easy anywhere, anyhow, even when you're wearing the right uniform. These Davidson High misfits were fucked. Andrew Farriss was bused to Killarney Heights High School, Davidson High's rival, where his uniform was akin to wearing a bull's-eye on his chest and a KICK ME sign on his back. "We had blue shorts, a white shirt, and a bright red jumper [pullover sweater] that was different from everyone else. Plus we had white socks and a tartan tie. And Killarney Heights' uniform was all gray!" Andrew says. "Some of my friends and I from primary school got served straightaway. We'd be out in the yard and the older boys would brand us with tennis balls. It was target practice for them. They'd just hit us in the head with them nonstop and they used tennis balls because they wouldn't leave bruises. Some kids were chased, and their heads dunked in toilets. It was horrible." The school wasn't much better—in those years the Australian government allowed physical punishment, so

*** If you've ever seen AC/DC, guitarist Angus Young's stage attire is a just representation of the average Aussie schoolboy (minus the hat).**

those who misbehaved were caned across their hands. "It was a terrible situation. Let me tell you, a cane across your hands really hurts."

The Davidson outcasts banded together like a rebel army that, as much as they could, held the Imperials at bay. They did have one advantage, one Paul Schofield, who, at nearly 6'1" was a formidable lad for his age. "I was picked on, but so many others had it worse than me," Andrew recalls. "But there were days that I would walk the four miles back home because I didn't want to get beaten up on the bus. In school we stuck together—my very good friend Paul Schofield would always back me up." One day in their second year, Andrew and his Davidson crew were outside in the school yard when they saw a new kid arrive who was clearly bound for a world of hurt. His name was Michael Hutchence. His family had just moved from Hong Kong and until now, he'd been educated in British schools. To the bullies of the world, particularly the overly hormonal high school wolf-pack variety, there is nothing more irresistible than an alien. Michael not only had an offshore accent to irritate the pubescent boors of Killarney High, he also bore a uniform as inexplicable as scuba gear in the desert. In short, he was doubly fucked.

In a matter of minutes, the bullies were on to him and it looked as if the scene would descend into the type of ridicule and carnage that was considered entertainment in the Middle Ages. "As soon as I saw Michael, I turned to my friend Paul Schofield and said, 'This guy is going to get so much trouble.' And then I decided I'd do something about it. I don't know what came over me because I've never been any kind of Robin Hood, but I got my friends and we went over and got in the middle of it and told them all to leave him alone." It worked and Michael was grateful. But the two didn't talk again after that for months, aside from occasional hallway salutations. "Then one day, he kind of found me and said, 'Look, do you want to come over to my house and meet my family?'" Andrew says. "I remember the first time being at their house, and looking at all the art and everything they'd brought from Hong Kong. I'd never seen anything like it."

The Hutchence family lived a short drive or a very long walk from the Farriss compound, at the end of a cul-de-sac in a house obscured by beautiful old trees. Michael's father was an importer, and Michael and his younger brother, Rhett, had grown up in Hong Kong, where his father's business was based. In Hong Kong the family had servants, and the boys attended private schools of a fashion closer to those of the English upper crust than the Australian middle class. As a teen, Michael was worldly, well-read, and interested in Eastern religion and culture. Like Andrew, he wasn't like his classmates, whose lives revolved around the beach, the opposite sex, and cars. Michael was into motorcycles and the two spent as many hours in the Hutchence family garage working on them as they did in the Farriss family garage while Andrew and Jon played music. "Michael and I would hang out for a while and then not see each other again for ages," Andrew says. "Isn't that what you do in high school? Maybe you're testing each other, but we'd always come around to each other again."

Michael's parents divorced in 1975, when he was fifteen, and his mother, a makeup artist, brought Michael to Los Angeles where he attended Beverly Hills High, an institution known for other rock alums like Slash and Lenny Kravitz. One year later, Michael and his mother returned to Australia, and the poet-in-the-rough that Andrew had known had grown. He'd also moved into a house a very short walk away from the Farriss's garage—so the two saw much more of each other. "He'd always been into philosophers like Hermann Hesse and he was already writing poetry before he went away," Andrew says. "But when he came back, we really had so much in common. He'd gotten into so much American music that I'd been listening to as well. We'd get stoned and listen to Eric Burdon and War and Pink Floyd for hours in his room." Michael and Andrew soon formed a band: Neil Sandon, a surfing buddy, was on drums, Andrew played keyboards and guitar, and a school friend named Kent Kearney played guitar. But the obvious was missing—a bass player. The boys did what they had to do—they placed an ad in the paper, and in so doing, found the final link in the chain that later became INXS.

Garry Beers attended the Forest High School with Tim and Kirk, but he didn't run with the same crowd. He was a surfer and had played school team rugby. "I was into surfing and still am today, but I wasn't like all the other surfers down on the beach," Garry says. "I was into music, I was into playing, and I was in a band. And the only reason I learned to play bass was because I lost a bet. We had two guitar players in my band and whoever lost the bet had to learn bass. That was me—and good thing I lost." Garry knew the Farriss family because he knew Tim and Kirk's band Guinness. "They were such a weird band. No one liked them at school because they were so different," he says. "They had that thirty-two-year-old pedal steel player and they did four-part harmonies. They were country music meets Yes—clearly very out there. Everyone at school was confused, but I have to hand it to them, they stuck to their guns, started recording stuff, and went for it until their pedal steel player went back to America."

According to Andrew, he found an ad that Garry had placed, advertising a bass player who also had a car, which, to a crew of teens, rockers or not, was worth more than musical chops. Garry recalls it differently. "I ran into Andrew at the local surf club and I approached him because I thought he was Tim—it was a very dark room—but we started talking and I told him I played bass and we arranged to jam the next day with Jon, who was eleven at the time. It was great, that was the first time I'd ever played with a drummer. And we played a complete load of crap." Jon didn't join the party on an official basis, but with Garry on bass, Andrew playing keyboards and guitar, Michael singing, Neil Sandon on drums, and Kent Kearney on guitar, they carried on, dubbing themselves Dr. Dolphin, learning covers and writing their own material. They intended to form a unit tight enough to play out—though the only venue that had them was Davidson High School.

Internally, it was soon clear, however, that unless Dr. Dolphin intended to jam through their metaphysical third eye, solely in the key of *whoa,* Neil needed to ease on down the road. "Neil was a very lovely guy, but he was a bit of an acid casualty kind of surfer character," Garry says. "He was just *so* mellow. He could only play one beat, which, looking back, was way ahead of its time. It was that loose hip-hop groove thing. But it was all that he could do. I remember one day we actually did get pretty rocking and Neil went into this serious drum roll and I couldn't believe it. Then he stopped cold, because all of that activity threw him into what looked like an acid flashback! He apologized, because he had to take a rest for a while. . . . God bless him wherever he is."

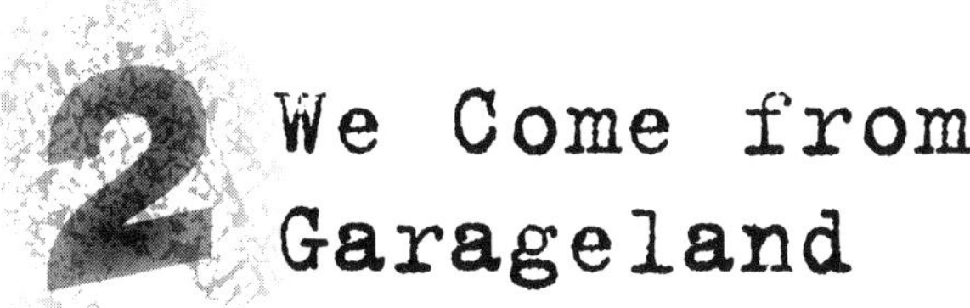

2 We Come from Garageland

BY THE END OF THE MID-SEVENTIES, the brothers Farriss and their new musical brothers were in separate bands—until genetics and illness brought them together.

The three Farriss boys had been mucking about in bands of their own design for a few years before Tim struck upon the notion that they should come together as one; a vision that came to him while laid up. Tim is burdened with a hereditary bone disease called Exostoses, and in 1977, the condition required a very painful surgical procedure to remove two bone spurs in his legs. Tim recuperated at the Farriss family's Belrose home for weeks, where, confined to his bed, he listened intently to his two brothers playing music, both in the family garage and their respective bedrooms. "I was in so much pain and just looking out the window, watching Andrew and his friends come over to play in the garage," Tim Farriss recalls. "I recognized Garry from school but I'd never thought he was cool because he hung out with the meat pies—the guys who only care about sports. But I lay there and listened to them play with Jonny on drums and not only did I wish I was well enough to get up and join them, I just thought, Why don't we just put this all together? I don't need to find a new band, it's all right here."

The others rocked the Farriss garage like never before and became so accomplished that they'd leave the door open so that the neighborhood might dig their jams. The family was blessed with tolerant neighbors, who stopped to look and listen more often than they asked the lads to lower the door. "Our neighbors were brilliant," father Dennis Farriss says. "In fact, they used to call me to tell me how pleasant it was to hear these kids practicing and going for it with all their lives instead of racing around the neighborhood misbehaving. There was one guy who rang us once, but to this day I think it was a put-on. He complained that his wife was experiencing migraines on a regular basis as a result of the boys' playing. When I asked him where he lived, he named a street about five miles away. I'm sure it was just one of the families on the street who'd finally had enough."

The Farriss family garage became a rock-and-roll science lab, home to Dr. Dolphin (Andrew, Michael, Garry, and others), as well as Tim and Kirk's evolving and revolving bands and a variety of young guns that Jon liked to jam with. There was always someone rocking in that two-car suburban space—and it was time that the local talent was harnessed. Tim had a vision and he knew how and where he could make it real.

While he and Kirk were in Guinness, they'd rented a storefront, formerly occupied by a vegetable vendor, in Avalon Beach, and turned it into a studio. They had built a separate control room and installed a state-of-the-art, four-track tape recorder, as top notch as their budget and the times could provide. It had been Guinness headquarters: they'd recorded, partied, rehearsed, and made that spot something special during the the last year that Guinness was together. When the band broke up, they rented it out to other bands, since that location had the equipment and convenience and the mojo that any local band could want.

Tim arranged for a meeting of the bands at Guinness's Avalon recording space. It was a fateful day, the first time that every member of what would become INXS ever played together. They just jammed; the song that brought them together, and that they recorded that day, was Bob Marley's "I Shot the Sheriff," though their version was closer to Eric Clapton's take on that classic ditty. They were joined in that endeavor by a piano player who Tim knew possessed more skill than most: he was armless and insanely adept at his instrument. "He was amazing, really amazing," Tim says. "He played with his feet, he ate with his feet, he did everything with his feet better than a lot of people I know can with their hands."

After that first session, most of the guys were decided upon keeping on as a band—all but Kirk. He was present for that first, fateful session, but after Guinness had disbanded he'd decided that his gigging days were done. "I was the singer and main songwriter in Guinness, but once David Stewart returned to California, I needed a break," Kirk says. "I just wasn't sure that I wanted to do anything musically at all. That day was great fun, but I still wasn't sure if it was what I wanted to do. But after six more months of constant pressure from Tim, I finally bought a Music Man combo amp and we built a small P.A. setup. And off we went."

The Guinness studio became the space where the boys played, recorded, and rehearsed until the lease ran out. Today, that space is situated in a quaint country-style, four-store strip mall you might miss if you blinked while driving. It is now Norma Jean's Hair, Nails, and Beauty, a business managed by a lovely woman named Liz who recalls the days when the veggie peddler was replaced by the studio, and remembers the scraggly boys who spent hours on end making noise in there. Oddly enough, Liz is also the aunt of James Morrison, a gifted trumpet player who recorded with INXS nearly two decades later. According to Aunt Liz, Morrison's parents did not exhibit the same degree of patience shown the fledgling Farriss boys in the years he honed his craft. When his brass racket became intolerable, his family sent him on an aquatic walkabout: he was exiled to the family dingy, ordered to row into the middle of the harbor that lay before the house, and blow like the wind once he was well out of range.

For obvious reasons, the band who would be INXS called themselves the Farriss Brothers back then and they soon did gigs, as fledgling musical units do, wherever they could. "I was sixteen at the time and Tim was well out of high school," Jon Farriss says. "He was working at a Toyota dealership, where Kirk worked too, so we did a gig on the back of a truck in their parking lot as a promotional thing once. I wonder how that affected their sales?"

The band's first real gig, however, was more like a night drive with Nick Nolte: wild, wasted, and swervy. It took place in a house high above

A promotional flyer for the newly formed Farriss Brothers band, circa 1977.

Whale Beach. Though it was only a short distance from the suburbs where the Farriss boys, Garry, and Michael grew up, it was at once half a world away. Sydney's Northern Beaches are a stretch of white sand, dramatic hills, lush foliage, and water as blue as the sky. The area has the funky 1950s hodgepodge architecture of the Hollywood Hills, the earthy pioneer spirit of the foothills of Vermont, the pristine, wide, surf beaches of Hawaii, and the type of foliage found in all three—all of which, somehow, makes impossible sense. Shadowy, narrow roads wind down the leafy hills, revealing glimpses of the sea every few turns; like small beach towns on the California coastline, the area is one part tree house, two parts beach shack. "In that era, that area was strictly a holiday destination for families or the community you'd retire to," Andrew says. "It wasn't at all where people would raise families. So the only other full-time residents who weren't retired were living what you might call an 'alternative lifestyle.'"

The Northern Beaches in the seventies was the kind of place where drugs were plentiful and a friend of Kirk and Tim's could smuggle primo hash into the country by stuffing it down the center seam of his surfboard. "There were a bunch of surfers who survived by selling pot, rather than go on the dole," says Kirk. "At one point, this group of guys we knew smuggled in all this Windowpane acid from the late sixties ✶ that had been on ice for almost a decade. That was the real-deal stuff, it was fucking awesome." The setting, the drugs, and the residents combined to create a scene where all was permissible, welcomed, and possible. "Everyone would be running

✶ **Windowpane acid is legendary in psychedelic lore. It is reputed to be the strongest, most transcendental form of LSD that the counterculture ever knew. It is, scientifically, a reacted solid allowed to crystallize. It was the stuff that Woodstock, Hendrix, the Grateful Dead, Timothy Leary, Aldous Huxley, and all those who were duly dosed in the era were dosed on.**

around naked all the time," Kirk says. "Or you'd be hanging out on the veranda, it would be foggy, you'd drop some acid and face northeast to watch the sun. We'd listen to music, or we'd sit around with guitars and practice harmonies. It was real hippie sort of stuff. Really trippy, actually."

The house where the Farriss Brothers played their first gig was a wee bit weird: a kooky, cozy cottage cut sharply into the tangled jungle hillside. It is still there, around a tight curve, at the bottom of a ski-slope-steep, vertigo-inducing set of stairs. The occasion was Tim Farriss's twentieth birthday, August 16, 1977, which is the day the band considers the moment their history began—coincidentally it is also the day Elvis died. (Conspiracy theory fans, feel free to start your cycle here.) Tim lived in the house along with a filmmaker and his girlfriend. Apparently said filmmaker had endured many accidents (some of which happened simply negotiating the steep stairs home) and had, along the way, found himself a Dr. Feelgood that prescribed an infinitely refillable prescription for Mandrax, a barbiturate-type sedative that was the mid-seventies Australian party pill du jour. The birthday revelers took advantage of the bottomless prescription, flinging pills hither and thither. "I realized pretty early in the night that I was the only sober person there," Garry recalls. "I was driving so I had to be. I had loaded all of the gear down these three hundred stairs and just watched as everyone just fell out while we played. I remember thinking, I'm in this pole house, built on a cliff, and there's four hundred people here completely fucked. It was weird." Mandrax made its takers silly then quickly turned them to human oatmeal, but before it did, a side-effect occurred: "It made people majorly horny," Kirk says. "You'd look around a party where everyone was on Mandrax and see people just start this orgy stuff that no one would remember afterward."

INXS has always been an astonishingly good live band, and though they were young and inexperienced then, there's a good chance that they rocked that house party. Of course even if they'd been utter crap, it is likely that their audience would have loved it anyway. Their audience that night would have loved anything and they loved what they heard so much that most of them didn't leave; in fact, most of them *couldn't* leave. There were so many Mandrax casualties by the end of the festivities that the living room, driveway, and particularly the steep steps up to the street were littered with bodies until sometime the next afternoon. "Our parents came to that party and I remember talking to my dad the next day," Jon says. "He said, 'Son, that was a great party. But I think you might want to add some pep to your show. All of you played very well, but I feel sorry, because your band made everyone fall asleep.'"

The Farriss Brothers were, after that night, officially a band and they began to gig wherever they could whenever they could. They were soon regulars in the beach communities in and around Avalon and Sydney's Northern Beaches, where the local surf clubs hosted live music each weekend. The surf clubs were much more than a place where lifeguards and wave riders met to discuss breaks and tubes; the clubs were then and are today akin to recreation centers for the whole town. So too were the Returned Services League clubs, government-run facilities for retired military men. The RSL's American equivalent is the VFW hall, except that the Australian version, on average, is much more fun: it's more like a well-worn neighborhood pub, a small time casino, a cafeteria, and a hotel ballroom combined. Both of these outlets were meeting points; they were and are places where locals of all ages meet, greet, and back in the seventies, got down to the sound of bands like the Farriss Brothers. At the time, the boys played covers by the best the seventies had to offer: Steely Dan, Roxy Music, Deep Purple, and Little Feat. They also, always, filled their set with their original compositions, which, in the beginning, ranged from Michael Franks–style jazz to ska.

The Farriss Brothers toured the beach towns, gigging at night and working, in part, by day for Bill Buckle, the proprietor of the Toyota car dealership. Tim, Kirk, Andrew, Garry, and Michael had graduated, while Jon slaved away at the books as a high school sophomore. Tim and Kirk had been employees for several years at Bill (did anyone call him "Seat" behind his back?) Buckle's and procured a job for Andrew, which he vastly preferred to his post as a cook, if you can call it that, at the local Kentucky Fried Chicken. "We did all sorts of things at the car dealership," Andrew says. "We were delivery boys, detailers, pretty much whatever needed to be done. The men we worked for were amazing to us. They had a prestige car division where they sold Mercedes-Benz and one of the dealers had his detailed one day. I was backing it up and ran it right into a post and really ru-

The Farriss Brothers band in 1977. *Left to right:* Garry, Michael, Jon, Andrew, Kirk, Tim.

ined the side of it. He walked over to me and very calmly said, 'Get out of the car and go away. I don't want to see you for the rest of the day. Maybe the rest of your life.'" Andrew's accidental solo smash-'em-up derby was forgiven and he remained an employee of Bill Buckle's for years afterward. Clearly the dealership was run by a patient man: as the Farriss Brothers' reputation grew and their number of gigs increased, so did the band boys' hours of sleep decrease. "We couldn't help it, some days we'd just be zombies," Kirk says. "I don't know if they thought we were stoned or not, but we weren't. It was sheer fatigue. One of my duties was starting all the cars in the yard to keep the batteries charged. So I'd start at one end and when all of them were running, I'd go back and start turning them off. A few times I'd be shaken awake by my boss because I'd fallen asleep in the seat of one of the cars with my foot all the way down on the gas." The staff at Bill Buckle let Kirk's naps slide because he fulfilled a greater need providing what we earthlings call lunch. "My clearest memory of that job is how important lunch was to the older guys that employed us," Kirk recalls. "They'd start talking about it first thing in the morning. Sometimes they'd send me miles to pick up their order from some restaurant. And because I could cook, once a week I had to make them a hot lunch—a leg of lamb and vegetables, all on this little electric burner thing. The general manager wasn't allowed to know about it, so I'd be cooking it up out in the yard, squatting between two rows of cars."

Bill Buckle and his entire staff from that era should be commended. Let it be known that these men, all of an entirely different generation than the band dudes they employed, were well aware that their young charges did not aspire to a career in automotive salesmanship. They knew that those band boys' musical ambitions came first and that as soon as they got served a snifter of success they'd fly off the lot faster than next year's import model, the fully loaded one with the sweet financing package. And yeah, they did fly, but not for success. That came later. They left for nearly a year, convinced that it was all going to happen, and when they returned broke and homeless, God bless Bill Buckle for giving the boys their old jobs back.

3 How the West Wasn't Won: To Live and Strive in Perth

IN EARLY 1978, THE FARRISS BROTHERS did something few bands would ever do: they moved approximately 2,500 miles (3,990 kilometers) . . . for their drummer. Jon Farriss, their youngest member, was still in high school, and was thus obliged to accompany his parents when they retired to Perth. Traditionally, drummers, despite their integral relevance in a musical unit of any genre (what, pray tell, is good music without tight rhythm?), are an afterthought. There is a reason why there are so many drummer jokes—example: What was the last thing the drummer said to the band? "Let's try one of my songs."—and that is because most drummers possess a near-autistic ability to be complex human timekeepers and nothing else. You have to hand it to them: each of their four limbs acts independently, holding sticks, striking skins, and pumping pedals in staggered intervals while connected to a larger rhythmic scale. It's an amazing accomplishment, but like genius-level autism, it's often the only arena many will ever rule. A technically perfect drummer is, in essence, like the Greenwich Meridian: a steadfast reality to which to set your watch.

The best drummers don't just keep time—they move it. And a band in their hands is as stable and free as astronauts and scuba divers—as a unit they can go forward, float freely, or pull 360s standing still.

When Jon moved to Perth with Mom and Dad, it wasn't just family ties that made his brothers, blood and non, follow him. His musical compatriots knew his worth and knew what they had when all of them played together—and there wasn't a distance they could measure worth letting that slide away. "All of us have made a lot of sacrifices to have done this," Jon says. "Looking back, even when I recognized things we did, as a band or as individuals, that were selfish, I can see that all of it sort of had to happen, whether we knew it at the time or not."

Perth is nearly as far from Sydney as New York is from Los Angeles, and between the two lies some of the gnarliest desert Australia—and the world—has to offer. The trek across the continent was the first of many marathons the band would run—and at the time, they were hardly well-equipped. Andrew owned a late sixties VW Bug, which he packed with gear, Garry, and Tim. Garry's Toyota Hi-Ace van was packed with gear and sent to Perth by train.

Kirk, Michael, and everything else they owned made the journey in Kirk's van, which was what is known around the world as a Shaggin' Wagon. "It was a red panel van—the kind without windows, so no one could see what was going on in the back," Kirk says. "It had no backseats so there was room to pack it with whatever you wanted to. When we moved to Perth, the other guys rode in the Vee-Dub and Michael and I filled the van with all the gear. During my last months at Bill Buckle's, one of the dealers, who wished that I'd expand my cooking repertoire, took me under his wing and let me attend these Chinese cooking courses he held at his house and I got really good at it." The drive from Sydney to Perth was a three-day affair, and after a midway stop at Kirk's grandmother's place in Adelaide, he put his Chinese know-how to work. With nothing but the stars, the fire, and the beady, glowing eyes of kangaroos and dingoes watching from the edge of the darkness, Kirk fired up a vegetable Szechuan surprise: "After a few bongs, we stopped in the middle of the desert, in the middle of the night, built a fire, and I cooked us a Chinese meal in a wok, with nothing and no one around for miles. It was amazing."

Perth is situated on the west coast of Australia, which in recent times has become a region known for its wonderful wines and heavenly beaches. It is a small community of middle-class and well-to-do families that prides itself on tradition and generally conservative values. It is a quiet locale that is far from cosmopolitan, which is considered an ideal place to raise a family.

When Dennis and Jill Farriss returned to Perth, all three of their sons, plus Garry, Michael, and Kirk, crashed at their home. Soon, the young musicians, like fungi on a damp log, became a stinky appendage in need of eradication. "Mrs. Farriss was wonderful and turned a blind eye to the fact that all six of us were living there, and allowing her to treat us with the utmost hospitality. She cooked for us, she did our laundry, everything," Garry says. "We started to realize eventually that she was sick of it. And who could blame her? But she never turned mean, she just told us in the best possible way. She'd take me aside and say, 'Garry, let me show you, this is how you properly wash clothes. And after they're dry, I'm going to show you how to iron them.'" Apparently what she didn't say, yet clearly implied, was that learning to wash and iron his clothes would be Garry's first lesson—the second he ought to learn was how to find his own apartment. Dennis and Jill Farriss did not retire to Perth solely to nurture their collective sons' creative endeavors, and so the oldest of the bunch arranged their own lodgings. Kirk, Tim, and Michael rented a house together, while Garry roomed with a guy named Mal Wark, who was a school friend of Andrew and Michael's. Andrew and Jon lived at home with the folks, taking full advantage of the family ties.

The boys lived there for nearly a year and during that time they accomplished a few things: they led Jon Farriss to complete academic ruin, they forged an everlasting band identity, they blatantly alienated the one and only booking agent in Perth, and as a result, were driven to gig in the nether regions of Australia—and had adventures that proved to be stranger than fiction. They also honed their playing and broadened their sound. "We had been, up to that point, very extreme, experimental, and naive," Jon says. "We were so eager to keep learning and we really did in Perth. Michael wasn't really a singer before then, but in those eight months he worked on getting his pitch, his intonation, and his phrasing right. He started to get it, but it wasn't until a few years later that he really bloomed. Garry and I worked together to tighten up the rhythm section and really give the band a true funk sound. Tim was playing these full-bodied chords, Kirk was noodling on lead guitar, and Andrew was on synth and guitar.

Later, we felt there was something soulful missing—saxophone. So Kirk just decided he'd do what it took to learn to play it. And he did."

The second house the band members inhabited was a tired shack that was never a home—it was a rehearsal space with corners to sleep in. Tim, Michael, Garry, and Kirk didn't even try; once Tim had convinced the owner to lease it to him month to month, they put mattresses over every wall in the living room, set up their gear, and lit into 'round-the-clock band practice. "We'd rehearse all day," Garry says. "We really started being serious about things. For the first time, we were all in it, we were together, and we were serious about writing original music as a band called the Farriss Brothers."

They practiced constantly and they gigged in every pub in town. One of their first engagements had little to do with how well they played. "We got an audition in one of the bigger pubs in Perth, strictly because the proprietor's daughter had a massive crush on Jon," Garry says. "We thought it was a proper gig but when we showed up, she was the only one. So we played four sets to this one girl who sat at the foot of the stage mooning at him like mad." Jon's good looks got them wherever that got them, but Tim Farriss's charm got them in the door of Perth's bigger pubs within weeks. Collectively the band looked upon their pilgrimage to Perth, the Farriss birthplace, as a spiritual journey and an artistic retreat from the Sydney scene where they could experiment freely and anchor a set of new fans. It didn't exactly work out that way. "The scene in Perth was very simple," Andrew Farriss says. "Unless a band was prepared to play cover songs and nothing else, they were not welcome."

The Farriss Brothers, as a band, had one thing going for them: they had a lot of friends who still lived in Perth, all of whom showed up to their gigs with little goading. They enjoyed what the boys dished out, which ranged from songs they knew to the groovy Steely-Dan-meets-the-Doobie-Brothers-on-a-surfboard jams they perfected daily.

The Farriss Brothers played every suburban pub they could, and soon found out that original music wasn't being nurtured in that part of the world. "The cover bands in Perth at that point were very heavy rock bands," Garry says. "It was all blues based. And we showed up playing weird, funky, Little Feat stuff. We could do that if we wanted. And we did to get by, but what we didn't do is go through the local booker to get our gigs." Tim talked them into a weekly residence at the Broadway Tavern, convincing

Peter Marsden, the one-armed proprietor, that they'd draw regular crowds. Marsden was as mercenary and unforgiving as a slot-machine; he was terrifying, donning tiny khaki shorts, pulled-up white socks, shiny black loafers, stained tank-tops, and a sour attitude, but he let them play away.

This residence at the pub became what their huge gigs did later: an event, an evening, that no one forgot. One night the band threw a costume party—they dressed up and everyone who showed up in costume got something special, called free admission. Andrew Farriss wore a chicken costume. "I remember opening the show, playing 'Long Train Running' by the Doobie Brothers, wearing this chicken suit. It really tested the limits of what I could handle. Not only was I dressed like a chicken, I was a drunk, stoned chicken, playing guitar with these wings attached to me." Kirk was a doormouse, Tim was Louis XVI, Jon was a jester, Garry was Henry VIII, and Michael was an Arab. "It was the only costume Michael would be," Andrew says. "You know, he had to look cool." The guy who looked least cool that night was a friend of the band who shall remain nameless. Said dude showed up suited up as Bugs Bunny, complete with feet sculpted of plaster of paris. Unlike Bugs, their bud lost his cool, got drunk, and fell out like Elmer Fudd on a bender. "When I walked outside after the gig, he was vomiting in the gutter," recalls Andrew. "It was so surreal. One of his feet was broken, but his ears were still on. His head was between his knees and he was making a huge scene."

Andrew was the only one who had done what most parents of boys in bands would encourage their sons to do: line up a career he could fall back on once his rockin' days were done. "I was going to get a business management degree at the Western Australian Institute of Technology," he says. "That was going to be my life and the band was going to be a part-time thing. I put it off when we moved to Perth, but later I was taking a class-by-mail kind of thing, earning credits toward a business degree. There was no way I was going to live in the house with the other guys. I didn't want that bohemian kind of existence, where it's all beer and girls. I was trying to keep a day job."

The house shared by Garry, Michael, Tim, and Kirk was basically a rock dorm. The living room was a mattress-insulated rehearsal bunker and the bedrooms were used, well, for what bedrooms are for. "You had to go through my room to get to Michael's room," Kirk recalls. "And he had this girlfriend who was a bit of a punk rocker and they'd just root like rabbits." Punk was the scene in Perth, though it was more for effect than cause. "A real punk in the late seventies was someone who lived in England and was part of the working class," Kirk says. "Anyone else in the world at that time was just acting the part. And there were plenty of them in Perth. I remember being at one party and watching some guy walk up to us, stick a safety pin through his cheek, stand there as it started to bleed, and walk off. There was a lot of that down there in those days."

There were also a lot of hard drugs, something the boys from the Northern Beaches had never seen before. They'd learned to love pot and all the mellowness it might lend them—but they'd find none of that in Western Australia. The drug of choice, which none of them chose to sample at the time, was heroin. The only other narcotic readily available was a strain of speed the local alchemists conjured out of medication prescribed to horses. It wasn't pretty and it made for unabashed parties at all times of day and night. Though it once laid their singer out ("Michael was once bedridden for three days because he'd done too much," Kirk says. "He just sat there awake but unable to move.") it also inspired furious rehearsals. "We used to take it and practice like madmen," Kirk says. "We'd go for hours and hours. It got so bad that we were eventually kicked out of our house. The guy next door died, and I'm sure we had nothing to do with that, but the landlord blamed us for it. He said that this man was well aware of all of the parties, the noise, and all of the schoolgirls coming around, who would spend a few hours in Michael's room before they'd ride their bikes home, which caused this man to die."

The boys were evicted from their house and soon after, they were, in essence, evicted from Perth. The Perth music scene was myopic, a place where innovation was intrusion, and tradition was law: covering the top pop songs of the day was the rule, and since they didn't follow suit, before long the Farriss Brothers were bounced out of the pub scene. They refused, as usual, to play by the rules—and the rule makers did not take to it kindly. For example, when the band was told that only cover bands got work, they'd play the most obscure B-sides Steely Dan, Traffic, and Todd Rundgren ever recorded. Their sets were so off the radar that the promoter and pub owners most often thought the original songs the band stubbornly kept in their show—hazy jams with names like "Hour in the Shower" were covers. "We'd really begun to develop our own sense of who we were and what we wanted to play," Andrew says. "That was the best thing about going to Perth. Unfortunately, it also meant we eventually had to leave."

Every local show in Perth was booked by one man, Dez Jose, who did not at all dig the Farriss Brothers. He soon refused to book them, leaving the band no option but to ignore him and go directly to the pub owners. Aside from their aforementioned weekly residency at the Broadway Tavern (the site of the infamous costume concert), and the odd one-off gig, Dez had blackballed them from playing anywhere else in town—and they were soon truly starving artists. It wasn't easy, but they made ends get close to meeting. Nothing's changed much in the Perth live scene since the late seventies: Dez, now quite an elderly fella, has only recently retired, but his booking company still has a monopoly over the local clubs. When he was contacted to arrange an interview for this book, he did not recognize the names of any of the members of INXS, nor did the band name ring a bell. He also seemed completely unaware that they have sold more albums than almost any other Australian rock band in history.

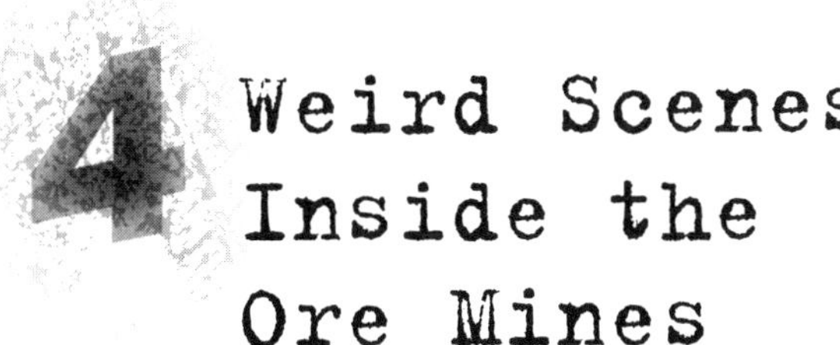

4 Weird Scenes Inside the Ore Mines

WITH PERTH CLOSED FOR BUSINESS, the boys were obliged to travel farther and farther from home to make a living, in which, on a good day, on the right corners, they might have hauled in as much cash pretending to be homeless. They'd drive hundreds of miles to play pubs, school dances, university gymnasiums—anywhere they could—and if they couldn't find friendly fans with ample floor space to loan them for the night, they'd endure the long haul home. They often did so anyway—on weeknights, they'd arrive back in Perth just in time to drop Jon off at school. "The poor guy, he was falling asleep at his desk all the time," Garry says. "He didn't stand a chance from the start—he was well on his way to failing out."

It didn't bode well for Jon's report card, but the group's travels did provide all of them the kind of Kerouacian education no schoolbook can deliver. Western Australia is rich with natural beauty and resources—it is where some of the nation's award-winning wines are produced, where the famous red-tinted deserts stretch for miles, where there are pristine surf breaks and so much impossibly gorgeous beach that you might find a new one to have to yourself each and every day. It is still high on unspoiled spaces and low on population, but in 1978, it was even more of a raw frontier, one where *Easy Rider* met *The Endless Summer.* "We used to play a pub called the

Busselton in Bunburry that was close to a fairly big oil refinery," Andrew says. "This town has a gorgeous coastline, so it drew all of the surfers, but there was also a very rough, industrial working-class population there."

One night, while the Farriss Brothers played, a notorious local biker gang showed up in the pub, causing the surf cats in the audience to ride the next crest right on home. "This very obvious change came over our audience," Jon says. "All of the surf locals, who always came to see us, started looking around the room and then started, sort of, casually leaving. It was getting on my nerves." The room thinned out and soon it was clear why—a very significant number of "bikies," as they're called, were in the house, all of whom were paying close attention to the band. A few of the scariest of them took chairs from the bar and planted themselves at the foot of the stage. "It was a bit like that scene from *Animal House* where the white kids walk into the black bar while Otis Day and the Knights are playing," Jon says. "They were all looking at us. I think one said, 'What you made of there, boy? You play country?'" They were willing to starve for their art, but they weren't willing to die for it—this was a fight-or-flight situation and luckily the boys knew enough songs to turn the pub into a biker barbeque. They knew to change the mood of their set without a formal band huddle, and their knowledge of classic rock covers kicked in—of course fear will do that too. "We knew enough Steve Miller Band songs, Elvis, and hard blues stuff to turn it around," Garry says. "It was such a bizarre, almost instant change from one audience to the other, but it turned out to be fun. Once they decided they liked us, they were cheering and really into it. I'm just glad we didn't get it wrong."

The true test of their mettle awaited the young bards inland some two thousand miles north of Perth, amid the most barren landscape on earth. At one of their increasingly rare Perth gigs, they met a man named Bob Matthews, who managed a strip mine in a desert expanse where the average temperature clocked in at around 40 degrees Celsius (104 degrees Fahrenheit). At the mines, driving trucks (whose tires were approximately fifteen feet high) down steep slopes of loose gravel was considered women's work: the men spent their days in the sun hacking at the earth with picks, shovels, and drills. Mine workers were one part mental patient and two parts outlaw, and to a crew of young band boys, they were altogether insane. The only civilization for hundreds of miles was the mining town—and like any human society on the edge of nowhere, it was utterly *Lord of the Flies.* It was entirely Australian, and far too *Mad Max.*

Mr. Matthews offered the boys three thousand dollars, which was a lot at the time (and a fortune to them), to be flown up to Mount Goldsworthy, where they'd stay for a week, and entertain the workers on two consecutive weekends. They would also be able to play another mining colony, Shay Gap, which was a hundred miles farther into the inland abyss. If they chose to drive themselves up, Bob would pay them five thousand dollars. They were young, ambitious, and poor, so the band unanimously decided to drive. It was a stupendously foolish decision, even in retrospect, even if you ask them, even though they survived.

They rented two vans and set out, with Kirk, who has always been the most obsessively organized and budget-minded (he was their uncontested accountant for years) of the group, plotting their course. "Kirk had mapped out a very direct way to go, but Tim grabbed the map and discovered that we could cut our travel miles in half if we took a smaller, local highway," Andrew says. "We thought it was a great idea, because the less gas we bought, the more money we made." Halfway into their trek, they realized that they were doomed by the scenic route, as they watched the quality of said highway, number 95, disintegrate until it was but a red dirt track pointed at the horizon. "It was so incredibly rough, just holes and rocks the entire way," Andrew says. "And we were too far to turn back, so we kept on." When the pilgrims were within drops of empty, they were lucky enough to find a gas station (rather a shack with a pump), where they slept until it opened. The three Farriss boys had sleeping bags, so they crashed on the dirt, and enjoyed the impossibly starry sky. "It really was amazing going to sleep out there," Jon says. "Except that I woke up in the morning to the most horrible smell and buzzing all around me. I rolled over, and I was staring at a dead kangaroo. It was so dark out there at night that we didn't even see that we'd gone to sleep directly beside a huge pile of dead kangaroos that they'd cleaned off the road."

The next day didn't prove much better. At one point, along a particularly bumpy stretch, the lead van's back doors flew open and despite fervent headlight blinking and horn honking, they didn't realize that all of the gear had fallen out onto the road, slowly and surely, for nearly a mile. "There weren't cell phones back then and we didn't have walkie-talkies,"

Andrew says. "We just had to wait until they realized what was going on." And later, the extreme band van tour took a potentially lethal turn when one vehicle got a flat tire. "I was nervous because we only had one spare between us, so if we got another flat, we'd be fucked," Andrew says. "We were in the middle of the desert where it is so hot that you can very easily die of exposure. There aren't gas stations very often and the only other people out there were truck drivers, who you'd see infrequently." While the tire was being changed, Andrew had the kind of mystical desert experience that made Jim Morrison the rock shaman he was. "We're all sitting there, worried about this little tire, and I look out into the horizon and I think it's a mirage, but I see this man walking toward us, out of the desert," he says. "He was an old Aboriginal man with a long beard and a spear walking in bare feet on this boiling hot sand. He was a hunter following the migratory paths his people had walked for hundreds of years." Andrew was transfixed. "He walked up to us, took us in, kind of nodded and turned at an angle away from the road and walked off into the desert. He was completely comfortable in this environment and I was amazed. I'm sitting there worried about a tire, nervous about where we're going, but what is this? Where is *he* going?"

They were going to a land that was simple and strange at once, a land with few, non-negotiable laws: 1) don't steal anything, 2) don't touch another man's wife, and 3) don't fight, because there aren't any rules if you do. Goldsworthy was an outpost where the American Wild West met the apocalypse: a giant mess hall, a long row of cell-like workers' quarters, and a shorter row of shacks that housed prostitutes. "Everyone lived in these little air-conditioned boxes, just enough room for a bed and that was it," Garry says. "There was a communal bathroom, and it was full of the biggest spiders I'd ever seen." There were no trees, no brush, no other mammals, just nothing but more nothing as far as the eye could see. The workers there were all on the run, either from the law, their family, or any number of insane entanglements—the kind only the bottom of a whiskey bottle could make sense of.

A band in town was a luxury; a welcome reprieve, or rather a fresh catalyst to the eating, drinking, fighting, and fucking that typically occupied the population's nonworking hours. The bands that made the trip were treated like royalty and were given, upon arrival, a Rastaman-sized bag of reefer. "It was great because we had a lot of time to kill all week," Garry says. "We could smoke pot and rehearse all day—when we weren't eating." The miners' work was incredibly dangerous, so they were paid well and treated well—including a catering setup worthy of Caligula. It was run around the clock, due to the staggered schedules of the camp's workers, which well suited the Farriss Brothers' spontaneous munchies. "It really was something out of the Old Testament," Andrew says. "There would be an entire cow on a spit, incredible fresh fish flown in from the coast each day, and just about any type of cuisine you might want."

The first night the band spent in Goldsworthy, they were grateful to have arrived alive and glad to see that they weren't given the typical town greeting. "There was an Irish guy who had arrived there a week before, and our first night, the other workers went around buying this guy drinks until he was completely unconscious," Andrew says. "Then they took him, shaved all of his hair—on his head, his body, everywhere—drove him into the desert and left him there to walk home once he woke up." The Irish are known for their strong stock and this man alone has sent their value up: he overcame deathly heat, flesh-searing sunburn (with a fair complexion, mind you), dermis-wide razor rash, and a hangover to sideline W. C. Fields. And he made it to work the next day.

The band enjoyed the sanctioned time to rehearse and the free meals, but they didn't always follow the rules. Michael, for one, had a hard time digesting the "Don't get with another man's wife" idea. "Michael nearly got himself killed," Kirk recalls. "He was with some guy's wife or girlfriend while this huge guy stood outside pounding on the door. The girl had to crawl through the tiny window above the air conditioner to get away, while the guy was basically breaking the door in." And it wasn't always Mike's fault: the female population of the mining towns was hornier than a pack of lager-filled soccer hooligans. "They were just so sexually aggressive," Garry says. "They'd be like, 'You! I've got an hour's break, come on, right now, let's get to it.'"

After one weekend set, the band was invited to a party at a small home on the outskirts of town where a strict admission policy was in effect. "This woman standing at the door would passionately kiss every man that came into the party," Garry says. "Later on her husband showed up, very drunk, and caught her kissing some guy, probably thinking that's the only guy she's kissed that night. He went crazy and they started to fight all through the house." They ended up in the kitchen, where Kirk and Garry were busy passing a bong. "A few days earlier we'd shaved Kirk's head because we were bored," Garry says. "So there we were, completely out of it, while these guys thrash each other across the stove and all around us." Apparently Kirk looked far too amused in the way that the cosmically high do, and the cuckolded drunk took offense, unaware of the fact that Kirk would have reacted the same way to a nearby nuclear explosion. "The guy said, 'Baldy, you're next!'" Garry says. "And I don't even know if Kirk heard him. He was singing along to the radio, which was playing 'Dreadlock Holiday' by 10cc, and he just kept pointing at the guy, singing the chorus, going, 'Oh, no.' He's a bit like that, sort of able to be in situations where he might die, but that fact never occurs to him. It's quite beautiful to watch, actually." Garry, the bong, and Kirk slipped out the back door before it got ugly, thank God, for the sake of the band, all that weed, and all that they had yet to do.

Goldsworthy was an intense town, but Shay Gap, a truly Martian aluminum bauxite operation six hours farther into the interior by van, was even more surreal. A row of shimmering white buildings surrounded by blood-red earth, the air was hot enough to paralyze and the powerful air-conditioning in the buildings akin to an oxygen tank underwater. The egglike colony was as odd and isolated as the space station existence depicted in the late seventies sci-fi series *Space 1999.* "You'd go outside and the air would just stop you in your tracks," Tim says. "It was like walking into a wall."

The band visited the two outland outposts twice, but they were smart enough to make the second trip by plane. They were grateful for the experience and for the chance to meet people the average human wouldn't believe existed. "There was one guy in Shay Gap who collected spiders," Jon says. "His room was full of them. Australia is home to many very large and very dangerous spiders, and this guy had some of the most venomous ones as pets. He'd always have one or two of them with him, too. I remember I was doing pull-ups on the diving board of the pool in the camp and a piece of fiberglass fell into my eye and I was blinded for a moment. This guy reached his hand out to help me and when I looked at him there on the end of it was a huge wolf spider, as big as his fist. I tried to stay calm, but when he opened his mouth and showed me the pet spider he had in there, I really lost it."

Spider man's freaky fetish was completely logical compared to that of a man we'll call Captain Thong.* "There was a guy in Shay Gap who had a thing for thongs," Garry says. "We first saw him at a party, standing near the door, approaching everyone he saw wearing thongs. He'd demand you give him your left thong and because he was a huge man, everyone did. He'd take a huge bite out of it, right by the toe, then give it back and chew on it like it was steak or something. I started to realize that he did it to everyone. You'd walk around town and every pair of thongs you'd see had this chunk missing."

*** On a quick cultural note, in Australia, what Americans call flip-flops are known as thongs, not to be confused with the undergarments known for their pantyline-eliminating qualities and sexy aura.**

It took eight months for the Farriss Brothers to milk what they could out of Perth: a band identity, a confidence in their musicianship earned through endless practice, and the balls to play to any crowd in any room, anywhere, at any time. After eight months it was also clear that their drummer, Jon Farriss, was going to fail out of high school, so before he did, he dropped out to devote himself to a career in rock and roll. With little else than the primitive but decent lighting system they'd saved enough to purchase with the money they'd earned in the mining towns, the band packed into Andrew's Volkswagen Bug and Kirk's van, putting Garry's van back on the train. They shoved off for Sydney, eager to take on the big city. They didn't want to return to rule the surfy suburbs they used to play—they wanted to conquer the urban heart of it all. They'd left as schoolmates, as unstudied adolescents, but they were returning with more miles under their belt than all of the peers they'd left behind. They'd taken a giant leap and they hadn't succeeded—the only music fans that missed them in Perth was their circle of friends. But their exile and isolation cemented their persona, resolve, and ambition in the face of all odds they might encounter. And they'd need it: they weren't like any other band in Perth and never cared, and when they returned to Sydney, they found they were just as different from every act playing the pubs. They were aliens who stayed true to their vision, and as much as they were shunned in the short term, their individuality proved itself essential to their success.

A renaissance was afoot in Sydney and Melbourne, the cultural loci of the country, which ushered in the Golden Age of Australian rock. In 1976, a Brisbane band called the Saints, led by the brilliant Chris Bailey, released a song called "I'm Stranded," which by all accounts is the first punk rock song ever written and recorded. Punk was the rallying cry for suppressed blue-collar English youth, but a hemisphere away, Bailey blew the horn. It seems odd, considering that the global highways of information that we take for granted today were, back then, at best, just amoebas nurtured by nerds. But to understand Australian pop culture is to understand two things: distance and osmosis—and the petri dish effect that kicks in when they're applied in tandem.

Australia is roughly 10,000 miles (16,093 kilometers) from England, and 9,000 miles (14,484 kilometers) from the West Coast of America, the two countries with which it shares the most pop cultural similarities. It was rare, particularly at the dawn of rock and roll—the fifties through the sixties—that musical acts toured Australia, simply due to the expense of traveling the distance. Instead, music seeped into the youth of the day in a manner far ahead of the times, through odd promotional videos played regularly on Australian television late at night. "That was how we first experienced bands visually," Tim Farriss says. "You'd see some dumb footage of the Kinks or the Beatles walking through a park while the song played. They wouldn't even be singing it all the time—they'd just be like, walking around." It was a medieval version of MTV.

At the same time, Australian radio fed eager ears a fertile hodgepodge of whatever, whenever—a programming philosophy that should be instituted in American radio immediately. "There weren't many stations to listen to then," Jon Farriss says. "But the great thing that happened was that they'd be a real melting pot. On the rock station you'd hear everything from Brian Eno to Led Zeppelin to disco to punk to whatever Australian bands they'd throw in, like Daddy Cool, Spectrum, and Billy Thorpe and the Aztecs. And there was a station that played Motown, jazz, and blues."

By the seventies, Australia was known for two pop music acts of note.* The Easybeats were Australia's contribution to the sixties

*** Australia haters might argue that none of these cultural icons is truly Australian. It is true, both the Easybeats and the Bee Gees included members who were not born in Australia, but both groups came together there and were aesthetically as Australian as can be.**

British Invasion sound, scoring several international hits (years later INXS covered their song "Good Times" with fellow Aussie Jimmy Barnes for the *Lost Boys* sound track in 1987). The Bee Gees (another wildly successful Australian brother trio) were born and got their start in England, though they truly blossomed into hit-making harmonists under Australian skies.

Both of those acts deftly replicated what was happening overseas. But in the seventies, Australian bands flipped the script: they didn't copy what came over the wire from the West; instead they listened, learned, took what they liked, and made it their own. The result was an incredible spectrum of music—so much of which never did get its due around the world. But the bands whose sound was powerful enough to travel the miles changed rock and roll forever. And they couldn't have been more diverse. Within years of each other, the raw ragged blues of AC/DC, the misanthropic goth of Nick Cave (with the Birthday Party and then the Bad Seeds), and the sexed-up New Wave R&B of INXS, emerged from the same fertile, hungry, inspired turf.

All of them shared one thing in common: the "rock finishing school" of the Australian pub circuit.* In Australia, pubs and their bigger, roomier sisters, the local hotels, are different animals altogether. A pub in Australia may also be a hotel and every hotel always contains a pub, and both entities are one-stop shopping for boozy revelry. Most hotels and pubs come complete with a bottle shop, where, once a patron has decided to leave, they may buy liquor to take home or to drink on the way. The hotels do have rooms, of course, but the spirit of these establishments is closer to that of a casino: there are well-worn bars, some type of stage for entertainment, pool tables, a smoky back room full of senior citizens and slot-machines, and a restaurant/bar. And if they choose to, any of these establishments are legally free to remain open twenty-four hours a day. "In Australia, the hotel, particularly in a country town, is a meaningful culture all its own," Andrew Farriss says. "It is an ultimate destination. It is where people meet, where stories are told, where you can learn about things. It is, in some places, the heart of the community."

*** In most places, a pub (short for "public," i.e., a public meeting, eating, and drinking establishment) is a bar that may or may not serve food, which usually should only be consumed in dire straits.**

Unfortunately, these days it isn't easy to find a hotel or pub quite like the venues that hosted AC/DC, Nick Cave, the Angels, the Saints, the Models, INXS, Midnight Oil, the Divinyls, and so many more. Today, though the amenities are the same, the vibe has gone a bit IKEA, presumably to stay abreast of our modern times, and live musical acts are more often a special event than a common occurrence. In the same rooms that witnessed nascent rock history, today there are dainty dangling halogen lights, blond wood, and salads. But in the seventies and eighties, those spaces were spartan, terribly carpeted, sweaty, smoky, weathered, and packed to the rafters. Fire codes were meaningless then and no one cared—if the room could hold three hundred but thirteen hundred showed up, the promoters and owners packed them in. Typically the bar manager would turn off the air-conditioning in an attempt to sell more beer. At good gigs the rooms were so stuffed that the smart fans in the house bought pitchers of beer for themselves to avoid renavigating the crowd—which, though the rooms were at best the size of a high school gymnasium—could take close to an hour. These feral conditions bred several things. One was an enormous pile of empty glassware in the middle of the floor as the night wore on. The second was a vertical pogo style of dancing necessitated by the extreme lack of personal space. The third was a humidity level that surpassed that of the equatorial rain forest in the wet season. The fourth was that, as a result of the previous three, the young, restless, and generally teen-to-twenty-whatever audience often enjoyed a good row. It is important to mention that these crowds were in no mood to endure sub-par entertainment. Quite simply, if you didn't rock, you generally left wounded.

The hotels and pubs of Australia were the epicenter of the do-it-yourself creativity that was blooming all across the land. "The pub rock scene in the late seventies and early eighties was one of the most fertile breeding grounds for performing bands that the country ever experienced, and frankly, I think that has ever happened anywhere in the world," says Peter Garrett, frontman for the powerful, political Midnight Oil. "It came about as a result of the burgeoning pride in Australian culture, a trend which coincided with the election of the Labor government under Prime Minister Edward Gough Whitlam. They championed Australian writers, filmmakers, and other creative artists. It also coincided with the rise of the punk scene, and the do-it-yourself attitude that arose out of that. Additionally, young bands had the benefit of many places to play. We'd approach the hotel owner and tell them they could make all the money from selling beer if we could take some of the money from the admission. It just grew like wildfire. A good band could play any night of the week and didn't need any kind of radio play or television support to win their audience. You relied on your capacity to get up in front of a bunch of people and make the whole place jump."

If there is one constant in the story of INXS it's that they were always brilliantly out of time: they played funk when the pub scene was hard rock, they made videos well in advance of MTV, they eclipsed almost every band they opened for, and booked opening bands on the cusp of their peak. They remixed rock songs long before any of their peers. They were the first sexy, all-male New Wave band, and it wasn't all about their looks: they infused the scene with the copulatory heat of rhythm and blues. And they did what so many Australian bands brazenly claimed they'd do and never did: they conquered the world. Their ingredients were correct, and like any massively successful success story, their timing was right. But that could only have gotten them so far. Their real secret weapon was earned the hard way, every night, all week long for two years, until they were too fit and too hungry for any conquest their native stomping grounds could provide.

5 The Miles, the Managers, and the Start of the Crusade

THE FARRISS BROTHERS RETURNED to Sydney from Perth in early 1979, to find a music scene hardened by punk rock and pumped up by the new Australian musical testosterone. "It was very hard edged," Andrew says. "The kind of beachy vibe we'd left wasn't the thing at all, even in the Northern Beaches. The bands up there had a sound that was somewhere between AC/DC and country music." In the city, naturally, it was even harder, inspired by bands like the Angels, Midnight Oil, and Cold Chisel, no-nonsense acts who dished out hard, heady three-chord bar rock. "It was an explosive mixture of teenagers, alcohol, cigarettes, and rock music," Jon says. "Everywhere you'd go, that's what you'd find—sex, fights, and great bands." Inspired by the scene around them, the band honed their innate funk to a razor-sharp edge that would be captured on their earliest records—a style closer in spirit to early Elvis Costello or Billy Idol's first band, Generation X, than to the groove of anything they'd done before. They sped up and tightened their sound, eliminating the vibey elements of their act, such as Tim Farriss's conga and percussion playing. "We were always our own animal," Andrew says. "We've never been in, especially back then, anyone else's tennis court. If I think of who we resembled at that time and in the years to come—and we're still talking about bands unlike each other or anyone else in their day—I'd put us alongside, if I had to, bands like the Cure and Midnight Oil, and later, R.E.M. and U2."

Broke as could be, Kirk, Andrew, and Tim returned to the North Shore—and their old haunts: they took up their posts tending cars for Bill Buckle, and acting band manager Tim lined up gigs for them all over town. "The pubs were just classic back then," Garry says. "You'd walk in and your feet were stuck to the floor by years of beer-stained carpet. You'd set up in the afternoon with all the regulars sitting there, drinking beer, watching horse racing, and giving you a hard time about it."

They began to build up residencies in nearby towns, taking advantage of the new highway that cut their driving times along the coast to a manageable three or four hours. It was a good thing, too, because in those days, the round-the-clock operating hours of the pubs meant that a band could play numerous gigs a night. "We'd be booked to play shows at midnight, three, and six in the morning," Garry says. "We'd do an early gig, drive a few hours, do another, and be back home by early morning."

Before long, they became regulars at the Manly Vale Hotel, which became their turf, their local—pub, stage, and living room all wrapped up in one. It was a beer barn of a building where, in the years to come, they experienced so many rock moments that even collectively they still can't recall all of the details. It was there that Gary Morris, the band's first manager, first saw them perform. Tim Farriss first met Morris in the parking lot of another hotel—the Newport Arms—where both of them were placing handbills on windshields that advertised their bands' upcoming shows. Morris had been managing Midnight Oil since 1977, and the night that he met Tim, the two spent more time talking about music than distributing ads. Tim's innate charm won Morris over and soon the man who was managing one of Australia's most successful acts checked out the Farriss Brothers' show at the Royal Antler. And soon after, Gary Morris began booking gigs for them.

Midnight Oil had quickly become an act that filled venues all along the coast with a thousand or more of their devoted. Their machine was running well, but Morris wanted to expand, and he'd found a band captivating enough to support the Oils as well as able to front their own tour, which would keep the Oils' road crew employed when his main priority required time off. In short, the Farriss Brothers were everything he was looking for.

He asked the Farriss Brothers to be the support band on a short Midnight Oil tour of the coast and soon usurped management duties from Tim. The only problem he had with them was their name, something he soon transformed through a mystical convergence of television, breakfast jelly, and joints. "I was watching TV, having a bit of a session with the lighting guy for the Oils, one day," Morris says. "And I saw a commercial for a brand of jam called IXL. Their ad featured a guy who said, 'I excel in all that I do.' I'd recently seen the English band XTC when they toured Australia, and I loved their name: XTC—Ecstasy. I'd also been telling Midnight Oil that the way they should market themselves as a group was to be inaccessible—just impenetrable beyond understanding." Morris's thoughts gelled in the way that supreme genius and its inverted reflection, drug-blind brilliance, typically do. His crystal vision was a bit of both. "In that moment, I put all those thoughts together. The name needed to be letters, but make a word. I put the IXL jam commercial together with XTC and the concept of a band that was inaccessible and I had it: INXS."

The name ruled and the band went for it. "It was an exciting new start," Jon Farriss says. "We had been playing together for two and a half years, but by changing our name, we were able to wipe ourselves clean of the past." But Morris didn't stop at the name—he had an aesthetic component to his epiphany that fell somewhere between Devo and the Village People. On stage, the "back line"—Garry, Jon, and Andrew—were to wear white overalls. Kirk was to dye his hair black, spike it, don a blue mechanic's jumpsuit, and affix a Band-Aid to the bridge of his square black glasses. He was also to spend every opportune moment making weird faces at the audience. "It was terrible," Kirk says. "It was so hot in the gigs that the dye would start running down my face by the third song. And I could only afford cheap dye, so I'd have to do it three times a week." Kirk had it easy compared to Tim, whose outfit, considering the swampy performance conditions, was sadistic: a yellow fisherman's slicker, clear plastic pants, and white underwear. "I never did wear it on stage," he says. "I broke a full sweat just trying it on." And then there was Michael, whose job it was to hammer home the message that INXS was a puzzling force to be pondered and adored from afar. "The idea was for INXS to be a band that came out, titillated the audience, and then disappeared," Morris says. "I told Michael that he needed to be strange on stage. He couldn't just be there, up front, he needed to be weird, he needed to make the audience think that he came from another place. So I gave him this idiosyncrasy to close the show. We cut the stage lights, put a spot on his face, and I told him to reach his hand out to the audience and to think of that as squeezing the crowd as he would a female butt. And then, as the band's final good-bye, he'd say, 'Koomooloomayo Yong Style.' It meant absolutely nothing. But it created a bit of mystique. And it worked, you know."

To drive the point home, Morris and his lighting man arranged stationary white spotlights aimed skyward along the perimeter of the stage. The beams were angled so that they encased the group in kind of a white light cage—symbolically encasing INXS in a space the audience could not enter and dared not understand. The lighting scheme was well-received by the band, far more than the onstage costumes Morris had devised for them. "Those of us in overalls kept those because they did look pretty cool," Jon says. "But the whole attitude where we weren't supposed to talk or even really acknowledge the audience didn't really work for us. Michael was only supposed to let them know if we were playing an original song or a cover and tell them he hoped that they were okay while we played inside our light prison."

It was as weird as it sounds in the retelling, but INXS's strange duds and white-light box did set the band apart. Morris even did one better: he landed them a gig opening up for Midnight Oil, the hottest band of the day. And the oddity that is INXS served them well on that mission.

Midnight Oil has always been a very straight-ahead band: they were, even then, never into drugs and drink, and have always been clear that the band is a platform to promote their political views. They are concerned with the rights of the Aboriginal population of Australia, the misuse of natural resources, and the plight of the underprivileged. They drew an audience that might never have gone to an INXS show—INXS's message was broader, speaking to universal human truths, with a goal no more complex than bringing joy through music. It wasn't a good match, in theory, but in the long run it worked: INXS was so good at winning over whatever crowd lay at their feet through sheer intensity, showmanship, and heart, that the Oils provided them with a chance to make new fans, even though the odds were against them.

For a time, Midnight Oil and INXS were both managed by Gary Morris, until a philosophical realignment changed everything. In 1979, Gary

Morris attended a Billy Graham Crusade outside of Sydney, where he saw the televangelist preach his holy trinity—Christ, conversion, and capitalism—on a sixty-foot stage before a flock of eighteen-thousand. At the time he noted that Graham's lighting rig, sound system, and audience were far bigger than Midnight Oil's. He was a skeptic then, listening in as the preacher man went on about heaven, hell, earth, sin, repentance, and how little time was left for those who had yet to join the home team. "I was used to the rock-and-roll, surf-and-sex culture and little else," Morris says. "I felt very out of place but was amazed by the reverence of these godly people."

When Graham asked the unconverted to gather on the grass of the arena, an intrigued Morris did, so as to engage one of Billy G's pamphlet-toting field scouts in a Socratic debate. "That guy couldn't answer any of my questions, and just walked off after a few minutes, so I stuck the piece of paper he'd given me in my pocket and didn't think about it again. I left after that and went to see the Oil's gig that night." But Christ wasn't done with Gary; in fact, J.C. was just getting started. "I began to wake up every morning with Christ on my mind," Morris says. "Everywhere I turned I'd see crosses, or stickers about Christ, or find myself in front of a church not knowing how I got there." As he tells it, a succession of events led Morris to a cemetery one night, where he raised his arms skyward and proclaimed that he'd been wrong, but now he believed. "It changed my whole outlook on life and I lost all desire to smoke dope, have sex, drink, and everything else I'd been doing. I was changed." Morris did his best to convert everyone else in his life: he dragged his girlfriend to church, he tried to talk his surf buddies off the board and into the pew, and he pitched his newfound faith to Midnight Oil. Everyone in his life regretfully declined.

INXS was, of course, among those Morris tried to enlist on behalf of Christ. "I remember the day Gary called us to come to his house for a band meeting," Garry Beers says. "We were so excited, we thought he had great news for us." The band showed up anticipating news of a record deal or at least a free meal. When Morris herded them into his car, they were nearly manic, anticipating good news and good times. Not quite. "We drove about two hundred feet," Andrew says. "We went out of his driveway and into a parking lot around the corner." Morris told them that from here on out, it was the Lord or bust. His way, or the highway. "He told us that unless we wanted to change our ways and become the world's biggest Christian band he could no longer manage us," Kirk says. "He wanted us to write songs about Christ and to promote a drug-and-alcohol free, no-sex-before-marriage, proper Christian lifestyle. He was very convincing and for a moment I think we might have done it. Then he got onto strange terrain. Once he started talking about ethereal beings and the kingdom of heaven, all of us, simultaneously, were like, 'Right . . . All right, then.' Which was followed by the sound of car doors opening."

Morris did what a Christian on a mission should do—he gave everything away, and in the case of INXS, earned double saint points by handing them to his worst enemy on a platter. "Chris Murphy was a young booking agent and he had long been my archrival," Morris says. "He was the agent we rejected for Midnight Oil, which started this war among a few young agencies at the time. The Oils were one of those bands who chose to cut the agencies out and book their gigs directly, and Murphy hated that. He was always a nasty fellow who tried to cross us whenever he could. But I knew he understood the business and I knew he would take good care of INXS." In the history of business transactions wherein one party cheerfully trades a tangible, untapped resource for a comically minute fraction of its worth, one bill of sale on par with Gary Morris's release of INXS comes to mind: the "sale" of Manhattan Island for sixty Dutch guilders, which, historians say, is equivalent to about twenty-four bucks.

"I wasn't sure that Gary Morris was serious," Chris Murphy says. "I was a booking agent and we'd worked together for years. We'd been rivals more often than not and out of nowhere he came to my office, talking about his conversion and asking me to take over INXS as their manager. I thought he was pulling some prank, so I went with him to see them play. . . . He said he'd just spent four hundred dollars on posters and if I reimbursed him, they were all mine. I wasn't even sure I wanted to be a manager to anyone, but who could refuse a band like that for four hundred bucks?" For four hundred dollars, Chris Murphy acquired what became one of the most successful bands that Australia ever produced, and for a time, the biggest band in the world.

With his earthly possessions redistributed, Morris set off on a spiritual quest, wandering Australia like a monk on a pilgrimage, relying on Christ and charity to get him through the day. His journey lasted two years, after which he strove to be of service in the Christian church, but was, to his dismay, not embraced. "They weren't inviting because they didn't really have a place for me," Morris says. "Like Jesus, I am more of a nomad who gives thanks to God on a daily basis in a way that doesn't fall into line with their institution." Instead, Morris found refuge in his former post managing Midnight Oil. And today he is a landscape developer. "I build organic communities for large private homes, rock star estates, and things like that," he says. "The Lord is the director of my life, and the bands and music business were the cross I bore in this life. And those twenty-seven years were the manure I used to fertilize my life's flower beds. They're right nice flower beds, mate. And I enjoy sitting back and smelling those roses each and every day."

Chris Murphy proved to be the seventh member INXS needed—a naive yet brazen, unrelenting business strategist with the brass balls it took to take the band from the trenches of Australia to the arenas of America. He learned as he went, blazing a trail in the business that was innovative, timely, and wildly successful. It wasn't easy and Murphy, both now and then, isn't known as one who always makes nice to make his point; he was often bombastic, uncompromising, and sometimes cruel. He left a line of enemies behind him as long as the line of friends in front of him, but over fifteen years Chris Murphy and INXS took it to the top, from a starting point that makes their journey that much more of a feat to be applauded.

Born into a family of talent agents, Chris Murphy was knee-deep in the business years before he grew short-hairs. "When I was ten years old, my dad took me out of school to go on tour with him. He told me that I'd learn more in those two weeks than I'd ever learn in school," Murphy says. The headliner on the tour was a comedian named Ray Seeger, the half-time entertainment was an exotic dancer named Uki, and the opener was a group of Russian acrobats. "I got to watch the acrobats and some of Seeger's act, until he got onto the dirty jokes," Murphy says. "But whenever it was Uki's turn to perform, my dad tapped me on the shoulder and sent me to a dressing room. I didn't understand it then because he called her a dancer and I couldn't figure out why I wasn't allowed to watch dancing." That trip changed Chris's life: he toured the country, learned to shoot kangaroos with

Band meeting. *Left to right:* Michael, Garry, Andrew, manager Chris Murphy, Jon, Kirk, Tim.

his dad, and got caught in ferocious dust storms crossing the desert regions. He got a taste for life outside of the box before he even knew there was one.

In the late seventies and early eighties, while still in his early twenties, Chris fell in to the family business, booking rock bands as the scene started to explode. He came from the surf scene and understood INXS's roots and vibe immediately. "The night Morris offered them to me, I told him that I'd take them midway through the third song. I stood there, thinking, 'This is pretty funky. This kid up front is weird. This band plays really, really well,'" Murphy says. "What Morris didn't realize was that I only intended to take them on as their booking agent. I didn't want to be a manager." Murphy went home that night and told his then wife, Wendy, the mother of his two daughters, about the band, and, since she was curious to see her husband's new charges, the couple went to see INXS a few nights later in Pembrook, a rural suburb an hour from Sydney. The venue was a rugby stadium, and on a big stage, Murphy saw the future. "They were really impressive that night," he says. "So I went backstage to meet them and they were really nice guys. I liked them even more when I found out they listened to stuff like the Average White Band. We had a meeting and I agreed to be their booking agent and take them to the next level, but I wasn't going to sign on as manager. I told them that when the time came I'd find them a manager. Then I remember, at the end of that meeting Tim said something that made me realize these guys, as people, were different. He said, 'Is it okay if, the next time we have a meeting, we do something more casual and friendly? We could have a barbeque together, don't you think?' That was the attraction for me, that mentality made me think that I should go for it."

Murphy booked the band in bigger venues, playing with established bands that drew dedicated audiences. INXS furthered his reputation as an agent with young, top talent, which soon attracted the attention of Michael Browning, a well-known manager keen on starting a record label. Browning had spent the late seventies in America managing AC/DC during their rise to riff iconoclasts, via albums like *High Voltage, Let There Be Rock,* and *Highway to Hell.* His goal upon his return home was to nurture the local scene—and find his next international act. "Chris gave me a cassette of two or three INXS tracks and one of them was 'Just Keep Walking,' which I thought was interesting," Browning says. "I went to see them play in an old converted movie theater in Sydney. Michael was so charismatic, he was this young Jagger even back then, but the band needed some direction. They were almost like a cabaret show. They'd change instruments and it was too showy. They were a group of talented people showing off their talent who needed a bit of direction. Whether or not it fit the song or the band, they'd play every instrument they knew how to play."

Browning saw raw talent in INXS, but he was much more interested in signing the other bands Murphy represented as a booking agent. The two settled upon a deal where each owned a piece of a record label they named Deluxe: Murphy brought the bands and Browning provided the cash to fund the recordings. INXS 's first single, "Simple Simon/We Are the Vegetables," charted in France and sparked the notion that the sound these Aussie boys were crafting might have more to do with the world at large than the scene at home.

It seemed that they were the only ones to think so when INXS recorded their first album, *INXS,* for Deluxe in early 1980. "I only had two directions for them artistically," Browning says. "One was to dirty it up a bit. They sounded too clean and nice back then. The other was to be more laid-back. They played everything so fast in the beginning. Other bands played fast punk and rock at the time, but that wasn't INXS—they were a groove-based rock band. I remember telling them, 'Get into a groove, slow down. You're recording a song called 'Just Keep Walking'; it's about walking. Imagine you're in a video, walking—not running.'" The album is INXS wired to the max: "On a Bus" and "Just Keep Walking" are taut post-punk stomps, as anthemic as the band would be, without the lush musicality they were capable of.

Deluxe Records gave INXS a budget of $10,000 to record the first album. To stay within the meager budget, they had to record from midnight to dawn at Trafalger Studios in Annandale, Sydney, usually after doing one or more gigs earlier that night. They were also only given a couple of weeks to record and mix the album. Most of the songs had been pretty well road tested and were put down live fairly quickly. The producer elect was a seasoned bass player named Duncan McGuire who, among other bands, was one of the founding members of the distinctive jazz/rock outfit, Ayers Rock. McGuire was a very gentle soul who had had his fair share of battles with demons over the years. His late night beverage of choice throughout the sessions was a large mug of coffee amply dosed with scotch. One night, Duncan was dramatically raising one of the faders on the mixing desk when he knocked his precious elixir all over—and through—it. Time was in short supply, so Duncan and the band had to painstakingly pull the mixing console apart and dry its innards with cotton balls before the session could go on.

Given that they recorded during the graveyard shift, there were a few times when Duncan's elixir was perhaps a bit too caffeine free: he literally fell asleep mid mix. On one of these occasions, close to sunrise, Tim and Kirk, the only band members still at the studio, were unable to wake Duncan. So they did what they could: Kirk hit the stop button on the tape machine and they went home, leaving Duncan blissfully asleep, face down on the mixing desk.

The resulting album was raw and managed to capture some of the energetic live sound the band was developing.

At Chris's insistence, the album's "authorship" was credited to the whole band. The self-titled debut was the only INXS album where the writing credits and royalties were split equally among the members.

Murphy and Browning set about increasing the band's exposure and making them the most popular act on the Aussie tour circuit. But they had their work cut out for them. "I know Chris will concur that they weren't immediately accepted," Browning says. "Sydney is often the same these days—if you're too good it actually works against you. You're considered pretentious." The duo had a few other groups on their label—the Numbers and a Perth group called the Dugites—that generated far more interest than the band that they knew had the most talent. "It was hard to get the media behind INXS," Browning says. "The media really didn't like them. The cool inner-city journalists and radio stations didn't care for them at all. They really were perceived to be uncool."

From the start, the band was never part of a scene, so they gigged like madmen until the world got the message. "I've never seen a band so intent on taking care of business, working really hard to make every gig the best it could be," Browning says. "They turned their house into a workshop: they'd rehearse there; they learned to fix their own gear. They'd go out to the neighborhoods where they had gigs days before the show to put up posters. People wonder why some bands make it and some don't. The answer is simple: hard work."

Murphy agrees with Browning on a few of those points, but remembers history a bit differently. "He'd managed AC/DC, so I thought he'd be a great mentor to me as I became a manager, but I don't think he ever liked INXS," Murphy says. "I don't think he got their chemistry as a band. He kept saying, 'I see Mick Jagger, but where are the Rolling Stones?' I used to tell him that they aren't a rock band and if they were, they'd have a five-year career. I saw them as having a groove-based, international sound more interesting than any band in Australia at the time. When I agreed to bring my best bands to the label, the one he was least concerned with was INXS."

The band and their new management/label machine were infused with the do-it-yourself ethic of the Australian rock scene of the day. It didn't matter that the press didn't like them—once their playing drew crowds too large to ignore, the critical tide, as it often does, turned in their favor. Murphy intuitively fell in with the band and did everything he could to further their growth. "After a year of playing pub gigs, I made sure that INXS only did tours, whether it was just a few cities or across the whole of Australia," Murphy says. "We chose a theme, made posters, printed T-shirts, and gave it a mood that created excitement. It made an INXS show into an event, not just another pub gig." One was the Fear and Loathing Tour, booked along coastal towns, aimed at winning fans among Murphy's old buddies. "I was a surfer and knew our band was perfect to break the surfing market," he says. "They were cool and cutting edge and everyone loved

Fear and Loathing in Las Vegas." To further bring surfers into the INXS fan club, Murphy introduced a tradition known as the moontan dance, in which they played a series of gigs booked for the first night of a full moon. In surfing circles, a moontan dance was a surf goof in which wave riders ran around under a full moon in all their glory. "You just ran around in the nude under a full moon," Murphy says. "I don't think everyone in the band knew what it was when they agreed to the name. But they liked it even more when they found out."

Murphy wasn't sure that he was willing to manage INXS full-time and leave his post as booking agent and burgeoning record executive. But he soon found that the band's camaraderie, excitement, mission, and vision were everything he'd been looking for. They were his vehicle, his future, his friends, and he realized he'd be a fool not to leave his office job to manage them. When he did, he informed Michael Browning that he could not be both INXS manager and a partner in their record label. Soon after, Murphy hired Gary Grant, a character he knew from the scene, to be his partner. Grant and Murphy were birds of a feather: music-loving surfers hungry to make a career of management. Grant and Murphy were the best of friends back then; they lived, breathed, and sweated INXS.

Most of the band's promotional innovations occurred in the management office, where Murphy and Grant literally cooked up ideas. "Everyone who worked for me worked like a dog—in at nine a.m., eat your lunch at your desk. But every night at six-thirty p.m., it was company policy that everyone was allowed to have a joint, some beer, some wine, or whatever they liked," Murphy says. "Most of INXS's tour campaigns were designed around a table after six-thirty." One of their classic ideas was the Una Brilliante Banda de Musica Amenizara Espectaculo tour, which was advertised on a poster featuring a bullfighter in action and the aforementioned title running as a border around the edge. In English, it roughly means, "A spectacular show by a brilliant musical band." And to further their cred, Murphy, through a talent agent friend in Los Angeles, got Cheech Marin to record a radio promo for the tour. "I had no money—I think I offered up one hundred bucks," Murphy says. "I just asked my friend to bring a tape recorder to his house and have him read the name of the tour in Spanish and do our ad. And he did it."

The History of Andrew Harriss

ANDREW FARRISS, by anyone's standards within INXS, is known as the quiet one. He's also, to some of them, the band's Brian Wilson: the shy multi-instrumentalist genius responsible for most of the music and none of the fanfare. He is the sensitive thinker who worries, analyzes, and considers the angles of everything endlessly. He is a control freak who never feels that he is ever doing enough for his band or his family, and who has a hard time enjoying success. When his band enjoyed their first Top 5 song in the United States, "What You Need," off *Listen Like Thieves* in 1986, Andrew pondered while everyone else celebrated. "It took me a while to figure out why I wasn't happy about it," he recalls. "The thing was, if you're at Number Five, you can still go up to Number One and that's something to look forward to. But after that the only direction you can go is down. And in order for us to do better than Number Five, we would have to write a song as good, if not *better* than, 'What You Need.' It struck me that in achieving your goals you're also losing something. It had felt like our career had been a game of cat and mouse, and suddenly we were catching the mouse. Or was the cat catching us?" Andrew's pensive trepidation also extends to

Alias*: Andrew Farriss

Born: March 27, 1959

Instruments: piano, synthesizers, guitar, harmonica, bass

Married: April 22, 1989, to Shelley Blanks

Children: Grace, Josephine, and Matthew

First Bands: Krauss, Merlin Circle, Dr. Dolphin

Sports: cricket, surfing, Tai Chi

* Andrew Harriss is the only known alias Andrew has ever used to hide his true identity when checking into a hotel. It's not very tricky, but apparently it always worked.

airplane and automobile travel—he is known for staying awake and sitting beside the bus driver during the band's overnight trips. He once became so panicked on a long plane flight that then manager Chris Murphy nearly had to pin him in his seat to keep Andrew from trying to jump out of the plane.

Andrew was a musician and songwriter at a very young age, perhaps because his mother gave him his own copy of the Beatles' "Hey Jude" for Christmas when he was eight. When he was nine he began to take piano lessons, and by his teens had led a succession of bands. He chose the name Krauss for his first band because, to his thirteen-year-old-mind, the word had a European sound to it that he believed would capture people's ears. Next came Merlin Circle, a short-lived affair, and finally, Dr. Dolphin, the group in which he and Michael Hutchence began to write and perform together. The first song Andrew can remember writing with Michael was called "River." Some of the other titles were "Those Four Boys," presumably about the four members of Dr. Dolphin, "In the City," "Your Room," the cryptically titled "Lyle Is a Dyfe," "Set Me Free," and the very precocious "Instrumental in E Minor."

Andrew and Michael were avid readers, and these early songs were informed by the knowledge they were picking up from Kahlil Gibran and Hermann Hesse. Andrew is such an avid reader that back then, his father had him pegged as a future professor. "I did think Andrew might become an academic," Dennis Farriss says. "After high school, he even enrolled in music at the University of Western Australia, while he was already touring with the band. He started classes, but he was a bit more streetwise than all the kids he met up there at Uni. He came home one day and said, 'Dad, I can't stand them. They're all puffed-up jokers. I can't get along with them.' And that was about as far as it went."

It's clear that Andrew isn't quiet because he's got nothing to say; quite the contrary: he's got so many thoughts coursing through his head that he remains silent until he's sorted it all out. And sometimes, the breakneck pace of life in a rock band doesn't always allow for ample time to reflect. "Andrew used to drive me crazy," Chris Murphy says. "For example, after we'd had a band meeting at my house and decided unanimously that we needed to go tour America to build on our success at MTV back in the early eighties, everyone left in high spirits. A few minutes later there was a knock on my door and it was Andrew. He'd driven around the block and come back and told me how he thought going to America was a risky choice. I'd just spent nine hours with him and the band and he hadn't said anything about it. But that's Andrew. I only got him to agree once I promised him that if I thought it wasn't working, he'd be the first to know."

A no-nonsense musician, composer, and performer at heart, Andrew was often opposed to some of the more cutting-edge musical excursions that his writing partner Michael Hutchence was intent on bringing into the band's repertoire. With *Dekadance,* a cassette-only EP released in Australia in 1984, following *The Swing,* INXS first experimented with dance remixes of their songs. Michael, who was into rap and dance music before most of his bandmates, worked with Chris Murphy to hire remixers to craft club cuts for the band on every album to follow, and they were one of the first bands of their stature to do so. Andrew, however, was entirely against it. "I almost threw Andrew in front of a train once," Chris Murphy says. "He doesn't know this, but he was that close to death. We were in Tokyo and I was so excited to tell him how we'd done all these club remixes of 'Original Sin' and how it would get INXS to a whole new audience. He hated the idea. He said it ruined the music and that he refused to sign off on it. I really could have killed him. It took forever but we talked him into it." Despite this, Murphy is the first to say that Andrew is dear to his heart. "He's a worrier, but a sweet worrier," Chris says. "There's never malice to it. And without Andrew, none of us would be here today."

Andrew is also a man known for speaking his mind. As a younger man, this was often problematic. Andrew, as primary songwriter, and Michael, as front man and primary lyricist, were charged with the chore of giving every interview in the early days—until Andrew let a stray thought loose on the radio. "I can't remember where it was, but Andrew was live on the radio and casually mentioned that the band could break up at a moment's notice, maybe even tomorrow," Chris Murphy says. "I started getting calls instantly. I had to quietly assure the record company that Andrew would no longer do interviews. I never told him that, so as the years went on, he'd always ask me why he didn't have a higher profile or why he didn't do more press. I told him the truth: 'You're really good at what you do. You shouldn't spend your free time doing press, you should spend your free time writing music.'"

Music has always been Andrew's passion, expression, and innate language. And in Michael Hutchence he met a most unlikely collaborator. The two men are complete opposites: Andrew is a homebody and Michael was a social butterfly. But that opposition brought the best out of both men. "Andrew is the musical engine room of the band," says his wife, Shelley. "He and Michael and Kirk were the ones driving the vision and Chris Murphy tied it all together. But Andrew was always the one filling in the gaps. He's a real control freak; there's a lot of ego tied up there and he's always been very tense about it. Michael used to always tell him to stop living like he was a sixty-year-old man. And Andrew would say, 'Yeah, well, I want to be sixty someday.' They were a couple of opposites, like Tom and Jerry, Bob Hope and Bing Crosby, or Fred Flintstone and Barney Rubble." In their creative relationship, Andrew was the responsible, consistently creative one, while Michael was the organic, intuitive shining star, who might be worthless one day and a genius the next.

Andrew is not the kind of man at home on the road. In fact, he'd rather endure a root canal without anesthesia than tour the world for two years nonstop again. He loves writing and performing and enjoys the knowledge that what he's written means so much to so many. But the months of his life he's spent traveling have always been a slice of hell on earth for him. "I think the entertainment lifestyle is full of sorrow," Andrew says. "I don't like it at all. I love music. And I love people who love music. But the lifestyle is very hard on people." As INXS grew in stature and Andrew grew into a man on the road, he began to wonder if he'd be able to reap the rewards of his work. He'd always wanted a family and quiet life, and as the demands of his career grew exponentially by the year, he began to believe that his calling had cost him those dreams. "When you are on tour long enough, you begin to lose a sense of yourself," he says. "You know nothing but a very unreal reality. You are no longer your own person with your own life. You lose touch with your friends, your normal social contacts. You are constantly in a controlled, professional working environment, so your world becomes wherever you are. And your behavior adjusts according to that environment. When you get off tour, back to normal society, it's very hard to adjust to it again. How can you, when you've been through so much and are so different, while what you return to is usually just the same?"

As they had more and more to celebrate, Andrew's bandmates often chided Andrew for his discontent with the endless touring. "Sometimes he comes across as really negative, and he's often really frustrated us," Kirk says. "I'd always try to get him to lighten up. I'd say, 'Andrew, what's wrong, matey? You've got a job where consuming drugs and alcohol in the workplace is not only allowed, it's rewarded! You keep your own hours more or less and you get to write songs, perform them, and make people happy. What is wrong with that?' But Andrew has to analyze everything over and over until he understands it completely. That's just how he is and at the end of the day, we love him for it."

After INXS hit their commercial peak with *Kick* in 1987, his dreams came true personally, as well. During some time off after a long tour, he met the love of his life, Shelley Blanks, whom he married in April 1989. They met by accident: Andrew was on a date with another girl who had invited Shelley along, thinking that a big group of people would be present to have dinner and go out. Shelley showed up at a Thai restaurant to find that she was the third wheel. "They were having this intimate dinner and the girl Andrew was with, who was a friend of mine, actually had another boyfriend at the time," Shelley says. "I was really uncomfortable, but Andrew just asked me to sit and have a glass of wine." She did and within minutes the two were talking nonstop. After dinner, the trio went off to see a performance by Jenny Morris, a singer for whom Andrew had done some writing and producing. When they showed up at the gig, he behaved a bit like a puffed-up peacock. "He said to me, 'Aren't you going to buy me a drink?'" Shelley says. "It was so Andrew. I just said, 'Why should I?'"

Andrew was intrigued by Shelley's background: she was in musical theater, had attended drama school, and had been touring as a primary player in a production of a Gilbert and Sullivan operetta. Their courtship began in earnest and shortly thereafter Shelley joined Andrew on a two-week tour of Northern Australia in late 1987. "I was fully thrust into this rock-and-roll lifestyle and I barely knew this guy," Shelley says. "One of the first nights, we were in a car with Michael and Jenny Morris, and we all started to sing. They got me to sing the operetta kind of stuff I could do and it was a lot of fun."

Shortly afterward, Andrew and the band returned to America, but it was soon very obvious that this was something serious to both of them: Andrew flew Shelley out to meet him on tour in Michigan, and that is when she fully grasped the magnitude of INXS's success. "I couldn't believe it,"

Andrew with wife, Shelley, at the MTV Video Music Awards.

Shelley says. "I remember going into a restaurant after a show and Quincy Jones sitting there, and him coming over to talk to Andrew, Michael, and Jon all night. It was then that I realized that Andrew, as the musical creator, *was* the band and how much responsibility he was shouldering. The band, as I saw it, was Andrew and Kirk musically, Michael as the face and the lyrics, and Chris Murphy holding it all together. I also realized that to be with Andrew, I was going to have to learn to be with everyone else in the band."

Andrew and Shelley were married in 1989 and their first child, Grace, was born in Sydney on June 10, 1991. Their second child, Josephine, was conceived in Rome, Italy, at the tail end of INXS's first sojourn in Capri during the recording of *Full Moon, Dirty Hearts.* Shelley and their daughter, Grace, joined Andrew on that journey, and witnessed an incident that Shelley, the one who knows him best, feels is most indicative of the complex brilliance that is Andrew Farriss. The band inhabited Capri during the wet season and weathered many a storm—both those brewed by nature and those brought on by Michael Hutchence. One night, while Shelley waited for Andrew to return from the studio, a tempestuous lightning storm rolled in off the sea. When Andrew showed up at the door to their villa, his hair was literally standing on end. "He looked like he'd seen a ghost and I could feel the energy around him," Shelley recalls. "He said, 'I almost got struck by lightning. It was . . . so close to me.' He'd nearly been swallowed by this white light all around him, he said. I told him that it was so typical of him. He always has to be where the action is. One time he insisted on fixing the tiles on the roof of our house to patch a leak during a lightning storm. He was nearly struck then, too. He insists on putting himself in the line of fire and thankfully he's got angels around him protecting him. Because Andrew's got a lot of faith."

During INXS's downtime in the late eighties and early nineties, Andrew spent his time writing and producing with other Australian musicians. One project that taught him more than he could ever have dreamed was producing a record for Yothu Yindi, Australia's premier

Aboriginal band; the result was *Garma.* Andrew is very well-read in Australian history and had long been interested in the culture of the indigenous people of his country. When his success offered him the opportunity to work with the group, he jumped at the chance. He tried to bring them into the studio, and set specific times to record, but found that his Western conditioning wasn't going to fly. "They showed up when they wanted to and they didn't want to record until they were ready," Andrew says. "I was trying to be an organized producer, informing band leader Mandawuy Yunupingu that they must record during their allotted studio time. He just looked at me and said, 'No we don't. We do it when we do it. What is time? The watch is a Western thing. You must come and live with us so that you'll understand.'"

Andrew did—he spent several weeks in the outback among the primitive towns the musicians call home. The first day he was there, Andrew was taught to fashion a spear from wood, and the second, he was taught to hunt. He learned how the Aboriginals live off the land, following centuries-old traditions. He returned with wisdom that changed his life. "The little time I spent among my Aboriginal friends taught me that, contrary to society's perception of them, they're not lazy; their culture is just very good at letting go of the problems that face them," Andrew says. "They don't believe that they're more important than the earth. They believe that they are here to maintain and look after it. I wish that modern culture took the same view, because they should—these people have been here for thousands of years. To them, land can't be owned or titled to one man by a piece of paper. To them, they are born with the right to walk the migratory trails of their ancestors, and no one can take that away from them."

Andrew Farriss has never been a rock star; he's a songwriter, a multi-instrumentalist, a deep thinker, and a compassionate, introverted family man. He lost a kindred spirit in Michael Hutchence, a reflection of himself he saw in someone he could never be. "Andrew went to the morgue to see Michael's body," Shelley says. "And when he approached the coffin at the funeral, he put a pen in Michael's hand." Looking to the future, Andrew is, of course, apprehensive, but he knows he's got a strong foundation to back him up, as do his brothers in INXS. "I can't put into words how much I respect my wife, Shelley, and how much she's supported me during my darkest moments. She's a great friend and we have a great relationship; I love her very much," Andrew says. "She's been through everything I've been through but without any of the glory. I wrote 'By My Side' for her, and it describes how I feel for her as well as reveals all of the flaws in my personality—particularly in the first verse. And I'm quite sure she'd be the first to point that out."

6 Recording Can Be Fun

IN APPROACHING INXS'S SECOND ALBUM, Chris Murphy thought his fledgling band could use some direction in the studio—a craftsmanship seminar that went beyond spontaneous jamming. He enlisted Richard Clapton, a gifted Australian legend, who came from the confessional, structured seventies school of songwriting inspired by Bob Dylan and attended by Jackson Browne and Bruce Springsteen. But Clapton was known to party like the Eagles wrapped up in one man. "Richard had never produced before and wasn't sure he wanted to," Murphy says. "I didn't care; I knew his songwriting capabilities would be a good influence to give INXS more structure. In the early days the band would jam in rehearsal until a song just happened. Then they'd stand in front of an audience and play that song and see whether or not the audience jumped around. Then they'd go back and chop it up until it worked. And if it continued to work live, they'd go in and record it."

INXS's eponymous first album was a straight-ahead new wave rock album, bursting with youth, energy, and a bit of inexperience. "Just Keep Walking" was a taut, strutting anthem, full of attitude, while tracks like "In Vain" and "Learn to Smile" hinted at the skewed funk and depth of musical interplay the band was capable of. The aesthetic vision of the record wasn't complex; its rapid-fire tempo and epic sweep lacked nuance—and that is what Murphy hoped to develop on the band's next effort, under Clapton's guidance.

Clapton first saw the band play at the Paddington Green Hotel in the eastern suburbs of Sydney at midnight—though he really didn't want to. "The way Chris was describing the band, they sounded like a British pop hairdresser band," Clapton says. "He got frustrated when I told him that and just demanded that I see them. They were playing a pub that was full of middle-aged drunks because it was the only one in that suburb open twenty-four hours a day. Murphy and I were the only two people there to see the band, but that didn't matter—they played with a passion and panache that blew me away." Clapton had been a successful touring musician for twelve years already and had played to his fair share of empty rooms. He'd played through it, like all bands do, but that night, he watched INXS rock their hardest to a room full of boozers with their backs to the stage. "They treated it as if it were their last gig," he says. "It was incredible. They had this song called 'On a Bus' that I thought was one of the greatest things I'd heard in ages."

Murphy arranged for INXS to record one song with Clapton to see how they all got along. The result was "The Loved One," a cover of a sixties classic by the Australian band the Loved Ones. The single broke the Australian Top 20 in 1980, and it was a natural choice for Clapton to helm the production of INXS's entire forthcoming album, the work where they truly settled into their early sound—*Underneath the Colours.* "I was completely enamored with them," Clapton says. "I really thought that they could become one of the biggest bands in the world, completely out of nowhere. I mean, at that point, they didn't even really have an audience." Recording the single was a wonderful new experience for Clapton, but when the band first showed up to begin work on the record, he wondered whether he'd bitten off much more than he could chew. The first day in the studio, Andrew Farriss showed up with a tape, raving to Clapton that he had the greatest collection of rough songs to play him. When they popped it in the deck, however, it was clear that most of the songs existed, as do many other things, nowhere else but in Andrew's head. "He had a bunch of very abbreviated ideas—they were keyboard melodies, really," Clapton says. "I was worried. But I soon realized the power of the Farriss Brothers band—and I'm not sure they even realized it themselves."

As everyone arrived one by one that day, each member picked up his instrument and found something to play, and before Clapton's eyes, the collective mind melded. "Jonny sat down and started bashing around the drum kit, and Tim showed up and started strumming away on guitar," Clapton says. "The song just started coming out of the ceiling. As a solo artist, I remember wishing I had catalysts like this in my life." After Garry and Kirk found their parts to play and the song became real, Michael, the last to show up, joined right in. "Hutch turned up half gone, just in party mode, much later in the night," Clapton says. "He heard the band playing and just went in and started singing phonetically—it was all gibberish that followed the melody and sounded good. He did that for a while, singing strange noises, then he'd stop and start scribbling things on bits of paper he'd hold up in front of him. Before you knew it, he had verses of lyrics—out of nowhere, just so naturally. Fuck, man, I was in awe of all of them."

The band and their producer more or less moved into 301 Studios, recording 24/7 to get it right, and also so that the band's singer knew where to end his night, or rather, begin his morning. "This was my first project as a producer, so I did try my best to be somewhat organized," Richard Clapton says. "It wasn't always a good thing that Michael knew where to go at the end of the night—after he'd been out partying until five or six o'clock, thrown out of every bar and party he'd been to, he'd come to the studio, because he knew we'd still be there working. Michael would show up with friends like Jimmy Barnes and whoever, and Jon would get really shitty.* He was like me, trying to hold the project together and be responsible."

For the most part, at the recording sessions they were fairly well behaved, as best they could be before the resident jester arrived with merry men in tow. "It was wild—Michael came in tripping all the time, wearing this crushed purple velvet cape like he was

*A quick and necessary cultural clarification: in Australia being "shitty" refers to being angry or pissed off, whereas in American vernacular, it is used to denote drunkenness. Furthermore, in Australia, drunkenness is, as it is in England, referred to as being "pissed," while in the U.S., it denotes anger. To sum up, from an American linguistic tradition, if you're shitty in Australia, you're pissed off, and if you're pissed in Australia, you're drunk. Conversely, Australians traveling to the U.S. should be aware that if someone says they're shitty or shit-faced, they should stop drinking, and if someone says that they're pissed, they should prepare to rumble. Perhaps this slang inversion is a side effect of the contrasting polarity that governs the direction that water spirals down the drain in each country. Regardless, it is important to note that if one is both shitty and pissed simultaneously in either locale, one is generally fucked indeed.

a prince," Clapton says. "He'd come flying, literally and figuratively, into the studio, like, 'Yeah! What are we doing? Let me do some backup vocals.' Usually the answer was, 'Not tonight, Mikey.' It worked out all right, because even with a bad hangover, Michael could give you what you needed. Well, not straightaway—a few recuperative measures were usually necessary."

It wasn't that Clapton was a Goody Two-Shoes—he was quite the opposite—he just took his job seriously and drove the band to record their best. He lent them his knowledge and formed lasting friendships, musical and otherwise, that spilled over into his own recordings, where various members of INXS lent a hand through the years. He also formed a lasting bond with Jon Farriss, for whom he wrote the song "Glory Road" years later.

All of that was to come, but before the end of his time as their producer, in the same caring, structured manner he nurtured the album's production, he also scheduled a full-on musical free-for-all. He knew the band wanted to make an album and party like rock stars, and he let them, in the way a good parent would—after they'd done their homework. "I tried to keep the partying in the studio to a minimum. We had a very small budget and only two or three weeks to do it. I knew that if we partied all the time, we'd end up with nothing," Clapton says. "Early on, I'd made the band stop bringing their friends around and it felt strange to me. It was hard to do, actually, because I'm a natural-born party animal myself. I hated it but I promised them that if they showed up and did what they had to do for most of the sessions that we'd cut loose later in the project."

There was one track that Clapton knew would benefit from the chaos of a studio full of hedonistic musicians and all the friends they could muster. It was the title track, "Underneath the Colours," a sprawling jam that sounds like a party in motion. "I knew that was the one we could get on tape properly while having a bit of a collective party," he says. "We'd tried the song in the cold light of day and it really didn't work. I told them, this is the one: bring all your friends, all your fucking stash, whatever you've got, because we're going for it. I still have the home video of that night."

The band invited twenty friends, amassed all the drugs and booze they could find, and had at it full bore. Twenty people might not seem like a lot, but consider, given the tight budget and the fact that the band was making roughly three hundred dollars a week playing live, the size of a studio in their price range was no larger than the cabin of a small sailboat. "There were people, like *everywhere,* even in the room while they were recording," Clapton says. "Everyone was wandering around, as the night went on, getting more bat-faced.* I don't even remember the end of the night." But Clapton does remember the next morning. He somehow made it home, but was awakened by his engineer, Alex Vertikoff, at 10 a.m. Though his initial response was "Fuck off, Alex," the fear in the young man's voice made Clapton realize something was amiss—something that might seem weird to those who've only known recording in the digital age. "We'd had such a big night that we'd left the tape we'd recorded to on the machines," Clapton says. "This particular lot of Ampex tape had gotten contaminated when it was shipped to Australia by tanker. The salt in the sea air combined with the chemicals in the tape to make some compound that completely destroyed the tape heads in the machine. So for all my efforts to keep things civilized, the one time I didn't, we really paid for it."

*** A genius Aussie idiom. A "bat-faced" individual is so inebriated on alcohol and/or narcotics that their facial expression has become twisted to the point that it more closely resembles a bat than the human it was mere hours before.**

They might not have gotten it on tape that first time, but the song "Underneath the Colours" was truly an evolution for INXS. It is a midtempo marching number that packed the wallop that the band's other slower songs never had; it is an anthem buoyed by a chant-along chorus, set into a loose, moody bluesy backdrop. The song's scratch guitar, deep lilting bass line, and skittering drum fills offset Michael's bedroom tenor, lending it a deeper sex appeal than ever before. Clapton did see something the band did not: by urging them to slow the tempo on their more complex, funky compositions, their strengths came to the surface. Only when they allowed their interplay to expand did it become clear that INXS was capable of so much more than rocking together in a tight line.

By the end of the studio time Michael Browning had paid for, INXS's album wasn't finished, and Mr. Browning wasn't willing to drop another dime on more recording. To recoup and regroup, INXS accompanied Clapton, who was one of Australia's most popular rockers, on a tour of the land, with an eye toward finishing the album afterward. By then they'd become close with Richard, and the fun he'd tried to control in the studio flowed freely on the road. "I was actually in a period where I was trying to behave myself and so was Jon Farriss," Clapton says. "We'd get to bed early, I was trying to quit cigarettes, and we were eating healthy, doing Tai Chi. But by the end of the tour we decided that we needed a night off—and we really went for it." Actually everyone went for it that night—and the town they were in never recovered.

It's called Kempsey RSL, and it's on the northeastern coast of New South Wales, where the bands played a local venue to about two thousand kids. "All of us arrived armed with goodies," Clapton says, chuckling at the memory. "INXS opened and after their set, started to party. I went on and midway through my set, it started to go haywire. We'd been ending each show doing encores together, so by the time they came back out with me, we were just a mess." The audience loved it: they were stomping on the floor, demanding more encores, refusing to let the night end—which, in this region of Australia, was a problem. "They had a curfew there and Michael wasn't having that," Clapton says. "He was up to mischief." After Clapton left the stage for the third time, the promoters cut the lights to let the audience know the show was over. "Michael grabbed me and dragged me down in front of the stage," Clapton says. "I was like, 'What the fuck's going on?' He just said, 'Richard, watch this!'"

When the lights came up, there they were—the other members of INXS and all of Clapton's band (including a lady)—flashing, as they say in Australia, their "brown eye." "Hutch had talked everyone into doing it, saying that he and I would be up there with them," Clapton says. "And he'd told the lighting guy to flash our spotlights on the stage a minute after they cut the house lights. So there they were—except for Kirk. He came out wearing only this great jacket that belonged to my guitar player, completely naked and facing the crowd." The audience went bananas—it was the best third encore they'd ever seen. "By this time, cops and parents were heading toward the venue and our tour manager was just standing there in the wings going, 'We're *fucked*,'" Clapton says. "But Michael wasn't done—he jumps on stage, stands in the spotlight, and invites all of these young pretty girls in the front to come up on stage and flash their tits and pussy to the audience, which they did—lots of them."

Their tour manager, a man named Neil, somehow ran the band out of the building and into the vans. He then ran them back to their hotel and into

Men in Black: INXS publicity still from *Listen Like Thieves*.

their rooms, urging them to gather their belongings like their life depended on it—because it did. They were literally chased out of town, pursued by a furious mob—kind of like Frankenstein. "It really was a scene out of an American comedy film," Clapton says. "We had a pack of cops and parents chasing us down the highway. About ten years later, I was planning a tour through that part of Australia and I suggested to my agent that we do a date there out of convenience. He looked at me and said, 'How fucking *dare* you? No one has played Kempsey ever since your last gig, the one with INXS.' And he wasn't kidding."

Underneath the Colours was INXS's second album and it catapulted them to the forefront of Australian rock in 1981. With two albums under their belt, an incredible live show, a nonstop tour schedule, and a reputation that began to precede them, INXS was building a foundation: they didn't fit in with the punk-influenced hard rock of their peers, but they were equally rebellious members of the renaissance that put Australia on the cultural map.

The closely knit Aussie communities provided the ideal setting for bands to take off—the pubs, hotels, and RSLs were open-minded in their spirit; places where, out of necessity or desire, war veterans and teenagers gathered regularly, to drink the night away and hit the slots or see a band and lose themselves. It says so much about the country, the people, and the era.

In Australia, the music scene fostered creativity, demanded musicality and performance, took no prisoners, and churned out some of the best live bands of the day. "That period of Australian music, if anything, was a bit feisty, but it was probably the best in the world," says Harry Della, a promoter who has arranged more Australian INXS tours than anyone else, as well as booking every band of note there since the seventies. "I used to go to England and America and no bands existed like ours did. A support band at that time could do three hundred to four hundred gigs a year just opening for headlining acts. You didn't see that abroad then and you don't now. You don't even see that here now. Top Australian bands today are booked for thirty-day tours—and that's a lot! Today bands here will be signed before they've even played thirty gigs—and they need two more years to even get good. Pubs used to book music at least six nights a week. They just don't do it anymore."

In the eighties, there were truly weird bands, ones that couldn't exist anywhere else—ones as rude, raw, honest, and uncompromising as a dingo in heat. A noteworthy one that opened for INXS held the honor of most excellent name—the Nicest People. "They were a hard-core ska band," Tim Farriss says. "The singer was shaved totally bald and he'd come out totally naked. The other members would wear women's lingerie, and the drummer had a huge Mohawk and he played turned sideways to the crowd. I always thought that was really cool to have the drummer in silhouette." The Nicest People were, well, nice, compared to another band often on the same bill called Jimmy and the Boys. "Their singer was called Ignatious Jones and he was a contortionist," Tim reports. "He'd be singing with his head under his butt and his arms twisted around him. They had a song called 'Raw Meat,' and he'd eat raw meat on stage. They once played a Hell's Angels party where he begged them to beat him up. And they did. And then he kept on playing. On stage he also liked to shit in a bowl and pass it around." He was Ozzy Osbourne, Iggy Pop, and GG Allin–rabid all rolled into one.

The members of INXS were road dogs for years, earning themselves a following as headliners and support acts for bands that were typically nothing like them—because at the time, no one was like them. "I knew early on that they were a unique band," Harry Della says. "There were then and there are today so many really good bands who are just too Australian. INXS wasn't—they had an international sound from day one. Every other band was guitar-based rock and roll, but they had a rhythm that no one else did. I've seen them play acoustic to a full house when the power blew out. I've seen them show up to play their third gig of the night at seven a.m. and they gave it their all like it was the first. They just had something. Part of it was this sex thing. They really were the first band of the day who drew crowds in the hundreds who got a girl following." INXS was the first band to swing, the first band with funk, who could rock as hard as the rest of them, but knew the primal power of rhythm—and how to harness it. "Jon is a phenomenal drummer, and that's coming from a huge fan of jazz," Della says. "And Michael was a star from the start, but without the rhythm of that band, he would've had nowhere to go. When you put that together, that's what got the girls going. That's what got everyone going! INXS was the first band to create a dancing scene at their gigs—and that was new."

They were deft performers, capable of taking their left-field brand of funk to the hardest audiences of their day, supporting straight-up rock bands like Midnight Oil and Cold Chisel, an act led by the infamous Scot Jimmy Barnes. Cold Chisel defined seventies Australian rock and roll until they disbanded in 1983. As raw as AC/DC and as notorious as Led Zeppelin, Cold Chisel set the bar by which all blues-based rockers were judged, not to mention raising the bar on raucous performance and legendary debauchery. Frontman and songwriter Jimmy Barnes, who has enjoyed continued success as a solo artist, remembers well the first time INXS supported Cold Chisel, on a tour of New Zealand in 1982. "Our audience was a little different from the kind of people going to see INXS. INXS was more of a pop band than Cold Chisel was," Barnes recalls. "But that didn't matter. They had the common thread you found in all the good Australian bands at that time—they had the ability to hold an audience. It came from playing beer barns every night for years. In a place like that you had to learn to work up a crowd, because the crowds you played to were a pack of wild drunks who wanted a good time. It takes energy and power to do that."

Barnes knew that INXS wasn't quite the typical fodder for Cold Chisel fans—and he loved it. "Michael had this whole animal presence on stage," he says. "And you know, the guys in the audience either loved it and the band, or they wanted to fucking kill him and hated them because of it. But you know what? Whatever their reason, they were watching."

Cold Chisel was such a huge act that drew so many fans that oxygen tanks were on their contract. "There'd always be around a thousand more people in these pubs than the place could physically hold," Barnes says. "No one could move, condensation would drip from the ceiling, and after you'd done three sets, if you're singing, you would need to lie on a fire escape with an oxygen tank to your mouth. By the third show that day, you'd be pretty lost, so it didn't seem strange at the time." INXS fell in very well on the tour, not only because they'd once turned a room of Perth bikers from foe to friend, but because they could—well, some of them at least—keep up with Jimmy Barnes.

"I am sure I am the one who gave them their first line of cocaine," Barnes says. "It was on that first tour of New Zealand and one day I was sick of my band so I spent the day driving to the next town in their bus. We were drinking, having a good time, and I broke it out and said, 'Here you go, boys, have some of this.'" The festivities continued through the afternoon, into the evening, through the gig and into the after-party, where enough damage was done to last through till dawn, noon the next day, and the evening after that. "At the hotel bar after the gig, our bands had a drinking competition," Barnes says. "All of the hard liquor bottles there hung upside down above the bar with taps on them. We decided that whoever could drink a shot from every bottle they had would win." First up was Phil Small, bassist for Cold Chisel, who slid along the sticky wooden bar, gulping everything from gin to tequila to scotch to cordials until, short of the finish line, he rolled over, tumbled across bar stools, and puked like a volcano.

Tim Farriss took up the challenge, was slid along the bar, and downed everything—without flinching. "It was bad," Barnes says. "We had to carry him around the rest of the night and we made the tour manager watch him to make sure he was all right." It didn't end there: with so much adrenaline and booze going around, the bands needed an activity, and suitably chose to destroy their rooms. In many lodging facilities, their actions would incite alarm, protest by the management and fellow guests, and potentially a visit from local law enforcement. Not so this night—the activity that pushed this party over the line was strictly carnal. "Sometime in the early morning the hotel manager turned up bashing on our door, because of an irate father at the main door of the hotel," Barnes says. "He was looking for his daughter, who was apparently sixteen. There were a few girls hanging around the band, who we knew were nineteen. Then we realized that she was the one we saw naked in the bathroom, going at it in there with Michael."

The next day, Tim was probably the only man on earth more sick than that girl's father. "Tim was drunk for two days after that," Kirk says. "His face was green, he threw up all day, he couldn't walk, he couldn't talk, and I think he finally sobered up to a manageable degree a few hours after the next night's show."

These were wild times, even in Australia, where a frontier mentality was still the norm—drunk-driving laws weren't widely enforced as they are today, and the youth of the day were spirited, to say the least. It was Australia's version of the sixties in America, and all the young dudes loved fucking with the Man. On a tour shortly after New Zealand, at a gig in Queensland, a region that, even then, was known for its conservative, police-state nature, INXS really went for it. On the way to the show, the band and their crew stopped to forage for psychedelic mushrooms in a cow pasture along the road—and they hit the jackpot. They harvested enough to fill a baseball cap, which the band and crew agreed would be more than enough to dose all of them. They also agreed that the magic 'shrooms would be saved for the post-show festivities.

The cap full o' fungi was left in road manager Gary Grant's room, but the door to the room was left open. Perhaps it was a mistake or perhaps it was deliberate, but everyone in the band and crew snuck into the room in secret and sucked up the 'shrooms. No one freely admitted to it, but by show time, everyone was well on their way to psychedelic bliss. "I remember seeing our road manager, Gary Grant, at the side of the stage, grinning at us as we went on," Garry Beers recalls. "He was like, 'I hope you guys are all right, because I've had some mushrooms. And I'm tripping right now!'"

The band took the stage, enjoying the rubbery mind-state of playing music on psychedelic drugs. "When we first got onstage, it was amazing," Garry says. "I had a fretless bass and all of us were just *so* into it." But the good times came to an abrupt halt at the end of the first song.

“Hi, how are you doing tonight?” Michael asked the audience, who answered with roaring applause. “That’s *great!* Us, *too*—because we’re all *tripping*!”

All along the back wall of the room, a row of uniformed heads popped up in unison—Hutch’s announcement had tweaked the ears of the Queensland policemen in the house. “It was horrible,” Garry says. “All of us went from completely loose to completely paranoid.” Needless to say, they didn’t do much of a meet-and-greet after the show.

It took five years of incubation to ready INXS for what came next. In that time, they did what they had to: they found an ambitious manager, a record label, and a following, and they learned all the lessons the wilds of Australia could teach them. By 1982, they’d grown, over thousands of miles and nearly as many gigs, from schoolboys to seasoned players on the brink of greatness. They were brought together by a familial bond and idealism as pure as it was when they were just kids playing in a garage. And in the years to come, as much as their world would change and their world would be changed by them, the chemistry they’d mixed in that small parking space in the suburbs of Sydney had fused them together forever.

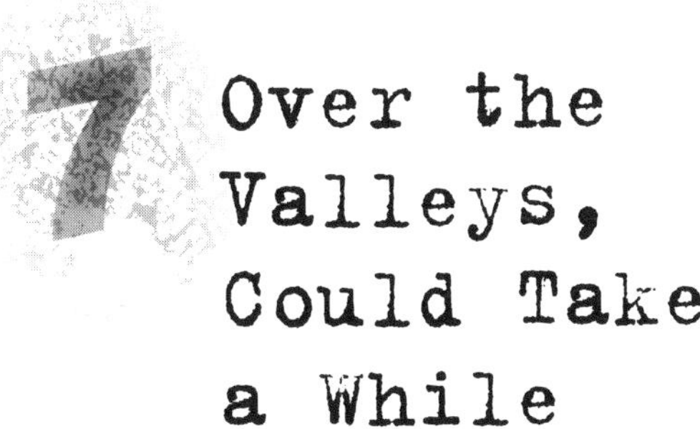

7 Over the Valleys, Could Take a While

BY THE END OF 1982, INXS had a solid foundation: a real, functioning management company, two solid records under their belt, gig offers to fill their year, and the hunger to push it further. Chris Murphy was their acting manager, their business mind, while the partner he'd taken on, Gary Grant, was their tour manager and presence in the trenches. He was a kindred soul who could balance work and play without losing the plot. Murphy offered Grant a piece of his management company, and according to their agreement, Chris would seek out and land the business deals while Gary looked after the band. The pair got on famously, furthering INXS's success beyond their wildest dreams, though their eventual split in the early nineties was far from amicable.

Murphy strove to build an INXS empire—and his first step was securing record deals and tours abroad. He'd face many obstacles, the first of which he found in his own backyard. Intent on broadening INXS's horizons, Murphy flew to England to land the band a European distribution deal for their next record as well as securing them an opening slot on a tour that would elevate their international profile. He succeeded on both points: he won over executives at RCA who agreed to distribute the band's next album, and convinced XTC's manager that INXS should support them on their upcoming tour of the U.K.*

Murphy had laid the groundwork for big things, but he needed some cash—twenty-five thousand dollars to pay for the band and their gear to be flown to and chauffeured around the U.K. to support XTC.

According to Murphy, he did what a manager should—he approached the band's record label to ask for the funds. In this case, Murphy met with his former partner in Deluxe Records, Michael Browning, the man to whom he'd seceded his shares in the company so that he might manage INXS full-time. Murphy remembers Browning, in more diplomatic terms, telling him to fuck off. He told Chris to request the funds from RCA, which he called "INXS's new record company."**

As far as Murphy remembers, the conversation went something like this: "I *am* asking the record company," Murphy informed Browning. "RCA is the distributor. *You* are the record company. You don't ask the distributor for the money to promote a tour, you ask the record company. I am the manager and you are the record company, right? So here I am, where I should be, asking you."

"Work it out on your own," Browning grumbled. "You'll get nothing from me."

Murphy was livid and incredulous, and though he is famous for his red-hot temper, in this instance he tapped a far more efficient trait of his: icy resolve.

"Okay, let me be sure I've got it right," Murphy said. "You're my band's record company for the entire world. I've just gone to England and landed a tour with XTC and a distribution deal with RCA. I've just made you money by going and doing your work for you. Now, all you have to do is fund the tour to make all of this happen, and you *don't* want to do that?"

"No," Browning spat.

*** At the time, XTC was more popular than asymetrical hair cuts: their single "Senses Working Overtime," off *English Settlement,* had established them as the Anglo version of Talking Heads, though lead singer Andy Partridge's mental breakdown a year later in 1983 sent the band in a different direction.**

**** RCA was not the band's record company at all. Deluxe represented the band and licensed the band's music for worldwide distribution—in essence they were the landlord who leased the record to RCA to sublet it throughout Europe. RCA paid for production and distribution; Deluxe remained the record company that nurtured and promoted the artist. Landing a distribution deal for foreign territories meant that a record company had nothing to do but collect a check and deliver an album they already owned.**

"Fan-tastic!" Murphy said, smirking.

And they never spoke again.

In the end, they were bought out of their deal with Deluxe Records, and Browning got more money than he'd ever invested in INXS. Browning went on to develop bands that did well momentarily in Australia and nowhere else. Murphy paid dearly for INXS's freedom, but lost the battle to win the war; within a few years he and the band were bigger and richer than they'd ever dreamed they'd be.

In the short run, to fund the XTC tour, Murphy did the only thing he could do: he sold the house his years as a successful booking agent had earned him. And to fund the band's next record, he took out a loan, and established a savvy INXS business tradition: rather than rely on a record company to pay for studio time, the band paid their way, and in return, took home a higher percentage of their sales revenue.

In his future negotiations with record labels, Murphy insisted on a business precedent ahead of its time, one that served the band well throughout their career. Instead of signing INXS to a label, thereby granting that corporation ownership of the albums, he negotiated licensing deals; in essence, renting the albums to the labels. It allowed the record companies to invest less in the band, while the band retained ownership and creative control over their material. The label was not responsible for covering the costs of recording or touring—simply the costs of production, promotion, marketing, and publicity for an agreed-upon number of albums.

It was a bold stance, particularly for a manager who'd never managed anyone, bargaining on behalf of a band hailing from as far from the capitals of the music industry—New York, Los Angeles, and London—as possible. In the eighties, the music industry was a well-oiled machine in which talent signed the rights to their work away to the record label in exchange for a few heady years of first-class travel and five-course dinners. Few realized that those high-life bonuses did not come for free: they were then, as they are today, billed back to the artist, on credit. *

*** The cost of making a music video, launching a tour, flying the artist first-class—all of it typically adds up to a giant IOU. Though they might be living like rock stars and touring the world, until an artist sells enough records to pay back their label, they have no cash to call their own. More often than not in the history of the music industry, artists never make enough to cover their tab—and find themselves at the company's mercy, either deemed profitable enough to justify the cost of funding another record or dropped from the roster with little afterthought.**

Taking all of that into account, it must be said that Chris Murphy had some set of balls. He was only in his twenties, but possessed the business acumen of a wizened banker. He set up a company in the band's name, an entity that served to copyright all of their music, videos, and merchandise. "They are one of the few bands in the world who have owned the rights to all of their videos from day one," Murphy says. "I told them, 'You're all going to have kids one day, so let's create a business around you now that will generate profit on its own for years to come. Because by the time your kids are grown, you're all going to be too old and fat to deal with it.'"

He also managed to cut separate deals with competing record labels—PolyGram in Europe, Warner Bros. in Australia, and Atlantic in North America—to distribute INXS's music, all the while (except for North America) allowing the band to retain ownership of their songs. And through the years, he played the labels against one another, to INXS's advantage. Murphy had never managed a band before, but it didn't matter—he'd clearly inherited his family's talent-agent edge. He also had an uncanny sense of timing, and an ambition as insatiable as the band's. He'd had a reputation as a cutthroat player in the Australian music scene, and after a few years at the helm of the good ship INXS, Chris Murphy became something else: an infamously uncompromising visionary respected more out of fear than admiration.

Business isn't pretty, and Chris Murphy was never in it to make friends. He loved the band, he loved the music, and he loved the combat, conquest, and contest of making INXS a money-making global brand. "It was smart thinking on his part to set the band up with direct signings in America and Europe," says his former partner Gary Grant. "Australia had great acts, but the fact is that Australians, when they could get them, always signed worldwide deals out of America. That meant that their album might be released, but they weren't guaranteed the promotional money to finance a tour in any of the company's territories. A direct signing meant that the record company was contractually responsible for promotional money, so the band was guaranteed a tour. That was all that we needed—if we had a stage, we knew INXS could blow any crowd away."

Tim and Michael meeting with producer Mark Opitz *(left)* and a Warner Bros. music executive, 1983.

The two albums that sent INXS's message worldwide were *Shabooh Shoobah* and *The Swing,* recorded, respectively, in 1982 and 1984. The two, consumed back to back, are a scrapbook of the band's musical DNA: they capture every bit of their intense complex musicality—and hint at the rich rhythmic vision they'd soon realize. *Shabooh Shoobah* was produced by Mark Opitz, an Australian musician who later turned producer after a stint as an A&R man for Warner Bros. Records. In 1982, Chris Murphy called him and sent him a tape of three raw INXS songs, asking him to pick the one he'd like to produce for the band. The songs were "Black and White," "Johnson's Aeroplane," and a ditty called "The One Thing," which in its origins bore little of the hypnotic carnal sensuality it grew to embody. "That was the only song I heard that I felt was important. But there were too many awkward bits—too many departures from the center of it," Opitz says. "I cut the original version in half and spoke to the band about it." Opitz produced that song, which evolved into three minutes and twenty-three seconds of slinky, jagged new wave sex, and tweaked the ears of trainspotters around the world. The song turned out so well that Murphy hired Opitz to produce three more songs. But he and the band weren't entirely convinced that their Australian compatriot could produce an entire album slick enough to hook the international audience they were after, so Michael, Kirk, and Andrew flew to England and America to meet with prospective producers. They took the band's rough demos and the tracks they'd just recorded with Opitz, playing them for heavy-hitters like Bob Clearmountain,* the engineer and mixing legend who'd

* Clearmountain did eventually work with INXS: he mixed *Kick* and *Welcome to Wherever You Are.*

worked with Chic, Roxy Music, and David Bowie. Opitz was none the wiser, but his work spoke for him: across the board, every producer the band approached respectfully told them not to mess with winning chemistry.

"Bob Clearmountain said to us, 'I love the music and I would definitely work with you guys,'" Kirk recalls, " 'but I don't have any ideas better than the guy who recorded these for you. The best advice I have for you is to go back to Australia and record the whole album with him.'" Opitz had produced about a half a dozen platinum albums in Australia by that time, but was still finding his way as an international producer. INXS provided him with an intangible he'd never before experienced. "They had spirit," he says. "There was a spirit in recording *Shabooh Shoobah*—we cried a lot, we had a lot of fun. It was like a self-taught master class in the process for all of us."

The album, recorded at Rhinoceros Recordings in Sydney, embodies the coveted crossroad where spontaneity, creativity, and kindred vision meet. The band had enjoyed success—and Top 20 singles—in Australia with their first two records. But to make it abroad, they knew this next album needed to capture the strongest, most international elements of their sound—it would have to hook fans, radio DJs, and booking agents worldwide. "They worked really hard on *Shabooh Shoobah,*" says the man who engineered the album, David Nicholas—better known to the band and many others as Chipper, due to his consistently sunny demeanor in the face of catastrophe. "It was all live playing, with very few overdubs. We were still recording on two-inch tape in those days. They were inspired, they didn't muck around in the studio at all—they were very serious about what they were there to do. Though after we were done working, all of us did engage in a fair share of carrying on." Some of that carrying on might have been due to the song from whence the album's title came. The phrase was a rhythmic chant born in the mind of Tim Farriss. In the very early stages of the song "Spy of Love," Tim began singing the phrase like a mantra as the band played. To the best of anyone's knowledge, it is nonsense in every language known to man.

The chant anchored the mood of the track but was later dropped in lieu of actual lyrics. Still, the wacky voodoo of the phrase remained—its sound and texture capture INXS then more than any two words in any dictionary ever could.

Shabooh Shoobah was the first rung up a ladder that INXS discovered was very tall. That album put them in touch, via cassette, vinyl, word-of-mouth, late-night videos, and watering-hole tours, with the musical evolution afoot overseas in the early eighties. Punk had gone supernova, but its brightest lights had evolved into something new. The members of INXS were eager fans of all that then, fans who had no idea that they would soon be the leaders of the next wave, defining a sound too young and new to name.

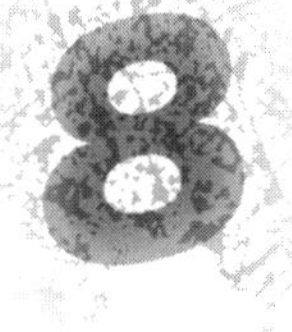

Have Accent, Will Travel: The New Wave Breaks on U.S. Shores

THE NEW WAVE THAT WON OVER American music fans, first as an underground college radio movement, then as the aesthetic behind nearly ten years of mainstream pop-chart hits, was born of seventies punk rock—both of the New York City and London, England, variety. New wave was the next level: it was where punk-rock experimentation met true musicality, where the spirit of three chords with attitude evolved. New wave artists followed the lead of punk's best bands, like the Clash and the Talking Heads, who infused punk with everything from reggae to funk to the myriad sounds afforded by synthesizers. New wave was more musically complicated than most punk rock and drew artists from around the world, though it was seen as an entirely British movement. Even those bands that weren't Brit, but bore the poncey hair, oddball or androgynous attire, and syncopated instrumentation of new wave were assumed to be crumpet-loving Englishmen.

INXS was precisely aligned to ride the new wave right to the top of the American—and world—charts in the eighties: they were unusual, sensual, and to the naked eye, British. In fact, Chris Murphy estimates that no members of the U.S. press even realized that INXS was Australian until their third or fourth tour.

New wave was the second coming of punk rock. Whatever you think of it, punk was an undeniable signpost that marked time. There is rock before and rock forever after punk.

Visionaries like the Clash, the Talking Heads, Blondie, and Elvis Costello bridged the gap between punk and new wave, while a slew of younger artists expanded the boundaries of the genre, acts born of punk rock's ethos, yet unlike punk rock itself. There is Robert Smith of the Cure, who, since the age of sixteen, had been writing introverted confessions so unique they have become a universe unto themselves. The Pretenders' spiked storytelling overturned gender roles in modern rock, and a little Irish band called U2 married Bono's bracing lyrical snapshots to the epic guitar panorama whittled by the Edge. In Australia, no one had a more unusual musical identity than INXS; they were intense, edgy, and progressive in their compositions, poetic in their storytelling, and romantic in their outlook.

These diverse artists, and many more as the eighties moved along, were encapsulated under the umbrella term new wave—and their creativity was exactly what American teens were after. New wave bands were something that their parents did not understand because they were nothing like the classic rock bands of the sixties and seventies. As the new wave movement grew more popular, it also became a sublimated stance against American society, as nearly all new wave bands were foreign or sounded so. Kids who rejected Ronald Reagan's America, didn't care for Top 40, and didn't relate to Lynyrd Skynyrd rock blocks had found a voice and identity in new wave that safely rejected American culture yet allowed them to enjoy all the benefits of living in America. There was no war on, but the youth culture was certainly demonstrating: they were defining themselves not by indigenous stereotypes, but via the cultural exports that washed ashore. No one with a sense of cool wanted to be pro-U.S., pro-Republican, or at all like Alex P. Keaton, the overtly yuppie high school kid played by Michael J. Fox on the sitcom *Family Ties.* They wanted to be like John Bender, Judd Nelson's character in *The Breakfast Club*—a take-no-shit rebel with a clue.

Those who found their identity in foreign music first heard it on college radio, which back then was as diverse as the Australian broadcasts INXS grew up on. College stations in those days played everything from funk to punk to jazz and soul back-to-back for those lucky enough to be in their range. College stations then were barely on the music industry, FCC, or even

On Three, Don't Smile. *Left to right:* Andrew, Kirk, Garry, Michael, Tim, Jon in 1985.

their local campus authorities' radar, which allowed their jocks unharnessed freedom. College radio brought new wave and hip-hop to the American suburbs, delivering visions of two entirely other realities: one cosmopolitan, funky, and mysterious; the other, just as foreign in its reportage of life in America's inner cities. To middle-class kids tuned in to college radio, far from urban culture, hip-hop and new wave were salvation: the music was raw, fresh, underground, and heroically unlike mainstream entertainment.

College radio truly was an influential educator at the time, one which, unfortunately, is now as formulaic and prone to record company control as the mainstream stations. College radio today is an established marketplace where record company dollars dictate play lists as they do along the nationwide network of FM radio stations owned by Clear Channel Communications. The only truly independent spirit is to be found on satellite and Internet radio stations, which of course is better than nothing at all.

Before there was an Internet, iTunes, or MTV, college radio stations were the best way to discover new music. They allowed many foreign bands to break in America without a major media campaign; a band could reach enough of an audience to sell out venues across the country, often without having released an album Stateside. Radio was crucial, but MTV was the medium made for and bred on new wave. The fledgling music channel emerged in 1982, infiltrated the foundation of the music industry like kudzu, and forever altered the way pop music is digested. It didn't matter that MTV's sets were shabbier than the basement backdrop of *Wayne's World* or that the production values were akin to a subpar film-school project, or that, at first, the VJs seemed as confused about their purpose as most people were about the channel. None of it mattered: every kid who laid eyes on MTV was instantly hooked. It was at once the dawn of a new age and the decline of Western civilization; MTV's hypnotic allure created a nation of flash-cut crackheads and ushered in ADD as a generational experience.

Music and video were nothing new in Australia, Europe, and everywhere else in the world, but in America, aside from a few stoney late-night shows in the late seventies and early eighties like USA Network's *Night Flight* and *Don Kirshner's Rock Concert* (which ran from 1973 to 1981 on ABC at 1 a.m. every Sunday) music and video were usually slapped together by accident, on a variety show or on wannabe dance parties like *American Bandstand, Soul Train,* and *Solid Gold.* MTV was the first 24/7 music-video channel. There were plenty of videos from years gone by to fill the hours, from the Beatles to Led Zeppelin to Parliament, but from the start, MTV adopted a new wave frame of mind, opting to play the same twenty or so clips endlessly: the Buggles' "Video Killed the Radio Star," the Police's "Roxanne," David Bowie's "Ashes to Ashes."

MTV was a subscription channel in the early days, one that was not included with basic cable. Cable television, for that matter, was a luxury in the early eighties—like any burgeoning technology it was expensive, exotic, and primitive. Early cable boxes had no remote control; the channels were tuned via a box with a row of switches, one per station—and at the time there were about ten stations available. Those with MTV were well-off enough to live in a home with cable television—and to convince their parents to subscribe. Those parents certainly reaped the benefits: MTV was better than videogames—it was a subscription to a babysitting service.

Record labels soon made the obvious connection that the kids who watched MTV, given that their parents could afford it, had access to enough disposable income to buy records. And so began the age when music was marketed to younger Americans more easily and more aggressively than it had ever been. Music video was, back then, not just the perfect marketing vehicle—it was also so new that innovation, vision, and diversity were the norm because there was no norm.

Chris Murphy was quick to see the new day dawning in America, and he knew that if he played his cards right, INXS could own the States. "In the early eighties in America you had fat, rich guys playing stadiums—the Eagles, Jackson Browne, Fleetwood Mac—all of them," he says. "They were just getting fatter and lazier. I knew that it was going to change—quickly. The bands from the U.K. who condensed punk and added to it would be the next thing—the Police, U2, the Pretenders. I knew that if we attacked it, we'd be part of that. But I knew we had to work hard. Punk and new wave was a U.K. phenomenon—coming out of Australia we meant nothing. At the time, to Americans, Australian rock meant AC/DC."

When Murphy heard about MTV, he was overjoyed—he couldn't have wished for a venue more suited to INXS. They'd cut videos for songs on each of their albums, and already had one in the can for *Shabooh Shoobah*—but before MTV, there were few opportunities for them to be seen outside of their homeland. All of that changed fast, and INXS's photogenic good looks advertised the band's music as well as their top-drawer live shows. INXS also stood out for their very suave, very heterosexual persona; next to the androgyny and alien otherness of new wave bands like the Talking Heads, Devo, and Flock of Seagulls, INXS brought masculine heat to the table.

Chris Murphy recalls the exact moment when he realized that INXS would take over the world. He attended a radio-industry conference in America, where the keynote speaker prophesied that within a year, an English music movement known as new wave would dominate commercial mainstream radio. Murphy left on the next flight to Sydney and ordered the band to meet him in his office at 6 a.m.

Completely confused, and still asleep, the members of INXS listened to their manager rave on about new wave and global domination and how they must go home and pack their bags immediately. "We're going to

America, like, *right now,*" he told them. "This is our chance. You see, there's this thing called MTV . . ."

Murphy had signed the band to a deal with Atco, a division of Atlantic Records founded by the Rolling Stones. He'd been offered more money by Columbia, but chose Atco because of one woman, Reen Nalli, who single-handedly barnstormed INXS onto the label's agenda. Chris, when he first set up shop in New York, was so broke that he literally relied on Reen to survive. "She'd call me and say, 'Would you like to meet over breakfast?' and I'd say yes, otherwise I wasn't going to eat more than a cup of coffee," he says. Another key player in INXS's conquest of America was Bill Elson, their booking agent at ICM, who set about landing them work as the opening act on a variety of tours.

Though the band wasn't exactly excited to start breaking a new territory after enjoying commendable success at home, they fell in line. "I knew that new wave was going to roll into America and that the radio people and MTV weren't going to know what was good and what wasn't—they were going to play everything," Murphy says. "I also knew that after a while, the new wave tide would recede, taking the crap bands with it and leaving those who were worthwhile and had established a beachhead. I remember asking them how they were different from Flock of Seagulls to American ears, and how we were too good to get washed out to sea. They didn't know what the fuck I was talking about."

He was right—INXS rode the new wave onto the beach and all the way to the bank in the eighties, as they were more than just an amazing band—they were the perfect new wave pop package. They filled the void in suburban American teens pining for something else. They were exotic, they were sexy, they could fucking play. And they had accents.

INXS's first video to air on MTV, "The One Thing," is a microcosm of every reason why America fell hard for them. The clip is a stylishly decadent, modern take on a Victorian banquet, a concept that reflected the band's persona more than they might have realized: they embodied the lush romance and yearning of the Romantic age with none of the wigs or inbreeding. Shot in Sydney, the band and various lovely well-coiffed models, among them Michael Hutchence's girlfriend Michele Bennett, tear meat from the bone, lustily feed each other, toss dishes, and devour figs with tangible carnal knowledge. The song reflected the band with Michael as their poet, their Lord Byron in leather pants, doing his part as vocal seducer, sketching scenes of sex, hope, and utopia.*

*** The British poet Lord Byron was born George Noel Gordon Byron in London on January 22, 1788, the same day that Michael Hutchence was born in 1960. Byron was a genius, known as much for his sexual conquests as the romantic poems that explored sex, lust, love, and loss in prose unlike any before him. In life, he created his own cult of personality—the Byronic hero, a defiant, brooding young man consumed by a mysterious past. He was a lover of women who required pursuit, both those spoken for or not—though he often lost interest once he'd achieved his goal. In his lifetime, Byron was involved in numerous public scandals resulting from his affairs with married women. At the time of his death, legend had it that Byron's conquests were in the thousands and that he'd bedded a woman in nearly every city in Europe. Like Michael, he was also five feet eight inches tall and died while still a young man. Lord Byron died in 1824, at the age of thirty-six; Michael in 1997 at the age of thirty-seven.**

Michael was the real deal, and his otherworldly persona predated and more accurately represented the inspiration of the so-called "New Romantic" eighties bands like Duran Duran and the Thompson Twins.

INXS's visual persona was already intact by the time Americans heard *Shabooh Shoobah*—it had been crafted as soon as the band left their original label, Deluxe Records. The intrepid staff at Warner Bros. Australia—Gibson Kemp, Joanne Petersen, and others—were essential in helping them find their public image. Art director Philip Mortlock, the designer responsible for the art on *Shabooh Shoobah, The Swing,* and *Listen Like Thieves,* was crucial. "From the start that band was tuned in to how important photography, album covers, and videos are," Mortlock says. "They wanted to be perceived as they were. They didn't want to turn up in outfits for their band photo—they'd only wear their own clothes. And they wanted their album art to reflect the music and the vibe of who they were. And Chris Murphy, though he wasn't to me, was a pain in the ass to a lot of people a lot of the time. He was a dynamic manager who, along with the band, had a real sense of the visual impact they wanted to have—and he knew how important that was internationally."

In 1982, on MTV "The One Thing" stood apart from clips like J. Geil's "Centerfold," Men at Work's "Down Under," and Michael Jackson's "Thriller" like oil in water. It set a standard for the band throughout the decade, as INXS's visual legacy was consistently innovative. For example, 1985's "What You Need," directed by Richard Lowenstein, was hand painted and animated from thousands of still photographs shot in succession. The video is grainy, sexy, raw, and elevated the medium. Lowenstein used simple cameras and developed the film at a local pharmacy in Melbourne. He then took two months to cut the photos into collage portraits, hand paint them, shoot the resulting stills onto film, and then edit them together to make them move.

The members of INXS were born to be video stars—it was as much an organic expression of their identity as their live show. From their first clip to their last, from "Don't Change" to "Suicide Blonde," INXS deftly projected every bit of romance, sensuality, melancholy, introspection, and exaltation that these six souls, when united as one, let loose in song.

INXS had one more asset that put them ahead of the stylish "hairdresser" U.K. synth-pop bands stirring up record company interest: years of gigs under their belt. And though they might have been confused when Chris Murphy insisted on packing them off to America in the early eighties to convert a vast country of strangers into fans, they did it without question—and to say the least, those miles served them very, very well.

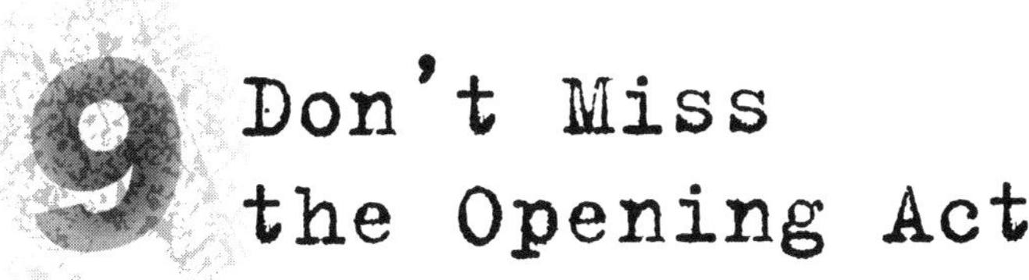

9 Don't Miss the Opening Act

IN AMERICA, VIDEO MADE THEM RADIO STARS, but concerts made them unstoppable. INXS spent the next five years nonstop on the road around the world, with two short months off per year for the holidays and brief breaks to record their next two albums—*The Swing* and *Listen Like Thieves.* Their achievement came in steady increments and the momentum never stopped, but there was no real guarantee that the pot of gold lay around the next corner. Five years of break-even touring and record sales is a commendable lifespan in rock and roll, but for INXS, it was just the beginning: in a classic case of being careful what you wish for, the success that came their way as a result tripled the demands placed on them. The tour schedules grew longer, the crowds grew louder, the venues grew larger, and for the first time INXS felt the heat of attention and the cult of celebrity—which nothing could have prepared them for. But it was meant to be. At Chris Murphy's semidemonic urging, the band had agreed to go big or go home: they signed on to open for the biggest acts that would have them, on any continent, anywhere, and when they had a day off, they'd play clubs along the way. They intended to keep at it until they were either adored and rich or loathed and destitute.

INXS's first hour on American soil was reason enough to turn back. They landed in L.A., in 1983, bound for a club gig in San Diego, after which they were to join Adam Ant as his opening band. They arrived a bit dazed, from the eighteen-hour flight, from the time-zone shift and the requisite trip back in time across the international date line (flying from Sydney to America leaves you off on the same day you leave, close to the same time, whereas flying from America to Sydney drops you two days after you left), and their first impressions of the U.S. were oddly familiar in a *Matrix* kind of way. "I remember looking at the traffic lights, the walk signs, the stores, the streets, and feeling like I'd been there before," recalls Jon Farriss. "It took me days to realize why—I recognized everything from growing up watching American television. I remember we stopped in to get some food and being so unnerved by cop cars going by with their sirens blasting. I remember being at some deli and trying to sort out the menu and getting to the front and the guy just yelling at me because I wasn't ready to order. I think I asked him a question about a sandwich and he asked me what the hell was wrong with me. Then I told him I wanted my order for take away, which means 'to go' in Australia, and he started yelling, 'What? Take what? What's your fucking problem?'"

The group's cultural immersion worsened quickly when their American van driver stopped at a local supermarket to procure some beer and rolling papers. After the driver left the van and his charges parked near the entrance, Jon's *Three's Company* perception of California quickly fishtailed into *Kojak* territory. Suddenly, two Latino males in a late-model American sedan skidded to a stop next to the van. Behind them, four cop cars screamed into the lot, sandwiching INXS and the suspects. The perpetrators and cops all drew guns, and the band, caught in the standoff, froze like a family of deer in headlights. "We'd been in America for less than an hour and we're now in a cross-fire situation with L.A. cops yelling at us through a megaphone to move our van," Garry says. "The guys in the car are aiming at the cops, the cops are aiming at them, and we're right in the middle."

Kirk was riding shotgun, so he jumped into the driver's seat and started the engine. In Australia, the cars and the drivers reside on the right side and it didn't help that the van was a manual shift. "Kirk puts the van in first and just kangaroo-hops it forward, right into a light post," Jon Farriss says. "We were out of the way, but we weren't going anywhere until this thing was over. There were cops blocking every exit. I looked out the back window and saw our driver as he came out of the store holding rolling papers and beer. He took one look at what was going on, turned right back around, and disappeared into the store." The bad guys eventually gave up and INXS's first tour of America was officially under way.

The Adam Ant tour was the first of several stints wherein INXS blew the headliner off the stage. They were men on a mission, one that Chris Murphy drove home each and every night. "He'd tell us, 'Get out there and fucking kill them!'" Kirk says. "And we'd be like, 'Chris, they're our friends, we don't want to do that.' And he'd say, 'This isn't about friendship, it's competition, and *they* are the competition.' He was right. Our motto became "Kill and Root," which, roughly translated from Australian, in the best terms, means something like "Take No Prisoners."

Slowly INXS became aware of a power of which they felt simultaneously proud and guilty. Surely it was talent and timing, but they began to wonder if they exuded some kind of innate Aussie voodoo: nearly every band that INXS supported on tour between 1982 and 1986 broke up shortly afterward. From the Stray Cats to Men at Work to Hall and Oates and the Go-Go's, INXS outshined their employers and seemingly rang the death knell on their bosses' careers.

Those opening tours proved that Chris Murphy was a truly savvy manager—INXS's time on the road earned them priceless exposure, made more precious given that they utilized every day off to play smaller clubs in cities along the way. "That's how we really broke into the American market," former comanager Gary Grant says. "Apart from the opening gigs on big tours, we always booked a few weeks of dates in smaller venues at the start and end of those tours. And it worked. Every time a music fan turned around, we were back in their city in one place or another. They'd see us in big venues as an opening band and then they had the chance to experience INXS on a more intimate level in the clubs."

INXS's plan didn't always go over so well with the headlining acts. Once they were more of a draw to concertgoers than the headliners, it didn't make for happy times on tour, particularly when INXS elicited encores—a truly rare phenomenon for an opening band. "We ran into quite a few situations where the headlining act—and this was common for us—would only allow us to use a fraction of the power of the stage P.A. and maybe one of the spotlights in the lighting rig," Gary Grant says. "That way we couldn't play very loud and we were in near darkness. So when the main act came on, utilizing all of the power and lights, they seemed that much louder and more impressive."

INXS's first gig as an opening act in America—for Adam Ant—resulted in a cold war on tour within a week. Adam quickly grew tired of watching his audience freak for INXS, so, being the reigning queen of his ant colony, he ordered his worker ants to turn the power down on INXS's set. But it didn't go as planned—the worker drones did not handicap their Australian friends' show for the sake of Ant's ego.

"Adam hated us but his crew loved us because we were just good, regular people, so they gave us more power than they were told to," Grant says. "It wouldn't have mattered anyway, Adam was so unpleasant to us that the band went out there every night determined to get encores and tear the house down." They succeeded to the tune of so many multiple encores that Adam Ant soon demanded that they stop playing them, no matter how loud the crowd shouted. "It wasn't the last time a headlining act wouldn't let us play encores," Grant says. "It was great, actually, because INXS would leave the stage with the audience wanting more. It left the crowd hungry, just thinking, 'Goddamn, that was great!' We always found that when we returned to those cities we'd left that way, we'd fill a bigger venue every time."

Grant is right: as INXS traveled across America, opening for artists whom they blew off the stage, they created pockets of fans who'd return to see them again and again. But the events of one winter night in 1983 nearly put an end to all of that—it was the first of a few close vehicular calls for INXS. The band was crossing the Midwest plains by bus, which was driven by a man whose ego eclipsed his abilities; by his account he was a Vietnam vet with an iron constitution who had driven from Boston to Barstow in one night without sleeping. "I've always been very concerned about who our drivers were, and I spent quite a bit of time talking to that first bus driver," Andrew Farriss recalls. "He told me how he'd driven across nearly half of America in one night and had never fallen asleep or had an accident. He said he'd been in Vietnam, and how he'd flown helicopters, and that I had nothing to worry about. He was very convincing. I worry about these things and he even convinced me."

Truth be told, Andrew is the band member who worries most—about everything—and predictably, likes travel least. Aside from his time onstage, he more or less abhors every variable part and parcel of touring—and after that night, he swore off sleeping on a tour bus forever.

"I finally got to sleep that night in my bunk, which is, really, like a small coffin," Andrew says, "when all of a sudden I awoke to a loud crash and was thrown out into the aisle. As I tried to get my bearings, smoke began to fill the cabin." The stalwart driver had fallen asleep at the wheel and the bus had drifted onto the right shoulder of the highway, launched off a snow bank, and landed on its side. The band, upside-down, sideways, and dazed, tumbled into the freezing midwestern night. "All I remember is feeling the bus turn onto its side as I woke up," Andrew says. "And then the smoke. All of us stumbled out into the snow, still half asleep." There was no way that was going to happen again—on every overnight bus trip the band has ever taken since, Andrew sits next to the driver, watching him, watching the road, and if the man behind the wheel threatens to lose his focus, Andrew finds a way to keep him awake until they've reached their destination.

Andrew's bus worries at their worst couldn't compare to the mental duress that Adam Ant endured with INXS on his tour, because what INXS wasn't stealing on stage, they were hijacking doubly afterward. Each night, Adam sent party pimps into the audience to bestow backstage passes upon the hottest girls in the house, so that his post-show fete would teem with the cream of the local crop. He started to notice that, a few too many times, the best girls never made it. "Adam's road manager would have all the good-looking girls in the hotel bar, trying to enforce another level of quality control before he chose which girls would go up to Adam's room," tour manager Gary Grant says. "They'd all be waiting around there for Adam until the guys from INXS walked in. It was hilarious; all of the girls would see them and be like, 'Fuck Adam Ant, we're going with them.' The whole room of them would follow INXS up to their floor of the hotel and the party would begin."

The proceedings continued to deteriorate nightly, so much so that INXS's tour manager Gary Grant was eventually summoned to Mr. Ant's chambers to discuss the "problem" the band had become. Adam, supine on the bed in a dandy smoking jacket and slippers, informed Grant that INXS

International Diplomats: INXS in November 1984.

would be dismissed for their ungrateful behavior if they did not cease and desist their chick-stealing ways immediately. "I explained that they were a bunch of working-class Australian guys and that they meant no disrespect by stealing Adam's girls each night. After about an hour of chatting away, I got him and his tour manager to agree to let us finish the remaining six weeks," Grant says. "He hadn't been friendly before, but let me tell you, after that, Adam didn't speak to us or even look at any of us ever again."

Despite his threats, there was no way Adam Ant was going to kick INXS off his tour. Adam wasn't stupid—INXS stole his show and his girls, but they brought an excitement that the tour couldn't do without: they were a band on the rise, an act on the verge of its prime. They were also newcomers unafraid of anyone—after Adam issued INXS a warning, they didn't back off; they took it as an invitational challenge.

"The night after Gary got his talking to, the band and I deliberately went up to the floor where Adam was having his after-party and took every available girl we could get our hands on," says Rick Sales, the band's no-nonsense American road manager at the time. The ensuing party downstairs was so out of bounds that Rick and Gary Grant, anticipating the arrival of hotel security, intercepted the hotel manager in the lobby. And given the circumstances, they did the only thing they could when the manager began to ask them questions about the party upstairs: they denied everything. "We blamed it all on Adam Ant," Rick says, "even when the elevator opened on our floor and the manager saw the boys in the band wave at us. We acted like we didn't know them and then we did what is known as a 'midnight checkout.' It's basically a fire drill for your group: you pack your bag, grab the girls, load up the bus, and find somewhere else to party."

INXS weren't the only ones who found Adam unbearable—so did his crew and backing band. Adam's haughty management style served to foster a relationship between INXS and his road crew that continued after the tour. As the relationship between Adam and his band members deteriorated, Adam's band vented their frustration with him to INXS. Maybe Adam saw that a mutiny was afoot, or maybe it was just his style, but he treated his backing players with the subtlety of a dictator in decline: the band members told INXS that Adam promised to fire them at the end of the tour. Unsurprisingly, his band took less pride in their work. By the end of their tour, they expressed themselves by sitting down during the very choreographed show's most upbeat moments.

Despite their differences, Adam Ant sent a case of champagne to INXS's dressing room to commemorate the end of the tour, along with a card that read something like, "You guys are great."

"I wasn't having that," says Andrew Farriss. "I wasn't having that at all. I told Adam's tour manager to take the champagne right back to Adam with a request from us that he shove it straight up his ass."

The Adam Ant tour built no bridges with Mr. Ant, but it did wonders for INXS's exposure, particularly via one historic gig they played just after the end of the tour, an experience they'll never forget—the legendary US Festival.*

* The events were held in 1982 and 1983, sponsored by Steve Jobs and Apple, and they entertained, on each occasion, approximately 250,000 people. The US Festivals were everything that Woodstock '94 and '99 were not: peaceful, diverse, and memorable for the right reasons. They took place over three days for two consecutive years and gathered a true cross-section of the brightest talents of the time, from the Clash to David Bowie to INXS to the Police.

The year INXS played the festival was divided by genre: along with the Divinyls, the English Beat, the Stray Cats, Wall of Voodoo, and Oingo Boingo, INXS supported one of the legends who'd inspired them for years, the Clash. The next day was metal heaven: Van Halen was the big draw, supported by Mötley Crüe, Ozzy Osbourne, Judas Priest, and the Scorpions.

That first tour was a great start in America for INXS—and a taste of what was to come. Their next big opening tour was a half-dozen shows on the West Coast for the Stray Cats in 1983, followed by a few shows with the Kinks on the East Coast—where one night, INXS discovered the hard way that some Kinks fans didn't care to hear new music. In New York, INXS was heckled so relentlessly by one fan that the entire theater turned to listen to him. Michael, as he always did in the face of adversity, turned the tables. He leapt offstage, wandered through the audience without missing a note, and serenaded the heckler directly, both of them caught in a spotlight. "Michael always knew to draw the attention to those types of people," Kirk says. "Invariably, with everyone watching them, those types would get shy. That Kinks fan, he just froze up. Then Michael hugged him and the guy couldn't help but hug him back."

Men at Work were next: they booked INXS on an American jaunt in 1984, during their follow-up to their "Who Can It Be Now?" instant stardom, supporting the not-so-embraced album *Cargo.***

** To their credit, the Men were as surprised at their overnight success as anyone else—they were in essence a kind of art-student side-project who became spokes-icons for Australia without logging the miles the average Aussie pub band did in a year. They made new wave pop out of Australian shtick, utilizing flags for backdrops, writing songs that referenced Vegemite, while lead singer Colin Hay did a kangaroo-hop onstage during the band's hit singles. Their label, CBS, gave them the full arena rock-star package, complete with a jet, emblazoned with their logo and the flag of their homeland.

Men at Work was a mellow live act that attracted a sedate, sedentary audience. Aside from their shared heritage, INXS couldn't have been more different—and though relations between the bands never faltered, the obvious aesthetic gap grew greater every night.

"It got to the point that there was a full house of young kids for INXS, most of whom would leave when the older crowd for Men at Work filed in," says tour manager Gary Grant. "INXS was basically blowing them off the stage, because Men at Work were never an awesome live band. We were blown away to travel on their plane instead of slogging it on a bus, but after a while, we felt bad about it. We'd be partying in the back of this jet, having a great time, while they'd be up front fighting among themselves. It was the beginning of the end for them. I believe at that stage the drummer had his own manager, which is never a good sign, and all the internal workings of the band were going to pieces." Indeed they did; after two founding members left the following year, the remaining Men released one more album and called it a day.

In 1985, after opening for Talk Talk, INXS won a slot as the warm-up band on Queen's U.K. tour, where they found that the crowd showed their eagerness to see Queen by pelting the opening band with debris. "Mostly it was bottles," Kirk says. "There were also tomatoes, loaves of bread, cans, lighters, coins, and anything else they could find. We wondered if it was us, but when we asked around, we found out that every opening band got the same treatment. Queen fans really just wanted to see Queen."

No disrespect to Queen, but when INXS got a last-minute offer to play their biggest American headlining gig to date—an outdoor twenty-thousand-capacity festival in Milwaukee—they jumped at the chance, and set about duping their employers. The gig was scheduled on a free day between gigs, but the venue was nearly two thousand miles away. It was possible, but it certainly wasn't easy—it was a roguish dare INXS couldn't resist. The band took the Concorde from London to JFK Airport in New York City, a helicopter to nearby LaGuardia Airport, and then caught a flight to Chicago, where they bumped into U2. "Bono was like, 'What the fuck are you doing here? Aren't you on tour with Queen?'" Andrew Farriss says. "We were like, 'Um, well, yeah. We are. Just not right now. But they think we are. Okay, bye! We'll see you, all right?'"

Leaving U2 and Chicago in the dust, the band motored to Milwaukee, ready to rock. The opening band was Jesus Jones, known best for their hits "Real, Real, Real," and "Right Here Right Now," * who finished a wonderful set just as a rainstorm of biblical proportions doused the grounds. "In a matter of minutes, there was a foot of water underneath the stage," Andrew says. "We sat and watched as the stage and lighting rigs started swaying. Then the promoter canceled the show and the cops ushered everyone out of there."

* **Jesus Jones merged samples, club rhythms, and dance music to platinum pop success, but failed to follow up with anything more substantial than the hits they're known for. Regardless, their moments of brilliance were proof that sample-driven club music and rock and roll can cohabitate beautifully.**

There was little time to mope—the weather was going to delay their return travel and they only had half a day to get back to Newcastle, England. They flew from Chicago to New York, New York to London, caught a shuttle flight, and arrived at the venue just a few hours before they were to perform.

They thought they'd made it, with no one the wiser, until Queen guitarist Brian May burst into INXS's dressing room wondering why their instruments weren't set up on stage. "Luckily, there was something else wrong that day. Apparently one of the truck drivers had stayed over in the last city to spend a night with his wife and hadn't left in time to make the gig," Andrew says. "Before we could come up with an excuse, Brian told us how crap it was that our gear hadn't arrived because it must be on that missing truck. Meanwhile it was actually parked in some New York airport."

INXS didn't play that night, which, according to Andrew, is one of only four gigs they've ever canceled or missed in twenty years. That is yet another of the band's amazing accomplishments: considering that their schedule averaged two hundred to three hundred gigs a year from 1980 to 1996, four cancellations is one brown blade on an acre of green grass. But according to Rick Parfitt, the guitarist for Status Quo, INXS played brilliantly that night. "He came to our dressing room and told us that we'd done an amazing set," Kirk says. "And when we told him that we hadn't played, he just kind of wandered off."

Down the hall in Queen's dressing room, ever the upstart, Michael couldn't help but tell Freddie Mercury of INXS's covert, thwarted mission. "Freddie loved it," Andrew says. "He thought we were hilarious. He invited us up to his room to party that night and as I recall he played some brand-new songs they'd recorded and sang them to us. It was amazing but quite surreal. He wanted Michael to sing with him, but Michael didn't know the words. And Freddy really got into it, he'd come right up to your face and belt it." Freddy's enthusiasm was partially fueled by the huge lines of cocaine road manager Rick Sales had provided Mr. Mercury upon his request—for which Rick, a man as tough and straight as they come, received a kiss on the lips. Rick didn't miss a beat—he turned Mercury's affection into an advantage for the opening band's staging. "Yes, I can say that Freddy Mercury kissed me, it's true," Rick says. "But I wasn't going to be satisfied with that. After he kissed me I said, 'So, I assume this means that we can use your drum riser during our set?' He laughed and said, 'Of course, darling!'"

Freddy Mercury serenading everyone in the room within inches of their face was an odd moment, but the party that celebrated the end of the tour was even more fittingly bizarre. Queen rented the entire penthouse of a London hotel and filled it with flamingos, midgets, mimes, sexual acrobats, and everything else to make the fete Fellini-esque.

Opening for the Go-Go's tour was a much more American affair—the bands toured together in the summer of 1984, playing outdoor festivals and more than a few amusement parks. Though the Go-Go's were headed for splitsville (they disbanded less than a year later), they did not take out their troubles on INXS, rather the two groups got along very well—almost too well. It was clear to both bands' road managers that if they could not locate a member of their band—say Michael Hutchence or Belinda Carlisle—they would usually find them in the bed or bus bunk of a member of the opposite band. And the days off on that tour were more tiring than work. "When we played a Six Flags, they'd let all of us ride the roller coaster for as long as we wanted after the show," Gary Grant says. "We would do big lines of coke and get on the roller coaster and go around and around and around. It's a miracle no one threw up."

10 The Takeover

DURING THE YEARS THEY SPENT winning fans around the world one stage at a time, INXS evolved, across three records, into a band like no other. Beginning in 1984, they focused their disparate influences—R&B, funk, disco, and punk—into a dance-rock hybrid that took the world by storm and inspired a slew of imitators. INXS was one of the first white bands to sound so much like a black funk band but without losing their edgy white rock roots; the resulting sound was a white version of Prince. INXS lent the automaton pop of new wave grit, depth, and atypical funk.

They also put forth an earthy, unmistakable heterosexuality, while popular and cutting-edge eighties synth-pop bands like Spandau Ballet, Human League, and Flock of Seagulls advertised androgyny, and acts like U2 and Midnight Oil preached politics. INXS were stylish boys who defined modern masculinity: smart, sensitive, cultured, and brazenly sexual. They evoked the past and present at once. They were utterly of the moment, yet they brought to mind the romanticism of days gone by; days when men *had* women, when passion was all consuming, and sex was a secret feast for the senses. Michael's lyrics, at their most seductive, echo the Romantic age, in all of the lust, yearning, and carnality of a bygone era's sensual poets—wordsmiths who were the rock stars of their day.

INXS's intensity is married to their musical complexity, one whose crescendos never lose the melody. They can blow the doors off without turning the amps up, and are truly a sum of their influences: the bands they emulated are the Rolling Stones, the Talking Heads, and Chic.

"In the eighties every white band in England was trying to sound like black funk musicians," *Swing* producer Nick Launay says. "Bands like the Chili Peppers and Faith No More carried that flag afterward. But INXS really did it first and did it best. It was very interesting, because there they were, this Australian band—and Australia is very, very white (and still is)—who really were tapping into a sound that the whole world wanted. That is why they were so successful. They were one of the few bands who had the direction right." The band's albums before *The Swing* (1984) were a mix of rock tempered with soul, colored by the music of their youth—Motown, 10cc, the Average White Band, the Clash, and Iggy Pop. *The Swing* changed all that, as INXS dove into the disco and funk ends of their influences. Producer Nick Launay was crucial to that evolution.

Launay is one of the most successful, visionary producers of the post-punk era who helmed seminal recordings by the bands that defined the fringes of rock after punk. Launay's hit list might not have made anyone millions, but his work foresaw the future: the sound of those albums are the single biggest influence on today's most popular alternative rock bands. From Franz Ferdinand to the Rapture to Bloc Party to the Killers, Launay's résumé is their blueprint. He produced Gang of Four's seminal *To Hell With Poverty!* EP, as well as Public Image Limited's *The Flowers of Romance,* Killing Joke's single "Follow the Leaders," as well as albums by the Birthday Party (*Junkyard* and *Release the Bats* EP), the Church, and Midnight Oil ("10, 9, 8, 7, 6, 5, 4, 3, 2, 1"—a massive chart hit in Australia). And he did all of it before he turned twenty-three.

INXS met Launay at Paradise Studios in Sydney while he was mixing an album for Melbourne's the Models. It was only years later, in print, that Launay learned what they really thought about him that day. "I remember reading in an interview with Michael and Kirk, I think, that they thought I was a junkie," Launay says. "I thought it was hilarious. I'm such an obsessive and back then when they met me, I was so consumed by the music that I would literally shake while doing a mix. They thought I was on drugs, but I was just so overwhelmed and consumed—and nervous—that I could not hold my hands steady."

They weren't too scared to hire Launay to produce their fourth album, *The Swing*—not only one of INXS's best works, but a pivotal point in their development. Every great band has their transitional album, the one that might not be perfect, or hang together just right, but is a document of a crucial place and time. Those albums are usually a dress rehearsal for their upcoming masterpiece. Such is *The Swing.*

"*The Swing* was supposed to be their Talking Heads album," Launay says. "It was supposed to be their *Remain in Light.* We didn't talk about it, but it was clear that that's what we were doing." The band, exhausted after months of touring, joined Launay, who was fatigued after months of recording the Models, in Oxford, England, at the Manor, an eighteen-bedroom, seventeenth-century estate complete with a lake, a go-kart race course, and a recording studio owned by Virgin CEO Richard Branson. They had just six weeks to get an album together, but it worked to their benefit: they wrote most of it on the spot, allowing all of the influences of the English music scene to shape the result.

"They wanted to make the record in England to lap up all of the feelings you get from being in other countries," Launay says. "But before we went off to the Manor to make the record, they did a tour of America, and that's when they met Nile Rodgers."*

Nile caught INXS in Canada opening for Men at Work on a night when it seemed that the audience had been dosed with Valium. "We were backstage talking about how weird and completely sedate the crowd was, when Nile Rodgers walks in," Andrew recalls. "We were discussing how terrible a show it was, when Nile bursts in and says, 'Man, was that crowd *weird* or what?' First of all, we were in shock to meet someone we'd idolized all our lives, and secondly, we were overjoyed to learn that he felt the same way we did."

*** Nile Rodgers's contribution to popular music can't be underestimated. As a youth of nineteen, Rodgers was the guitarist in the house band in Harlem's world-famous Apollo Theater. He soon grew bored of playing the pitch-perfect guitar line in sixties soul classics, and learned to turn his instrument into a rhythm outlet, perfecting the polyrhythmic scratch sound that made disco dirty. With Chic, he made history, via tracks like "Le Freak" and "Good Times." As a producer, Rodgers's work is exemplary; Madonna's *Like a Virgin* and David Bowie's comeback album, *Let's Dance,* set the sound bar for eighties pop music very high.**

Nile wasn't there by accident—he'd heard "The One Thing" and *Shabooh Shoobah,* and was intrigued. It was decided on the spot that he and INXS should work together and would meet up in New York to collaborate on a track. Chris Murphy wasn't going to let that promise dissipate—INXS had a shot at working with, quite simply, the most respected and successful producer of the day. "I proceeded to call Nile on a daily basis," Chris Murphy says. "I completely harassed him. I was not going to let this opportunity slip by. I knew that if we did a track with a producer of his status that it would elevate the band's reputation tremendously. Once other producers and other musicians saw that Nile had worked with us, they'd take us altogether seriously."

Murphy locked Nile into a two-day session during the band's next swing through New York, but a week or so beforehand, Rodgers called him in a panic. "He wanted to know what we planned to record," Murphy says. "He'd heard the records, but he wanted some new music to listen to before we met. So I ordered Andrew to give me something, immediately." Andrew and Michael had been working on a speedy rock song called "Original Sin" that they felt good about. Murphy sent it off to Nile—and in Mr. Rodgers's hands, the song blossomed into a slinky, seductive, hot slice of pop. Anchored to a rich, strolling bass line, the steamy horns, coy funk guitar, and Michael's come-hither vocals are pure sex and transcendence. It didn't hurt one bit to have the exquisite backing vocals of Kirk Pengilly and Darryl Hall of Hall and Oates harmonizing on the chorus.

"Nile Rodgers was the biggest record producer in the world at the time. He'd done Madonna's 'Like a Prayer,' David Bowie's 'Let's Dance,'—the two biggest records of the day—and INXS had recorded with him in the same studio, using the same engineers who'd done 'Let's Dance,'" Nick Launay recalls. "INXS had suddenly gone from this up-and-coming band who was edgy and interesting to an act that had worked with Nile Rodgers—they were suddenly a very serious band to watch. 'Original Sin' was so incredible that when I heard it, I just thought, 'How on earth am I going to follow this?'" Launay's challenge began in the middle of autumn, in Oxford, England, in 1983. Sitting on worn-in antique furniture, around a huge fireplace at the Manor, INXS brought out the demos they'd been working on. "Andrew had this amazing demo of 'Burn for You,' that he'd recorded all by himself, playing every instrument, on the tour bus." Kirk had a song called

"Face the Change," and Tim had a number called "Melting in the Sun." The band was also keen to rework an old demo called "Johnson's Aeroplane." All in all, they had a start, but they had a lot of work to do.

Aside from those songs, the album was written in the studio (apart from a bit of work back in Sydney at Rhinoceros Recordings), which allowed them to be completely organic: they corralled the funk and disco influences they'd tapped with "Original Sin," and incorporated them into their taut rock lexicon. Launay and Garry Beers listened intently to Japan, an English synth-based band featuring Mick Karn, a fretless bass player whose nimble style and elastic, buoyant tone was considered one of the best in the world. At the time, synthesizer acts like Human League, Depeche Mode, and Soft Cell had brought the fringe to the mainstream. "Those bands were, at the time, very alternative, but they found a way to make it catchy and completely pop," Launay says. "One weekend, Human League was up at the Manor when INXS had a day off, and they heard 'I Send a Message' and were totally blown away. It made sense; there was INXS, playing music as catchy as those bands, but they were still this rock band who could really play their instruments." INXS, by bridging the black funk tradition with white rock and roll, tapped into a cocktail that defined the times. "There were a lot of white guys in England and Australia wanting to play as well as black musicians and wanting to sound like black musicians. INXS had just come from working with Nile Rodgers, one of the greatest funk musicians who ever lived—so naturally, every guitar and bass line on *The Swing* is funk based. Yet, it's rock as well. And it was also important to them that the beats be four-on-the-floor dance beats. They wanted, from the start, to make it a dance record. And, truthfully, it was one of the first records to be done that way, blending black and white influences over completely straight-ahead dance rhythms. The only band who'd done it before, in those days, was the Talking Heads."

INXS was a band at the top of their abilities after so many years on the road—and they had to be to meld all of their influences so naturally. *The Swing* is a true snapshot of the times: it's black and white, light and dark, embracing everything from the down-wave descent of "Melting in the Sun," to the pensive pogo of "I Send a Message," to the blissful, romantic elation of "Burn for You." "INXS, more than any band, drew influences from everywhere in the world," Nick Launay says. "On that album, they tapped into the funk-dance thing in America, hit on the black and white soul style that was huge in England, and because they are such great players, made it all work within the parameters of a rock band. It was a truly international sound."

The Swing was put together in a very stylized way: the songs are symphonies of syncopation; the instruments and the sounds play off one another very deliberately. "I was very meticulous about the arrangement," Launay says. "Everything was short bits of sound that come one right after the other that all fit together like a very strange puzzle. It wasn't about playing the guitar freely—everything was very controlled. And that is what the eighties was. I'd say INXS invented the eighties through their records and the influence they had. And the thing is, it came out of punk, but it was also anti-punk. Punk rock is simple chords played with incredible feeling—mostly because a lot of the punk musicians couldn't play more than those few chords and were doing the best they could. The music that came along in the eighties was pretty clever stuff. You had to be a good musician to pull it off."

INXS was more than gifted enough to make the vision a reality—they were also wise enough to love technology. *The Swing* is the first album released worldwide that featured drum sounds enriched by triggered samples of the same drum—an effect that is commonly used today. But at the time, it was alien territory and none too easy to achieve. Nick Launay used the second generation of a simple sampler—a device that could record less than one second of sound and play it back when triggered. By today's standards, it's like writing an essay with a quill and inkwell instead of a computer. "The first sampler I ever had was this little black box called an AMS 1580 that could retain six hundred milliseconds of sound," Nick Launay says. "When we did *The Swing* I had the next generation of that and what I did was feed Jon's snare sound into it, then set it up so that every time he hit the drum live, it would play this minirecording of his drum sound. It gave the drums a bigger, fuller sound when he played—and huge drums were very important in the eighties. That album, to my knowledge, was the very first one to feature any kind of triggered drums. *Let's Dance* didn't have it, and I hadn't heard any record that had. Of course after *The Swing* came out, just about every record released treated the drums that way. And it's almost funny to talk about it, because these days, triggering drums to get that effect is par for the course."

Launay and the band also used that little black sampling box to alter guitars, synths, and anything else that might be more unusual after a tweak.

"It really hadn't been done before," Launay says. "We had this weird bit of technology and any way I'd think to use it, the band would completely be like, 'Yeah! Let's try it.'" INXS was also the lucky recipient of one of the very first two Yamaha DX7 synthesizers ever produced, and they used it extensively on *The Swing.* *

"We were really lucky to have that," Launay says. "It was straight from Japan—all of the writing on the keyboard and in the manual were in Japanese, so Andrew learned to use it intuitively. It was literally the first one off the factory line. I think the other one went to Duran Duran."

On *The Swing,* INXS fully embraced the day's top technology, wielding it as another instrument, one that augmented but never outshone the band's playing. They knew the union of true musicianship, so to them, the malleable sounds afforded by digital technology was yet another means of expression. Forever after, INXS utilized digital sound technology to push the limits on record as well as in concert, well before the equipment was suited to the conditions. "They were the first band to go out and tour with an Akai MPC-60 as part of their stage setup," Launay says. "They'd use it to load the sound set for each song, play the song, then load the sound set for the next song. They really were the first to do it that way. They were at the very forefront and I don't think anyone realized it. INXS took huge risks and I'm sure it backfired occasionally, but it was very, very adventurous." * *

Of course, today, musicians can make computers do whatever

*** The Yamaha DX7 is, arguably, the most influential instrument in eighties music. Released in 1983, it is one of the most popular, affordable digital synthesizers ever produced. It relied on frequency modulation dramatically unlike the analog units that had come before. It was notoriously difficult to program, but the DX7 came with enough preprogrammed sounds and the ability to manipulate them that eighties artists easily coaxed strange, metallic, percussive noise from it. The DX7 quickly became a staple of every keyboardist's arsenal and is still coveted today, by everyone from Nine Inch Nails to the Chemical Brothers to U2 to the Beastie Boys.**

*** * The Akai MPC-60, released in 1988, is a legendary mini-music production studio that remains one of the most utilized pieces of equipment today. The MPC-60 is the machine that made hip-hop possible and sampling an art form. It is an all-in-one sequencer and sampler designed by Roger Linn, the mastermind behind the Linn Drum—the first industry standard in drum machines. The MPC-60 is versatile and portable; it can record and store programmed beats made in real-time as well as samples of anything—all of which can be edited and looped with ease. It's no wonder that hip-hop artists from OutKast to Jay-Z to Eminem won't enter a studio without one.**

they want on or off stage—since the introduction of Pro Tools in the nineties, a few clicks of a mouse can make a guitar sound like a tuba, a drum sound like a flute, or a singer sing in tune—but in 1984, those possibilities were far off and technology was still a trial-and-error affair. INXS paved the way.

The Swing isn't the most even INXS record; it is at once as dark and edgy as the Manor in winter and as sunny and ethereal as Sydney in summer. It is a marriage of opposites—the contrast that is INXS. "Recording *The Swing* was an exhausting, stressed, amazing time," Launay recalls. "The band drew from so many cool places. It was all recorded live, as albums should be, done half at the Manor and half in Sydney—and you can hear the result, which was literally half winter and half summer. I think it says so much about INXS that they put out an album with one song—'Original Sin'—done by Nile Rodgers, the top producer of the day, and one of the greatest funk guitar players of all time, while the rest of the record was produced by me, this guy known for working with the most left-of-center, dark alternative bands. That's just weird. And that's just great. And that's how they continued to do things." *The Swing* was the band's biggest album in Australia: it debuted at Number 1, and lingered in the album charts for well over a year. It even eclipsed the sales of *Kick*—the band's most successful album internationally—on their native soil. To date, *The Swing* ranks as one of the Top 10 best-selling albums of all time in Australia.

Unfortunately, it wasn't as embraced elsewhere in the world, particularly in America. Chris Murphy and the band knew that they had an amazing single in "Original Sin," a tune positioned to be the global hit to push INXS into the top tier of popular music. "They'd done what so many groups were trying to do. A group of white Australians recorded this incredible fusion of black funk and hard rock on a song about black and white relations that was produced by the top man of the day—who, incidentally, was black," Launay says. "That one song summed up everything there is to say about those subjects at that time, subjects that weren't honestly talked about. It should have been bigger than 'Let's Dance.' But it wasn't, because the lyrics were interpreted entirely wrong."

When the executives at Atco (the Atlantic Records subsidiary), INXS's American label, heard the song, they were perplexed by the band's new musical direction and its lyrical implications. They were, actually, unsure of what to do. "Atlantic didn't want to release it," Murphy says. "They said it was too controversial. They'd sent it to radio stations across the country and all of Middle America refused to play it." The song was taken for a ditty about a taboo love affair between a white boy and a black girl, and as such was deemed too hot and too wrong for U.S. airwaves. "The label basically asked me what the hell we were doing," Murphy says. "They asked, 'Why are you working with Nile Rodgers? Why are you doing black music? What is this supposed to be, some kind of R&B track? INXS is a rock band.'"

Through persistence and charisma, Murphy managed to get the single released, and after it was, INXS, Atlantic Records, and almost every radio station that played it received death threats and hate mail. At one gig in Texas, someone threw a loaded pistol onstage with a cryptic note attached that read, "In appreciation of your music." "We weren't exactly sure how to take that, or what the message was precisely," Kirk says. "Did it mean that the person who tossed us the gun appreciated it and felt that we might need protection from those who didn't? Was it entirely sarcastic and threatening? We weren't sure, but we were unanimously in agreement that whatever the message was, it wasn't good."

The truth is, "Original Sin" isn't even about an interracial tryst, as a cursory perusal of the lyrics will reveal. For all of its steamy sonic suggestion, the song's message is closer to Martin Luther King Jr.'s vision of interracial harmony than R. Kelly's bedroom manifestos. Michael was inspired to jot most of the song's lyrics down during his first drive through Harlem. While his car was stopped at a traffic light next to a city park, he watched black and white children playing together and was struck by the loss of innocence and the acquisition of race awareness that come with age. The original sin he wrote about wasn't a call to taste the great "taboo" of interracial sex, it was an ode to mankind's shortcomings, a lament for our fall from grace and the shortsighted prejudice that keeps us apart, when, in truth, we're all one.

Perhaps it's predictable, maybe it's ironic, or it might be as inexplicable as their love of Jerry Lewis, but while "Original Sin" offended Americans everywhere in 1984, it thrilled the French. INXS's marketing rep in France was utterly moved by the song, and in the years to come, he always seemed to understand the band's creative direction when no one else did. "There were several times over the years when Jacques's enthusiasm was the only thing that kept me going," Chris Murphy says. "When none of the record companies we were signed to seemed to get what we were doing and I was desperate, Jacques always seemed to phone me at precisely the right time. He'd say, 'Chris! I love this single. This 'Original Sin,' I love what Andrew and Michael are doing. It's brilliant!' "

Never one to let something like adversity or public opinion get in his way, Murphy spun the American controversy into European gold by putting two record labels at odds, all to the band's benefit. "I told the European label that the Americans were banning the song, and I told the Americans that the Europeans loved it," Murphy says cheerfully. "It drove both of them crazy. And it ensured that both labels got behind the single stronger than before."

Mr. Murphy got his rocks off successfully stirring up recording corporations while "Original Sin" took off of its own accord: it hit Number 1 in France, Australia, Argentina, and Italy and became a naughty, must-have piece of vinyl in America. "On the twenty-fifth of January, 1984, 'Original Sin' went Number One in France and I was informed by phone very early in the morning," recalls tour manager Gary Grant. Grant was in Rome, crashed out in a two-bedroom suite with his primary responsibility, Michael Hutchence. That morning, the pair was recovering from the previous evening's festivities, which had lasted well past dawn in honor of a very well received tour of Italy. Grant was duly dazed when he answered the phone and heard the news. He fumbled for his glasses and stumbled headlong into Michael's room.

"It took a lot to wake Michael when he was out—I mean a lot. It wasn't easy, but I shook him that morning, just repeating, "Michael, 'Original Sin' is Number One, 'Original Sin' is Number One!' " Once Hutchence perked up, he tumbled into a rock star moment worthy of the greatest golden gods: "When he finally understood what I was saying to him, Michael jumped out of bed, completely naked, and began singing, 'We're Number One! We're Number One!' at the top of his lungs. He was marching around the room with one arm raised, bellowing as loud as he could. He strode right onto the balcony and directly across from our room, on the roof of a church, a dozen nuns were kneeling there, saying their prayers that morning. It was amazing—I don't know if they heard him before they saw him, but all of them stopped their prayers and turned in unison to look at him, just completely stunned. It stopped Michael in his tracks for a moment. Then he just smiled, waved at them, and shouted, 'We're Number One!'"

The Swing is also a pivotal album in the history of INXS because it was the reason why they met Richard Lowenstein, the man responsible for the band's greatest moments in music video. Lowenstein is from Melbourne, the town that inspired Nick Cave, the Models, Hunters and Collectors, and many more. Lowenstein was not at all familiar with the byways and sunny coastal highways INXS had traveled. After seeing one of Lowenstein's darker videos for the band Hunters and Collectors, INXS decided that Lowenstein should make their next video. Of course they did: on the surface, INXS and Lowenstein had nothing in common, but INXS knew that Richard was an experimental kindred spirit.

Chris Murphy arranged for Lowenstein to join the band on the Northern Australian coast during their summer tour. The pasty, black-clad director

Michael Hutchence and music-video director Richard Lowenstein.

and his crew met them poolside at a hotel in a surf town where spring break never stopped. "We walked up and there they were, these tan beach guys drinking piña coladas on their lounge chairs around the hotel pool," Lowenstein says. "Chris Murphy had talked me into doing this—he's so convincing that I thought it was the right thing to do. But at that moment when I laid eyes on them, I remember thinking that I'd made a *huge* mistake. I didn't know what we'd have in common. But then, all of a sudden, this guy, this ball of energy, bounced over to me and said, 'Hi, I'm Michael Hutchence. How are you?' He was so gracious and nothing at all that I expected." From the outside, Michael and Richard couldn't have looked more different: Hutchence was a long-haired, skinny, sun-baked, sexy urchin and Lowenstein was a pale, pensive, particular artiste. But they saw a bit of themselves in each other, and that first video marked the start of a lifelong friendship. "We immediately started talking about what we could do for the song, which was 'Burn for You,'" Lowenstein says. "I found out right away that he and I did see things alike. And that was it—I was sold. It was the start of a long friendship that changed my life."

"Burn for You" was shot over one week, and the video is as beautiful as the love song it accompanies. It is a rosy slice of time; a home movie of the band on tour in Australia that captures the warmth of their inner family. Lowenstein's later efforts, groundbreaking clips like "What You Need," "Need You Tonight," and "Never Tear Us Apart," got heavy rotation around the world, but "Burn for You" is a priceless portrait of INXS in their youth, in their prime and on the verge of becoming the biggest band in the world. The clip captures an ethereal moment in all its glory: Michael's first love, Michele Bennett, was on that tour, as was Karen Hutchinson, the mother of Kirk's daughter, April, as was Tim's wife, Buffy, as well as Jenny Morris, a gifted vocalist and longtime friend of the band. Richard Lowenstein had just met them and had no idea what he was walking into, but he got what they were about and captured them openly and honestly. That tour, in the minds of those who were there, was perfect, the last time of that kind they'd ever know. It was the end of an era—their last moments of perfect innocence, the last taste of the past before the future arrived. That video is what everyone wishes their home movies to be: warm memories captured forever; memories of moments that flicker by too fast.

The History of Lester Histermine

KIRK PENGILLY was born in Melbourne, a city known for its dark, bohemian nature, though Kirk is as bright and carefree as sun-drenched Sydney. He is one of three boys whose father, an advertising man, helmed his own company by his thirties. Each year, for two weeks, he took the family to Sydney, where they'd charter a thirty-six-foot boat and, starting at a town called Bobbin Head just north of Sydney Harbor, cruise the waterway inland. "We'd live on the water, just fish and knock about," Kirk says. "We'd moor where we liked, with mountains and bush and wild animals all around, and no one else anywhere in sight." During one of those trips, the family passed through Cottage Point, a tiny township situated amid untouched national parkland. They spied a house for sale—and that was that. "Dad saw it and said, 'That's it, we're moving,'" Kirk says. "He sold his business, which was very successful, and Mum reluctantly packed us up and moved us out there."

The Pengillys' new waterside compound was unique; the home was cut

Alias: Kirk Pengilly

Born: July 4, 1958

Instruments: guitar, sax, vocals, programming

Married: December 30, 1993, to singer Deni Hines

Children: April, born April 12, 1988, with former girlfriend Karen Hutchinson

Divorced: 1996

First Band: Guinness

Alternate Aliases: Andy Clockwise, Barry Tone, Ken Nuggets

Other Interests: cooking, boating/sailing, movies

into a massive rock and powered by a generator. Rainwater, collected in a tank, fueled their plumbing and provided drinking water. There was no garbage collection, and the nearest town was seven miles away—the first three of which were a dirt road. "Our house was built around this giant rock that came through the middle of it and extended out into the water," Kirk's brother Drew says. "There was a cave cut through it—our parents' room was at one end of it and the room that Kirk and I shared was at the other end." They also had a dog named Randy who loved beer and constantly ran away to hang with three local dudes who loved to watch Randy lap lager from a can. "We'd hear a splash outside late at night and it would be Randy coming home," Kirk says. "He'd be so drunk that he'd fall into the swimming pool on his way to the house."

Kirk's oldest brother, Mark, played music and encouraged Kirk to take up guitar at just nine years old. "My dad used to let Mark's band practice occasionally at our house; he'd let them fire up the generator during the day," Kirk says. "I'd watch them and that was a huge influence on me. Mark used to play records all the time: Bob Dylan, Van Morrison, Gordon Lightfoot—that's the first music I remember." For some reason, Mark also assigned musical homework. He elected himself the family Elvis expert, middle brother Drew the Pengilly authority on Roy Orbison, and Kirk the steward of all things Cliff Richard, Britain's answer to Elvis. Kirk religiously collected Cliff Richard singles but he moved on from there to Carole King's *Tapestry,* James Taylor, and later Glen Campbell. Mark, in his late teens by then, got a job in advertising, took off to pursue a music career in London, but left Kirk a significant gift—a flamenco guitar restrung with steel strings.

Kirk taught himself to play it, and as he did, he took in music from a writer's perspective. He no longer heard songs; he heard chord structures. He stopped listening to lyrics and started listening to harmonics; he dove deep into many a Yes album on his path to becoming a young singer-songwriter, and worked out the chord progressions by ear.

Kirk made his first record in 1969 at age eleven, when his friend Michael Sheridan from Melbourne, a fellow guitar player, came to visit. "We used this old reel-to-reel tape recorder that my dad had used in his advertising business," Kirk recalls. "We did three songs: the Beatles' 'Yellow Submarine,' the Animals' 'House of the Rising Sun,' and my original 'I Need You,' a big hit. It was massive in Cottage Point."

It's an exclusive, developed, secluded community now, but at the time, Cottage Point was a seasonal getaway with less than ten full-time residents.

According to Kirk, one of them was "a weird nerdy guy who had one of those machines they once used to cut records, 78s, actually." He would record their favorite songs off the radio, then they'd give the guy a couple of bucks to make bootleg compilations for them. "He was the original Napster," Kirk says. "I still have that record somewhere—it's got a little yellow label with a misspelled title—called 'Kirk Ben Gilly and His Gang.'"

Kirk met Tim Farriss in high school, and they became instant friends and musical collaborators. Kirk began to spend most weekends at the Farriss house, out of convenience and friendship; his lengthy trek from Cottage Point took ages, while the Farriss boys lived a few short minutes away from his school. Once Kirk set his mind to playing music, he cared about little else. "Kirk was never interested in sports like I was," his brother Drew says. "As an adult he's bought gym memberships, gone in for a few training sessions, and never gone again. He just wanted to play guitar. We used to call him Flab, because every time there was a chore for us boys to do around the house, Kirk was never around for the manual labor."

After Kirk finished high school, he moved into a house in Whale Beach with Tim and the members of Guinness. "Kirk pretty much wasn't around after that," Drew says. "And once they formed the Farriss Brothers, they really took off and did their thing. They were so devoted. Once it got going, it was very obvious that this was going to be a big band." But in case it wasn't, they had a backup plan. "It's a good thing it worked out because I can't imagine him doing much else," Drew says. "When they were still young and making their way they did have this very detailed high idea that if it didn't all work out, they'd collectively found this Mexican chip factory. There was all this talk about going into business with some investor. They intended to produce the Australian equivalent of Doritos."

Kirk is the most regimented, anal, and organized member of INXS—and proud of it. He's kept detailed journals of his life since the late seventies; contained in twenty worn books and a few computer disks, they're legible, clearly dated, and proved invaluable to the writing of this book. Keeping a daily diary of an ordinary life is tough enough; maintaining an accurate record, as it happens, of a life like Kirk's is just shy of fanatical. It's so very Pengilly: Kirk is the type of man who, even as a teenager in a rock band, made his bed with precision every morning. "Kirk is a unique guy," former INXS tour manager Bruce Patron (who shares Kirk's birthday) says. "During the *Kick* tour, at the very height of their popularity, you'd go into Kirk's room and find a string across his bathtub with his socks and underpants hung out to dry. I couldn't believe it. I'd say, 'Kirk, come on, you know they've got laundry service here, don't you? We send runners out with laundry every day.' He didn't care, that is just how he does it."

Kirk is a skilled guitarist, able to fill in on rhythm as deftly as he conjures solos. Before the Farriss Brothers became INXS, they decided that a horn was needed to add color to their sound, and Kirk volunteered to learn it. "Tim, Jon, and I lived in a house together at that time, and I drove Tim crazy for three months," Kirk says. "I followed him from room to room trying to get some feedback. All I could play were these simple sax lines. I soon lost interest, but later, once Chris Murphy started managing the band and we really became INXS, I picked it up again at his urging." Over the years, Kirk's self-taught mastery of the instrument became a cornerstone of INXS's sound.

In concert, Kirk's side of the stage is very much his own. His monitors only reflect his playing—a bold testament to how tuned in to the music he is.

"He's always had it that way—he only likes to hear himself," Garry Beers says. "It's not a selfish thing at all, it's what he's used to. Kirk is a Cancer and he's the most Cancerian person I've ever met; he's set in his ways. It's weird, though, as a fellow band member: you go over to his side of the stage and you can't hear anything you're doing or anyone else is doing. He's been playing with us all this time but he's got no idea what the band sounds like onstage while it's happening. But it works! I often felt like Kirk was always behind the beat, but when I'd listen back to the recording, I realized that he was fine."

It might be odd on stage, but Kirk's meticulous nature also helps the band live and in the studio. "Kirk is a true perfectionist," INXS producer Mark Opitz says. "He was always a great judge of the band's gigs and that's very hard to do. At the end of a show he knows exactly where he's made mistakes. He's a guitarist and the band's devil's advocate all at once." Kirk also always knew what would work. Dave Nicholas, the band's longtime engineer, is always impressed by Kirk's intuitive musicality. "The real chemistry of INXS was Michael Hutchence and the band working together," he says. "But to make that happen, the players had to bring it all together. And what Kirk did, which I'm not sure everyone realized, was come from the left. He always brought ideas that no one else did, and those ideas were often what made it all work."

As concentrated and controlled as he is, Kirk is equally loose and experimental. He's a bohemian at heart and, like his bandmates, he loves to defy the norm. He certainly did so back in the day when he and his boys showed up for lunch with Kirk's parents—on acid. On one of their many trips between Sydney and Melbourne for gigs, they planned to lunch with the Pengillys, who then lived on a farm about a third of the way to Melbourne. A friend had dosed them with LSD, and they arrived chez Pengilly with the situation barely under control. As the drugs took hold and the guys started to grin and cackle like madmen, they were glad that Kirk's dad, Jack, who passed away in 2002, liked to tell corny jokes. He *loved* to tell corny jokes, actually, and had amassed quite a repertoire. That day, Jack's son found a new appreciation for his father's sense of humor—his friends laughed so heartily that the man shared every joke he'd ever heard. "We were hysterical and were goading him on," Kirk says. "He didn't realize at all that we were out of it. He just thought he was absolutely hilarious. Each of his jokes gave us a reason to laugh, which we needed very badly. It was insane." Each boy—all of them poor and undernourished then—could barely eat the food that Pat, Kirk's mom, had prepared that day, arousing much suspicion in Mum. She couldn't quite figure out what was wrong with them, and as she pondered it, the sight of her husband breaking out his record player distracted her. To the boys' utter bemusement, Mr. Pengilly started dancing. "We were listening to music, all of us red-faced, I'm sure," Kirk says. "We got my dad to dance, which nearly killed us from laughter. He was dancing so hard that he kept making the record player skip, and every time it did, we were pitched into another round of hysterics. I still don't know how we ever got out of there."

Like Buddy Holly and Elvis Costello, Kirk Pengilly is a rock star with glasses—a condition prone to chronic occupational hazards. In the early days, Kirk was pushed to work his spectacles for all their worth; with tape around the bridge of his thick black frames, he became the band's resident nerd, known for his spastic expressions and weird onstage demeanor. Kirk got into it by spiking his hair, donning oddball outfits, and making faces, but his bottle-bottom specs became a totem—one that he couldn't do without. "I learned to carry spare glasses with me on tour because they were stolen a number of times," he says. "I'd jump into the audience and someone would pull them off. I hated that, because I'm truly blind without them."

Even though Kirk secured them with a tight band around his head, zealous fans who didn't realize or care that he actually needed them to see loved to peel them away. One night in Salt Lake City circa *Kick*, Kirk had had enough. He was in pain, a bit boozy, and fed the fuck up.

The day before, friends took Kirk skiing for the first time and cruelly set him loose at the top of Park City, Utah's premier ski resort. "Our managers told us specifically not to go skiing," Kirk says. "So of course, I did. I fell so many times just trying to get back down to the bottom that I banged up the right side of my head, my right shoulder, a few ribs, and severely bent back my right thumb. I was taken to the hospital, X-rayed, and was in a lot of pain, but the whole time I had to pretend to the band that nothing had happened."

During that tour, Michael had taken to pushing Kirk into the audience mid-guitar solo; usually Kirk would be caught by the crowd, passed around, and returned to the stage, playing all the while. That night, Michael took a running start from the back of the stage and body-checked Kirk, sending him sailing far above the heads of their fans. "It was a long stage, so he got a real

good start," Kirk says. "And the crowd didn't catch me—they parted and I fell flat on my back. Then they kind of swarmed me and someone stole my glasses." Furious, and a few drinks deep, Kirk got back to the stage, completely unable to see. "I grabbed the mike and said something terrible, like, 'I'm going to kill the fucking cunt who stole my glasses! The show is over if you don't return them right now!'" The culprits didn't and the show went on, but later backstage, Kirk and his specs were reunited. "Three girls, all of them about twelve, came up and gave them to me and apologized," he says. "I felt awful for saying what I did. But no one should steal a man's glasses."

Kirk's corrective lenses didn't always make his vision clear, however. During a sound check at Rock in Rio in the nineties, Kirk asked his guitar tech to remove a loitering hippie from the stage. "This guy was just hanging around, checking out my rack and all of my equipment," Kirk says. "We're running through a few songs and he is just hovering, inspecting our setup. He was freaking me out. So I got him kicked offstage. And once we were done I learned that he was Carlos Santana. Whoops."

The dizzying heights of success changed everyone in INXS, even keep-it-real Kirk. He got over it quickly, but his brother Drew reports that for a moment or two, Kirk became one of those Hollywood types who scan the room while they're talking to you and seem disinterested in any conversation not about them. "Work for those guys was twenty-four hours a day at that time, so I think they found anyone not involved with what they were doing uninteresting," Drew says. "But Kirk never truly lost his head. I remember one time he told me that in three months he had spent on entertainment what the average person earned in a year. He wasn't bragging, he was just amazed by it."

Kirk has learned many things about himself over the years, and here's one he'd like to share: Kirk Pengilly abhors limos. He's lived much of his life in them, and he still thinks they're silly. That said, ladies, listen to his advice on how to properly exit one—several paparazzi shots of her privates are proof that even heiress Paris Hilton has no idea how to alight from a stretch in a miniskirt. "I've always preferred to arrive anywhere in a town car or a van," Kirk says. "I prefer vans, actually, because you step down out of them, which is easier for girls. Limos are a challenge for them. There's only one way to do it right: the girl must swivel on an axis, keeping her legs together until her feet are on the ground. Then she gets up. God, what a pain in the ass."

Kirk Pengilly is either protected by guardian angels or blessed with natural luck, because the man has repeatedly, inadvertently traversed the globe with narcotics on his person and never been caught. After a lengthy tour of South America, where the cocaine flew as free as a bird you cannot change, the band's minders reminded them to dispose of their dust prior to their departure. With characters like Michael and Tim to worry about, no one—including Kirk—thought that Kirk might leave with enough cocaine to jail him forever. "I basically flew around the globe nonstop to get home," he says. "I had several connections and went through customs in a number of countries. And when I got back to Sydney and started to sort out my dirty laundry, I pulled four grams of coke out of the back pocket of my jeans. I couldn't believe how lucky I was not to get caught. Well, there was only one thing to do at that point—celebrate! There was no jet lag happening that day. I was unpacked in no time."

Kirk was equally lucky—and equally surprised—at the end of a tour of America, when he opened a gift from a professional magician, who was a staple at INXS shows in the Northeast in the mid-eighties. He'd befriended the band and gave Kirk an envelope in token of his esteem. Kirk dropped it in his carry-on bag and amid the travel and chaos of the tour, completely forgot about it. The band gigged across America, Canada, and Europe, and when Kirk landed in Australia for the holidays, he finally emptied his luggage. The magician's envelope tumbled out and inside, he found a plump bag of pot. "I'd carried it all over the world," he says. "The bag had been through countless X-ray machines and I'd not been caught, thank God."

Kirk's first true, long-term girlfriend was Karen Hutchinson, a hair stylist from Melbourne who helped shape the band's look in the early days and often came on tour with them. In 1988, they had a daughter, April, who is now an up-and-coming model. They were together for ten years and are very close to this day. They're also devoted to raising their daughter as best they can, and clearly they're doing it right, because April is a charming, bright, beautiful, extraordinary girl.

Kirk's life after Karen took its turns and suffered its peaks and valleys. He married Australian singer Deni Hines in 1993, and after just two years was separated. The nineties were as much a period of tumult and transition for INXS as they were for Kirk. His next relationship, with Sydney DJ Louise Hegarty, was an intense time. They were together for seven years. "Louise and I had a very dramatic and crazy relationship," Kirk says. "There were a lot of problems, and it was never easy, but we had a lot of fun as well, and in the end we both survived." In 2002, three months after the relationship ended, Jack Pengilly (Kirk's dad) suddenly passed away from cancer. "This period was one of the lowest points in my life," Kirk recalls.

But as fate would have it, happiness was just around the corner. Kirk met his match—a woman as different from him as could be. "I'm nocturnal and she's day-turnal." Layne Beachley is, truly, the greatest professional female surfer who's ever lived: she's won six consecutive world championship titles and still ranks in the top five in the world. She's an amazing athlete and a free-spirited soul who managed to get Kirk into the sun, onto a beach, into the water, and onto a board, which he says was a "harrowing experience." She has also inspired him to lead a healthy lifestyle and, to say the least, he can't thank her enough.

All That and Then Some

THE SWING WAS A MASSIVE ALBUM in Australia and parts of Europe, and it boosted INXS's profile, but it was their next album, which swung back toward big-anthem rock and roll, that won the war in America. *Listen Like Thieves* (1985) was ideal for mainstream American radio—it is straight-ahead foot-stomping, and fist-pumping rock, the kind that Australian bands (AC/DC, Midnight Oil) do so well. It was the band's American breakthrough, but it is significant for another reason: it is the last album to feature songs written by a combination of band members. Andrew Farriss and Michael Hutchence wrote the top-selling singles on the album, and they became the primary songwriters in the band in the years to follow.

Farriss and Hutchence are two men who could not have been more different. Andrew is shy, introverted, and though he loves the rush of playing the music he's written to an adoring audience, he has always preferred privacy to celebrity. Michael was his foil: he was an insecure, aloof youth, who grew into a rock star without equal. They were a bit alike as teenagers, but grew into very different men. Andrew, always the solitary type, found his soul mate and became a happily married family man, while Michael blossomed into a social butterfly whose home was the road and who brought the road home with him. But their opposing chemistry made the music: An-

Chris Thomas, the producer of INXS's three biggest albums, and Michael.

drew is proficient on piano, guitar, bass, harmonica, and anything he puts his mind to, while Michael played nothing at all. Yet together, they shared an unspoken language. Andrew could sit at a piano and bang out chords that set Michael to humming melodies and scribbling lyrics. More than a few times it was clear that they were on the same page without saying a word. Andrew would show up with a demo tape of a new song that he hadn't yet discussed with Michael, and within an hour his partner would have mapped out the words. Andrew's meticulous methodology was exactly the framework Hutchence needed for his spontaneous creativity.

Listen Like Thieves, Kick, and *X* are INXS's most well-known, commercially successful records. They are, to most of the world, INXS's legacy—and to some, the only albums in the band's catalog. All three are collections of powerhouse singles—and were conceived as such—that showcase INXS's range, from their rock side to their funk side. They're also a testament to the songwriting prowess of Andrew Farriss and Michael Hutchence, which always gracefully strode the line between perfect pop and the cutting edge. INXS could not have achieved these heights without two things: what they'd learned via experimentation recording *The Swing* with Nick Launay, and the wisdom of Chris Thomas, the producer who helmed all three of their biggest albums.

Even before he worked with INXS, Thomas was a legend. Thomas learned to produce from the Beatles' master mixer George Martin—he even played keyboards on the White Album. Thomas assisted mixing Pink Floyd's *Dark Side of the Moon,* produced Brian Eno's *Here Come the Warm Jets,* and forged a long-standing relationship with Roxy Music, producing their landmark albums *For Your Pleasure* and *Siren.* That is achievement aplenty for one life, but that was just his opening act. Thomas produced the Sex Pistols' *Never Mind the Bollocks,* and then began to work with the Pretenders, with whom he created their breakout album, *Learning to Crawl,* in 1984, among others.

Around that time, Thomas heard "Original Sin" and "I Send a Message," and felt he'd found his next muse in INXS. Everyone in the band knew about him well before Michael had met Chris coincidentally, at a gig by the Japanese band Sandii and the Sunsetz.*

* Founded by Sandii Ai and Makoto Kubota, the Japanese new wave band Sandii and the Sunsetz was embraced by everyone from David Bowie to INXS, the Pretenders, Eurythmics, and the Talking Heads, and supported most of them on tours throughout Asia and Europe. The band was huge in Australia, adored for their nonsensical English lyrics (particularly on the hit single "Sticky Music" in 1983) as they were for Sandii's coy, coquettish vocal style. Sandii, who had spent her teenage years in Hawaii, opened a hula dancing studio in Japan in 2001.

"I was in Australia with Elton John and we bumped into Michael," Thomas says. "*The Swing* was a huge album in Australia at the time and I loved 'Original Sin.' I'd wanted to meet him and was happy that INXS wanted to work with me. I left a message with his management, but I didn't hear from them for seven months. I don't know what that was about—I don't think Chris Murphy wanted me on board at first."

Half a year later, Thomas met the entire band after their gig at the Hollywood Bowl in Los Angeles. They agreed to work together and Thomas had a plan: he felt that what he'd heard on record fell short of the high-energy spectacle he'd just witnessed. "To me, *The Swing* had nothing to do with what the band was doing live," Thomas says. "That album doesn't sound like a rock-and-roll show at all. The gig I saw at the Hollywood Bowl was a dangerous concert—grown women were throwing themselves at the stage. I couldn't believe it. I hadn't seen a gig that exciting or a band having that kind of effect on people in years."

Thomas certainly did capture the fireworks. *Listen Like Thieves* blazes from start to finish, glowing as hot as the album cover's montage: a flaming sunset, a humid crowd, and Michael's silhouette within the band's logo. The album opens with a taut snare-drum roll that sparks the fuse on a seductive bomb called "What You Need"—the song that made INXS American radio stars. It is the funkiest cut on the album, followed by a string of floor-stomping anthems, from the title track, to "Biting Bullets," "This Time," all the way through to the record's closer, the evocative, blistering "Red Red Sun." *Listen Like Thieves* was INXS's most cohesive work to date, a journey as ragged as the peaks, valleys, and endless expanses they'd traversed.

Listen Like Thieves went Gold in the U.S. a few months after its release, because its taut, melodic refrains connected with American audiences more than the hybrid funk of *The Swing.* And given the success of the singles "What You Need," "This Time," and "Kiss the Dirt"—all of them penned by Andrew himself or Andrew with Michael—Chris Murphy, Chris Thomas, and the band decided that the next album should make the most of the momentum. INXS's next would be nothing but singles written entirely by Andrew and Michael.

"That was the fundamental difference on *Kick,*" Thomas says. "That songwriting partnership certainly worked—and it worked better than ever on that album. The massive success of 'What You Need' gave Andrew and Michael the optimism and confidence they needed to go further. They needed to see that they weren't just getting bigger and bigger in Australia with bits of success abroad—and they did." The band gathered at the Sydney Opera House in 1986 to rehearse the songs Andrew and Michael had written for their next album. From the start, the proceedings were history in the making. "This was a band that was really on the up, and all of us knew it," Thomas says. "There was a sense that everything we were doing was moving toward a logical conclusion and that they were going to be a really big band."

Nonetheless, the genesis of *Kick* was nothing like the result. The demo of "Never Tear Us Apart," for one, bore none of the gorgeous orchestral majesty it does on record. Initially it was a piano ballad closer in tempo to the moody bounce of "Mystify" than the pensive ballad it became. " 'Never Tear Us Apart' was a piano song originally," Thomas says. "It was a Fats Domino, bluesy, kind of Rolling Stonesy, early sixties song. I heard it and thought we could do more and came up with the idea to substitute strings for the piano. That changed everything. It was what the song deserved, because in structure and lyrics it was so strong already."

Management had booked a European tour to follow the recording of *Kick,* but there was just one problem—at the end of the sessions, producer Chris Thomas felt that something was missing. "They had an incredible momentum building and were gaining fans all the time. There was an audience waiting for the product," Thomas says. "But I decided that they didn't have the right songs yet—we needed more. I fought very strongly for that and I was very unpopular with Chris Murphy. But I insisted that we keep working. We'd done the same thing with *Listen Like Thieves*—'What You Need' was the last song recorded for the album—and it was the biggest single." Indeed, that song hit the Top 5 in the U.S.—a first for INXS.

There wasn't much time, so Andrew and Michael were exiled to Michael and Jon Farriss's apartment in Hong Kong under orders to create a hit single in two weeks. The plan was to do the European tour, then finish the album over six weeks in Paris. "We were under an incredible amount of pressure," Andrew says. "We'd been in the studio and working so hard and were already tired. To have only two weeks to come up with what we were told must be the first single was not easy." They had to top themselves on command and luckily, divine inspiration intervened. Andrew came up with the guitar riff of "Need You Tonight," the undeniably catchy single they needed, minutes before he left home to join Michael in Hong Kong. "I was actually sitting in the back of the car that was taking me to the airport," he says. "Just before the guy could pull away, I heard the guitar line in my head, told the guy I'd forgotten something, and ran upstairs." He returned forty minutes later with a cassette in his hand and a pissed-off driver in the front seat. In that time, he'd recorded the song's unforgettable shimmering rhythm guitar, hopping bass line, and a simple drum beat. The moment he landed, he gave the tape to Michael and the result was their creative union at its best. "Michael loved it," Andrew says. "He listened to it for a few hours, then went into his room for about ten minutes and came out with nearly all of the lyrics. It was one of those incredible moments that we were lucky enough to have a few of."

At the end of their two sequestered weeks, Andrew and Michael had penned "Need You Tonight," "Kick," and "Calling All Nations." When Thomas heard the demos, he knew that the album was done. The band knew it too—and after their tour of Europe, they met Thomas in Paris, set to celebrate the completion of an album they were already proud of.

Thomas's engineer on *Kick,* at INXS's behest, was David Nicholas, who co-owned Rhinoceros Recordings, the studio INXS had used so often that they eventually just bought it. Nicholas is responsible for one of *Kick*'s most interesting moments—combining "Need You Tonight" with its stream-of-consciousness coda "Mediate." "Andrew came in with a demo of 'Mediate' that was much longer than the final version. He had about four pages of lyrics that follow that rhyme pattern. The day he came in and played the demo, 'Need You Tonight' was playing in the background and the idea hit me. I rewound his tape and hit PLAY just as 'Need You Tonight' ended and it synced up so perfectly that I actually thought something was wrong. It was one of those very spooky studio moments where you aren't sure what is happening." The result was truly innovative for a pop album in 1987: whether heard as two separate songs (as many radio DJs chose to play them) or as a whole, it engagingly melds two moods—seductive heat and detached introspection. The songs are powerful on their own, and together they tell a story: they are a one-night stand and the reflective dawn of the morning-after, woven into seven minutes of music.

The final *Kick* sessions in Paris were made more raucous by the presence of the band's friend and collaborator, *Underneath the Colours* producer Richard Clapton. Clapton was deep into the recording of one of his greatest albums, *Glory Road,* in the very same studio. That album was very much tied up with INXS: every member played on it in the end, and the title track was inspired by Clapton's close friendship with Jon Farriss, who produced the album and played drums on most of it. Richard had watched Jon, who was still just twenty-five at the time, grow from a teen into a young man in the spotlight, and he knew what Jon might not have at the time—that he was on the verge of both his greatest success and his most trying period. Clapton wrote a song about Jon, a song about a young man embarking on a life-changing journey.

For six weeks, both camps shacked up in a five-star Parisian hotel where the stuffy staff treated them like naughty schoolboys—with good reason. "It became fairly common that the management would call us with noise complaints," Clapton says. "And there were so many nights that really were out of control. The second night we were there was outstanding, really. I'm not sure if that's the same one where Michael threw all of the furniture in his room out of the window . . . it might have been . . . I really can't remember."

The night that Clapton does recall was indeed out of bounds and, to the best of everyone's recollection, here's how it went. It began at the studio. After a day of recording *Kick,* INXS went next door to work with Clapton in the evening. Michael was there to do backing vocals, Jon Farriss was there producing and playing drums, and Gary Grant, who'd begun managing Clapton after leaving his post as comanager of INXS, was there too. As the night wore on, Michael sought some cocaine to perk him up. "We had a studio assistant named Phillipe Lefont, who was this little gay Frenchman we immediately christened 'Fifi,'" Clapton says. "Over the course of two hours, Michael kept asking Fifi to find us some coke." English wasn't Fifi's strong suit and an Australian accent was a particular challenge, so Fifi did what he could: he met Michael's requests with smiles, nods, and nothing more. Eventually, Hutchence's patience faded. "He went up to Fifi and said, 'Hey, mate, you know, coke, right? I'm talking about coke. Don't you understand? Coke? Coke—we want coke. You know, *cocaine?*' And Fifi says, 'Ooh la-la, *cocaine!* Why didn't you say so?'" Fifi dashed over to the studio's mixing board and began to disassemble it, confusing everyone.

"You want cocaine? Okay! You know The Stones were here just before you last week," Fifi says. "I think maybe underneath here we find five, six grams of dust. We have plenty of coke!"

True to form in those days, the mixing board during the Stones's sessions had doubled as a chopping block. But halting the recording to take the studio to pieces in search of their scraps was madness, so Clapton stopped Fifi and somehow communicated that he should go off and procure fresh coke for them. The work continued and the drinks flowed and when Fifi came back, the lines blew freely. It was soon clear that the day's labor was nearly done, and so friends were phoned and the invited dropped in. Michael handed out Ecstasy to everyone, but Clapton put him to work before Hutchy got too happy. "I got mad at him, actually," Clapton says. "I told him, 'Will you please just lay these vocals down?' Michael was like, 'Would you just chill, man? You're always so serious, Richard. I can still do it. These pills are like having a joint.'" Clapton didn't believe him and tossed him into the vocal booth before the drugs took hold. "His vocals were great, and they're on the album, just the way he sang them that night."

And then, the party started right. Everyone was fully blitzed by midnight, when it was decided that more good times were in store back at the hotel. Readers, this is where the facts, by everyone's account, get blurry. Bear with us, the details have been re-created as accurately as possible.

Predictably, the festivities quickly elicited numerous noise complaints from the hotel management. Half of the revelers opted to relocate to a friend's apartment nearby, a few went home, and Clapton did something in between. "Earlier in the night, I'd started indulging in everything Michael had in his candy bag—there's a reason why I used to call him the Candy Man," he says. "All I know is that sometime near dawn the hotel staff found me in the fetal position in the middle of one of their long hallways." Four hotel staffers slid a blanket under Clapton, lifted him, and toted him, like a comatose Cleopatra, to his bed. "I remember nothing," he says. "But I didn't have to because they never let me forget it. Every time I passed through the lobby for the next six weeks, one of them would say to me, 'Hey, Richard, will you be all right tonight? Will you need us to tucky-tucky you in?'"

Clapton's exit was actually the most graceful of the evening. When the others arrived at their friend's apartment, INXS's engineer David "Chipper" Nicholas made an entrance by drunkenly bouncing off the door frame, the walls of the foyer, and falling ass-first through a glass coffee table. In the way of the truly inebriated, he sprang to his feet, uninjured and completely unaware of what he'd just done. He had awoken an elderly neighbor downstairs, however, who called Les Gendarmes—the French police.

Les Gendarmes are no joke—they're not beat cops hooked on pain au chocolat and café au lait. They're like underused, agitated marines—overarmed and seemingly ready to slay to keep the peace. That night, upon arrival, Les Authorities found about ten completely wasted party-people, most half dressed, the rest nude, lewd, and orgiastic. Gary Grant snapped out of a compromising position and did his best to manage the situation, disregarding the fact that his nudity undercut his authority. "I wasn't there, but from what I understand Gary was very obnoxious—and very naked," Clapton says. "So the Gendarmes handcuffed him to a chair."

A moment later, Michael emerged from a bedroom, naked, unlit cigarette in hand. He wandered over to Gary and asked for a light, as unconcerned that Grant was bound to a chair as he was that the men in uniform were not there to party.

"Michael, I do *not* have a light," Grant said, incredulous. "As you can fucking see, I'm sitting here naked, cuffed to a fucking chair, you *fucking idiot*!"

"Hey, no need to snap, man," Michael said blissfully. "*God* we're bitchy tonight." Then he strolled over to the nearest Gendarme and, giggling, asked him for a light. He was promptly cuffed to a chair beside Grant.

The whole lot was hauled to jail. But Grant—a manager to the end—put a positive spin on the night: he told the authorities that he was Richard Clapton. Yes, he was wasted, but he knew the value a good rock-and-roll arrest would do Clapton's public image in the months leading up to the release of his album. He didn't, however, inform his client upon his release from jail. Unsure of how he made it home, Clapton awoke with a crippling hangover to a phone call from his girlfriend back in Australia, who broke up with him on the spot. "It was already all over the news back home that Michael Hutchence and I had been arrested naked and on drugs, in Paris, in the midst of an orgy. And I really did have no idea what she was talking about," Clapton says. "I was so hungover that at first I thought it was true because I couldn't remember. But once I got my bearings, it didn't matter, no matter what I said, she never believed me, and she never came back. And the funny thing is, in Australia, nearly everyone still believes that I was there that night."

Kick is the album that crossed into the mainstream and made INXS a household name. Their most accessible work, it's still complex, a polished version of *The Swing*. Chris Thomas felt that *The Swing* didn't capture INXS's energy, so on *Kick*, he labored to infuse the funk-soul of that album with the rock bombast of *Listen Like Thieves*. "*The Swing* was a rehearsal for *Kick*," *Swing* producer Nick Launay says. "They'd leaned toward funk on *The Swing* and then they'd leaned toward rock on *Thieves* to make it in America. By the time *Kick* came around, it was time to lean toward funk again. When I heard that album, I thought, Wow, they got it right."

From Michael's intimate whisper on "Need You Tonight" to the soaring, lovelorn "Never Tear Us Apart" to the kinetic shuffle of "New Sensation," the record is pure energy and emotion—it's at once a party and a dizzying seduction. The production is exemplary: Thomas isolated each member's gifts and sewed them together seamlessly. Everything is stark and clean: Kirk and Tim's guitar lines shine brilliantly, Garry's bass resounds like the snapping of a giant rubber band, Jon's drumming is a contained earthquake, and Michael's vocals are laid bare atop of it all, captured in all of their rich delicacy.

"I was very jealous of Chris Thomas's production on *Kick*, because they had finally found their groove and were very innovative with the production," U2 frontman, Bono, says. "And Michael's vocals were so incredible. They were just dry, and really up close, you know. And Michael could whisper—boy could he."

"The funkier direction of *Kick* was born from the songs, but there had always been an underlying funk element in their sound," producer Chris Thomas says. "Jon Farriss's drumming came from a funk background. And Michael was interested, particularly in that period, in the dance movement that was emerging in England in the late eighties. And we'd all been moved by Prince, who was a huge influence as well. They moved away from a rock-guitar sound on *Kick*—and they did it like only they could."

Once *Kick* was complete, all involved tried to be objective—and they all still thought it was a masterpiece. Chris Murphy flew to New York immediately to play it for the top executives of Atlantic Records—who rejected it wholeheartedly. "They hated it, absolutely *hated* it," he says. "They said there was no way they could get this music on rock radio. They said it was suited for black radio but they didn't want to promote the band that way. The president of the label told me that he'd give us one million dollars to go back to Australia and make another album. I was speechless. I could not reconcile what they were saying with what I knew was so right about the music. And I didn't know what I was going to do. I never told the band—the only people that know this are the three people who were in that room." Chris's longtime ally at Atlantic, Reen Nalli, had left the label by then, and though he'd not gotten on too well with the others in power, he never thought, in light of INXS's growing success, that he'd be received so coldly. It was a conundrum: the band had never been offered a million dollars to record. But the album was the top of their mountain, the ideal realization of their aesthetic. The money could never repair the insecurity that rerecording would cause the band.

Chris Murphy left that meeting and wandered around Manhattan in a daze so thick that he was nearly hit by a cab. But by sundown, he had a plan—he'd play the album for the band's European and Australian labels, hoping they'd understand it. They didn't. "I had never spoken to the president of our European record company," Murphy says. "But he was so incensed by the album I sent him that he called me the next day. He said, 'What are Michael and Andrew *doing*? What happened to them? This album is a disaster.'" Neither label even suggested a song they might release, upon revision, as a single.

It's black comedy, sad reality, and an early indication of the nearsighted stupidity that has castrated the music industry that teams of executives at the world's top labels unanimously decided, independently of each other, that *Kick* was commercially useless. They were stupendously wrong: five songs off *Kick* went on to hit the American Top 10, even more so did globally. The album sold millions worldwide, inspired a bevy of imitators, and remained on the American and world album charts for over a year. And even though *Kick* did little back home in Australia in the short run, it remained a top seller for the next two years.

Kick was INXS's biggest challenge—they had to convince the entire world that they were right. "We had an album that every single one of our record companies hated," Murphy says. "I don't know where I got the strength, but I woke up in Manhattan that next day and said, from the depths of my soul, 'Fuck it. Fuck it all. I'll do this myself. I don't give a shit.'" Murphy called the band's accountant and took inventory of their assets, from the equity of recording advances, to the value of their mutually held real estate. Without informing the band, he made an executive decision to gamble it all. He knew that if they won in America, the rest of the world would follow, but Chris needed to budget carefully and needed one motherfucker of a spin for this agenda.

Murphy knew that replicating the resources of a major record label was financial suicide: hiring a promotional team alone would cost hundreds of thousands of dollars. Instead, he used guerrilla tactics, pursuing a divide-and-conquer strategy within the ranks of Atlantic Records. He broke accepted protocol and, unbeknownst to label brass, arranged a meeting with the radio promotions staff to play them "Need You Tonight," even though the label hadn't formally agreed to release the song or anything else off *Kick*. Most of the radio reps were baffled—the rock department didn't understand the song at all and the R&B people didn't think they could get it any black radio play. The only one who loved it was Andrea Guinness, the head of college radio promotions. She loved it to death, in fact, and told Murphy she'd crusade to make it a hit on the college charts.

"It was the first time I'd heard anything nice," Murphy says. "I kept saying to her, 'Do you really mean it? *Honestly?*' I had never met her before, and I couldn't thank her enough." Murphy now had his in: if American college radio got behind the record, that's where they'd start building their platform. Murphy needed interest in just one market, enough to book a tour, because he knew the band could do the rest. With no formal commitment from Atlantic Records to release *Kick,* Murphy locked in a string of concerts at colleges to create, he hoped, a demand in advance of the supply.

He spent all of the band's money to finance it, and to wisely hire a few independent PR agents to promote it. With whatever was left, he bought as many college radio ads as he could. Murphy pitched the excursion to the band as a no-nonsense endeavor to show America their pub rock roots. They played college bars and university auditoriums and did what they always had: they sold them out and blew their audiences away. Their initiative won over Atlantic Records, sort of. Midway through the tour, the label added the album to their release schedule, but agreed to little in the way of promotion: it seemed that Atlantic's decision makers realized that INXS would do, and spend, whatever it took to make *Kick* a success—and they took full advantage. "I had to sign a merchandising deal with some company just to fund the tour," Murphy says. "We had to create our own promotional team. We had to pay independent PR people about two grand a week. We did interviews at every radio station in every city. We worked like fucking dogs. Thank *God* it worked."

The band had no idea what was going on behind the scenes—and Murphy elected to keep it that way. He knew that they'd be unable to be their best live if they knew how much was on the line. "The band didn't know then and they'll probably only find out when they read this: I risked every dollar they had and every dollar I had on that tour. If it failed there would have been a mutiny. It would have been the end of everything and I knew it."

It didn't matter—the INXS college tour was a smash success. "Need You Tonight" devoured the college charts while the second single, "Devil

Inside," crossed over onto classic rock play lists and made INXS a mainstay of Top 40 radio. Over the course of four consecutive Top 5 singles, *Kick* struck a nerve with American fans, from the fringe to the center. It's amazing to think that respected figures of the industry thought it was crap. It's amazing to think that it might never have come out. And it's amazing to think that it was all just beginning.

Do As the Romans Do: Postcards from the Success Tsunami

IN 1987 AND 1988, INXS WAS the biggest band in the world. With no help from the label, and in spite of the market-share predictions of music industry executives, *Kick* went platinum in America within a year. It went Double platinum four months later and Triple platinum by the end of 1988. Two years after its release, *Kick* had sold nearly 10 million copies internationally and yielded numerous Top 10 singles globally. "Mystify" reached Number 14 at the very end of 1988 when it was released as a U.K.-only single. And the band won awards everywhere—a pile of MTV Video Music Awards, *Billboard* Awards, and American Music Awards. They toured for fourteen months, tried to remember what their homes looked like, missed their families, and finally took some time off in 1989. And in 1990, once their next album was written and recorded, the whole process began again.

The *Kick* and *X* tours were globe-trotting circuses—the band's gear, lighting, crew, wardrobe, and entourage filled a fleet of semitrucks stuffed with hundreds of gear cases, enough to pack the cargo bay of a 747. They logged, conservatively, a hundred thousand miles, nearly twice the distance around the globe, in two years.

INXS had worked long and hard but mega success still came quickly. *Kick* captured an international sound that reflected the style of the times—it was a moment and a movement that crossed all borders. It spawned a litter of imitators, who capitalized and bastardized INXS; in 1988, it spurred every major label to seek out and sign some kind of slinky, sexy, romantic, rock and rhythm-and-blues band. They found them all all right, crap or not, from the Fine Young Cannibals to General Public to Faith No More to the Red Hot Chili Peppers to the Fixx. INXS put punk, funk, soul, and rock together better than those bands could ever hope to, for one simple reason: INXS could and still can play them into oblivion.

Kick was an Australian miracle: a band from Oz had tripled the spoils of six years of respectable, gradual success in one fell swoop. They'd been well-known in Australia for years, but it couldn't compare to 1987, the year the band got its first taste of celebrity, American style. Suddenly, their anonymous U.S. shopping trips were impossible.

INXS was dubbed the INXSexies in Australia way back when because, well, they were sexy, but in the late eighties, the intensity of their female fan base got a bit ridiculous. And it was a bit too-much-too-late, as by then, most of the boys couldn't care less. Tim Farriss was married in 1981, Kirk was in a committed relationship, as was Jon, and though all were appreciative of the amorous intentions, they didn't usually go the distance—which often meant sprinting to their hotel rooms and bolting the door.

It worked out well, however, for those in the band who were ready and able to enjoy such fruits of their labor—and if no one else was up to it, Michael could certainly handle *all* of it. "To me, it seemed that there was a major power struggle between American men and women in those days," Garry Beers says. "Women were becoming executives and receiving equal pay and fighting for their due. American males didn't seem to know how to react to that. It was obvious that women hated insensitive jocks, so I think that American guys tried too hard to be sensitive—which wasn't what women wanted either. That's why they loved us. It was simple, we were just like, 'Hello! We're Australian, we're men, we're confident, and we love to fuck. How are you tonight?' Of course the accent didn't hurt either.

So many nights I met girls who wouldn't say a word. It was weird. They'd look at me and say, 'Just *talk*.'"

Perhaps it was their generally wholesome upbringing, perhaps it is the positive, conscious cultural condition of being Australian, but, call them what you will—INXS wasn't nearly as base as they could have been. Where so many rock bands of less worth, skill, and success celebrated behavior worthy of arrest, INXS never turned their privilege turgid. It threw Rick Sales for a loop. Sales was their first American road manager, and he's a keen, merciless wit who spent his years before and after INXS tending to heavy-metal bands (he's managed Slayer for the last decade).

INXS seemed weird to Rick; in 1987, he'd road managed in a tour world where his gear arrangement, room assignment, and general ass-kicking duties took up his daytime, and at night he was required to procure free drugs and sex for his charges. His bands had passes to sort it all out, particularly to label the special ladies in the house. Those stickers adhered to any fabric and were easy-to-read; they said DICK LICKER. Backstage, everyone would know which girls were road-tested and ready.

INXS didn't dig that at all—they didn't even get it. They didn't see the point: there was no challenge. To them, why would anyone want to stake an unearned claim? Who are those who boldly go where so many have gone before? "I never understood the pleasure to be had in that groupie thing," Kirk says. "Why would anyone want to be with someone who'd been with a few other guys that same night? I mean, think about it, if that's one night for her, who else has she been with that *week*?" No one had CC'd Rick Sales on that memo, so the first night he spent in INXS's employ, Rick did what was usually expected and ushered a pair of hookerly looking ladies backstage. The band treated them like the friends of friends you find drunk at your party and you're not sure how they got there or how they're getting home. They did what they could—they let them hang until closing time.

INXS had so many high times in the last years of the eighties that it takes Kirk Pengilly's meticulous journals, every living band member, two former tour managers, a tape recorder, and several outside sources to make sense of it all. If sense is to be made of it all.

South America, 1984

FROM KIRK'S DIARY: *INXS's first Number 1 here, "Original Sin." In town to headline Rock in Rio festival, in Brazil and become the first international band to stage a major concert in Buenos Aires, Argentina, following the junta.*

Gary Grant, Michael Hutchence, and Tim Farriss got here two days before the rest of us to do press. They trekked 29 hours by plane. Airline lost their luggage but gave them 100 U.S. dollars a day per diem. 100 U.S. dollars went a long way.

"Our label rep for PolyGram was named Carlos, who referred to everything he recommended as 'very famous,'" Gary Grant says. "Each night, Carlos said, 'I take you to a restaurant, very famous, very famous restaurant.'" Carlos was promptly asked to procure something South America is very, *very* famous for—cocaine. The boys gave Carlos their three hundred airline sponsored dollars, because to them, drugs were more important than clean underwear.

Carlos's eyes grew wide, "You want three hundred dollars' worth? Okay . . . Eh, okay! I get for you, from very famous man."

A few hours later, Carlos returned with a sugar-bag of blow. In Australia cocaine cost $200 a gram and barely worked, diluted by too many connecting flights from Colombia. In South America, given the exchange rate, it was $1 a gram. A night of fun back home cost the same as enough snow to ski on in Brazil. "We had so much we were throwing it off the balcony of the hotel," Grant says. "Dinner was out of the question. We apologized to Carlos because there was no way we were going to the very, very famous restaurant. I don't think we were hungry again for three days."

FROM KIRK'S DIARY: Two days later. *Buenos Aires, Argentina, the concert becomes a riot. INXS headlining third night of a three-day festival. Find out later that ten births and five deaths occur during the festival. Rained for days before the show, kids are up to their ankles in mud. Complete chaos. Learned that concert P.A. is the one used at Woodstock. Some local promoter bought it years ago. Makes sense, it sounds like an antique. Festival is the first time this city has partied since the new government came to power. It's the government's gesture of goodwill.*

The festival was held in the José Amalfitani Stadium, a massive arena that holds fifty thousand, which had been used as a site of mass executions during the seven-year junta that began on March 24, 1976. The stadium was a place where enemies of the state "disappeared" to. The assassinations were plentiful and more cultural than political in nature; the junta's perceived "enemies" were the intelligentsia—doctors, lawyers, artists, musicians, poets, writers, and anyone connected to them by blood or belief. Musicians and writers were killed for creating works even vaguely critical of the government. When the junta arrested someone, they'd confiscate their address book, interrogate their neighbors, and arrest everyone in that person's circle of family, colleagues, and friends they deemed a threat. In the end, over thirty thousand people "disappeared" and never returned. It is estimated that five hundred or more children were born to mothers kept alive in captivity only until their offspring could be given to the families of high-ranking military officers. There were approximately 350 known detention centers and concentration camps, and more than a thousand military personnel involved in the abduction and physical and psychological torture of citizens deemed "enemies of the state." In 1985, five of the nine rulers of the junta were convicted—two received life sentences; one seventeen years, one eight years, and one four and a half years. According to an investigatory commission assembled by the succeeding government led by civilian-elected leader President Raúl Alfonsín, those men were responsible for the unjust documented deaths of nine thousand citizens.

FROM KIRK'S DIARY: *It's incredible to watch the crowd. This festival and celebration is taking place on the same ground where 1000s of their friends, families, and countrymen were assassinated.*

The emotional intensity was tangible because the local bands on the bill and the crowd were at once joyful to be free of the violence, hollow from losing so many loved ones, and awed by the knowledge of all the blood which soiled the soil they stood upon just a year ago. The new government ensured that should their measure of goodwill get out of hand, the mob would not: they erected sheet-metal barricades at the front of the stage, enforced by military police along the top. The metal was not ergonomic, however—it blocked the sightline of the first thirty rows of fans.

A nasty game ensued over the course of the festival: when audience members jumped up and grabbed hold of the barricade in an effort to see the show, the police hit them with gun butts and clubs until they let go. INXS took the stage that third and final night to a frenzied mob going for broke—or broken. The audience pulled the metal barrier down in the first half hour of their set, and the guards bashed back indiscriminately, bloodying all within reach. It was too much for Michael Hutchence—he smashed a policeman with his microphone stand after watching him brutally assault a fan. And then he took control of the situation.

"Stop! Stop!" he shouted to the crowd. "Stop this! No one needs to be hurt. Stop this now."

The military guards insisted that the band leave the stage and halted the show. As INXS exited, shook and upset, a muddy, bloodied young man hopped the remains of the wall, evaded the guards, vaulted on stage, and ran up to Michael. He bled from his head and swayed in place, visibly in shock from the blows he'd endured.

"Hi! I'm from Melbourne!" he shouted, grasping for Michael's shirt as the guards dragged him away. "I'm from *Melbourne*!"

> FROM KIRK'S DIARY: ***It was the first of many trips all through South America. INXS truly pioneered—opening doors that forever put South America on the tour map for international bands.***

South America, 1988–1989

The band headlined Rock in Rio in Brazil again, the same year Billy Idol and George Michael did. A few weeks before the show, wealthy tourists were kidnapped for ransom—a seasonal local blight—so the Department of Foreign Affairs provided the visiting foreign musicians with armed guards. Considering the rampant institutional corruption at the time in that country, this gesture was not necessarily a plus.

INXS wasn't too worried, they'd come armed. They brought Jeff Pope, a respected member of Australia's top-ranked tactical police—the nation's top S.W.A.T. team. Pope, a scientifically affable, problem-solving block of chiseled muscle, fit the bill: his quiet, even demeanor is unshakeable. "George Michael was held up on that trip, while he was out seeing some Incan ruins," Pope says. "There was a standoff because his security were British army and they just held the kidnappers at bay until an airlift could be flown in. He was all right in the end."

Pope never let the band know what went into ensuring their safety—he maintained a don't ask, don't worry policy. "Andrew Farriss doesn't like guns, so when he asked me if our security were armed, I'd tell him that we weren't," Pope says. "I didn't like lying to him, but I had to. Truth is, our men were always armed to the armpits."

The one-dollar grams of cocaine and bountiful beautiful women were often overwhelming to the hardiest of souls. "There were moments when we played South America—Rio, Peru, Argentina—when I had to turn my back to the audience," Kirk says. "Women would have their tops off and they're the most beautiful women in the world. I'd look down into the first few rows and see so many gorgeous half-naked women that I couldn't play. I just couldn't play at all. So I'd turn around until I got control of myself again." On occasion, one or another of the local delicacies sent a band member or two AWOL. "We lost Jon Farriss and Michael Hutchence for thirty-six hours down there once," Jeff Pope recalls. "They'd made off with some señoritas and wouldn't make contact with base. They had quite a party, it seems. They were up all that time—in every sense of the word as I understand. They slept for two days straight afterward."

On a flight from one South American country to another, Michael nearly turned the youngest of the lot, Jon Farriss, prematurely gray. The two were seated facing each other, along with several famous guests who've requested that they remain nameless, in the front lounge of the band's private jet. As the plane drew closer to its destination, Michael asked Jon for his theory on the probability of a customs search that day. "I was like, yeah, we'll probably have one," Jon says. "Michael just grins at me and says, 'Okay.'"

As the plane made its descent, Michael asked Jon again if customs might come on the plane.

“Probably, mate,” Jon said, suddenly nervous. “Look, mate, what’s the matter?”

“Nothing, mate, nothing,” Michael said, shifting in his seat.

“*Mate,* if there’s something I should know, can you fucking run it by me? *What* have you *got*?” Jon said.

“Nothing, mate, no worries,” Michael said, with a warm, false grin.

The jet landed and taxied and Jon began to seriously worry. Michael was seated with his back to the front of the plane. He didn’t have the best eyesight and wasn’t known for his awareness of his surroundings. Jon spied two jeeps of customs agents buzzing across the tarmac to meet the plane.

“There are *customs* cars out there, Michael,” he said desperately.

“Yeah, okay,” Michael said, mischievously. “Do you think they have dogs?”

The plane leaned to the left as the cabin door was opened. The authorities’ boots resounded on the metal stairs and a dog barked.

“Yeah, they’ve *got dogs,* Michael,” Jon spat in his friend’s ear. “Now *really* is the time to tell me what you’ve got, mate.”

Michael pulled a bag of coke out of his jacket, roughly enough to blast everyone in sight to the rafters.

“Oh, *come on, mate*!” Jon whispered, trying to avoid attention. “What the fuck have you been doing with that all this time?”

Michael charmingly smiled at him, opened the bag, and shoveled all of it up his face in two mighty snorts. It was so strong and plentiful that he coughed a giant white cloud out of his mouth. Jon tried to play it cool, fanning the air and wiping the white dust off Michael’s face as two customs agents marched down the aisle. Jon did what he could, but Michael still looked like he’d gorged himself on powdered donuts. He did know enough to hide under his hair and calmly hand over his passport.

“I was freaking out,” Jon recalls. “Fucking freaking! I’m wiping it off his face and out of his hair but there’s this white cloud just floating around him that I could do nothing about.”

“*Gracias,*” the officer said, perusing Michael’s papers. He handed them back, turned around, and left the plane.

“The funniest part of it all was that we had to go directly from the airport to sound check,” Jon says. “We went through a few songs and the whole time Michael's trying to sing, grinning like his jaw might come off and belting out every song twice as fast and much too loud."

Germany, 1988

FROM KIRK'S DIARY: *Frauleins of the Forest—played with Dave Stewart who requested 'anything white.' K.P. handed out roofies. Tim found the frauleins.*

Germany has beer, bratwurst, big blondes, and according to Tim Farriss, fräuleins running wild in the Black Forest. INXS played a gig in 1988, during which Dave Stewart of Eurythmics joined them onstage for their encore, then rode with them to their next destination. During the trip, one of the bad kids in the back of the bus wanted to party and demanded that those on board who could, must produce "anything white." Kirk had been suffering from insomnia and jet lag on that tour and a crew member recovering from a heroin addiction gave him a stash of Rohypnol. He told Kirk that it would definitely help him sleep* but Kirk didn't see how: he'd watched the guy pop roofies regularly, as if they were multivitamins. Kirk passed his supply around and they were sucked down with strong cocktails as the bus rolled on.

* Rohypnol is a benzodiazepine sedative drug that is liberally prescribed in Europe but not in America. It has been widely abused in the States and labeled the "date-rape" drug because of the sleepy, hypnotic, drunk feeling it induces for up to eight hours. The pills are white and dissolve easily and tastelessly in alcohol, allowing sinister manipulators to dose their hapless victims. Thankfully, Hoffman-LaRoche, the drug's manufacturer, has phased in a green version that retains its color when dissolved.

FROM KIRK'S DIARY: *Debate over which man on the bus is most attractive to the female population of Germany. Many arguments made. No consensus reached.*

The bus pulled over on a highway somewhere in the Black Forest so that the musicians might pee. Tim Farriss wandered into those woods, a simple man in search of bladder relief, but he returned der Schwindler.**

"I'm in this stretch of the Bavarian Black Forest with my dick out, having a pee, when these two beautiful girls materialize in front of me," Tim says. "They waltz out of the woods and I tuck them under each of my arms. It was

** der Schwindler: German for "a confident man."

clear to everyone right away that I had won that bet. I walked the ladies onto the bus and said, 'Hello, mates, meet the fräuleins of the forest!'"

They weren't midsummer night faeries, and they didn't live in the boughs of a spruce; they emerged from one of the many cars of fans trailing the bus. Tim had no idea of that, of course: he thought they were mystical blond beings. In truth, they were stalkers. And they got pissed when every guy on the bus passed out in a roofie haze nose-down in their cocktails shortly after their arrival. When the party posse arrived at the hotel, Michael and Tim were so far gone that a hardy crew member had to carry them into the hotel. The girls were shooed off the bus—none too easily.

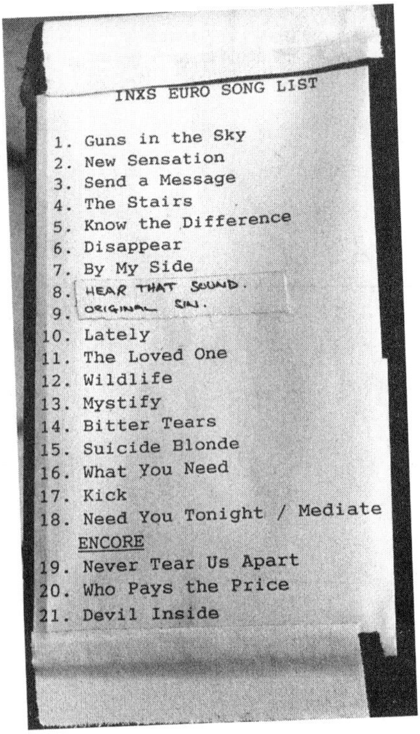

INXS EURO SONG LIST

1. Guns in the Sky
2. New Sensation
3. Send a Message
4. The Stairs
5. Know the Difference
6. Disappear
7. By My Side
8. HEAR THAT SOUND.
9. ORIGINAL SIN.
10. Lately
11. The Loved One
12. Wildlife
13. Mystify
14. Bitter Tears
15. Suicide Blonde
16. What You Need
17. Kick
18. Need You Tonight / Mediate

ENCORE

19. Never Tear Us Apart
20. Who Pays the Price
21. Devil Inside

With a half-conscious Tim under one arm and an immobile Michael under the other, their minder made his way to the elevator, where while trying to prop Tim against the wall, he dropped Hutchence. Hutch slumped to the floor, and didn't flinch at all as the elevator door repeatedly closed then opened, then closed then opened, then closed again, on his head.

The poor soul burdened with getting Michael and Tim to their rooms finally dragged them upstairs, laid Michael out on his bed, the door still ajar, and wrestled Tim, who, semiconscious and giggly, playfully fought him all the way to his room. He dumped Tim on the bed and returned to lock Michael in and discovered that Michael wasn't alone—he caught one of the fräuleins attempting genital resuscitation. He dislodged her from Michael's crotch and tossed her down the hallway, as nicely as he could. Once Michael, who was so unconscious that surgery would have been painless, was tucked in, the fateful babysitter returned to Tim's room and experienced déjà vu: Tim was comatose and the other fräulein, on bended knee, was engaged in the same procedure. She was similarly removed, both of them finally eradicated like a rough case of Black Forest fungi.

Cover of INXS's first single, "Simple Simon," 1980.

Opposite: Michael Hutchence at the "Baby Don't Cry" video shoot, 1992.

Right: INXS, 1991.

Below: The final tour with Michael, 1997.

Overleaf: Candid shots from the road.

(Photo by Grant Matthews, courtesy of the authors)

(Photo by Nick Egan, courtesy of the authors)

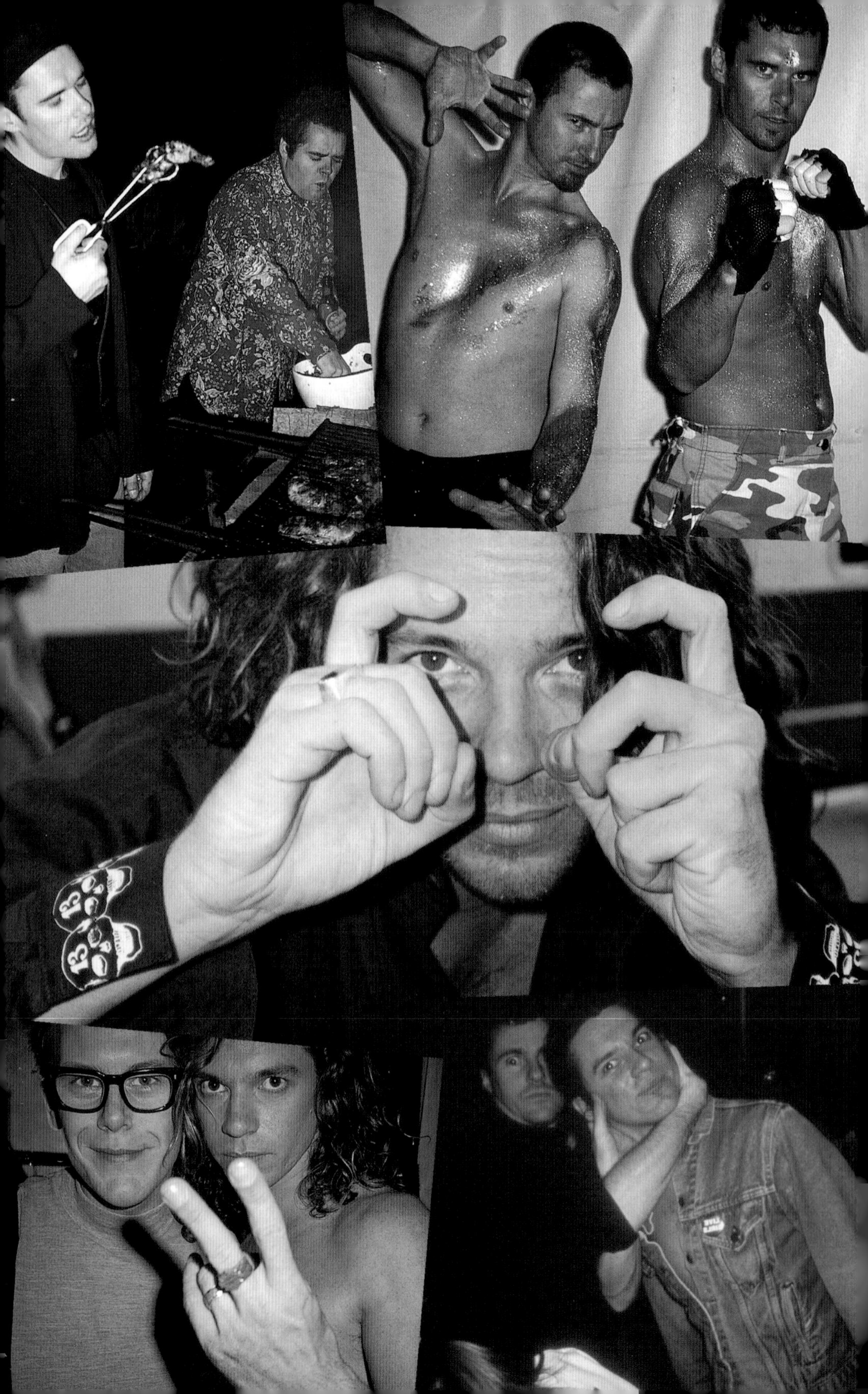

MTV
MUSIC TELEVISIO

(Photo by Yan Gamblin, courtesy of the authors)

(Photo by Pierre Winther, courtesy of the authors)

(Photo by Pierre Winther, courtesy of the authors)

(Photo by James Minchin, courtesy of the authors)

Opposite: **The band mugging with a surfboard.**

Top: **Shooting the "Baby Don't Cry" video, 1992.**

Above: **Shooting the *Elegantly Wasted* album cover, 1996.**

Right: **INXS in 1997.**

(Photo by Serge Thomann, courtesy of the authors

INXS live in concert.

Years later, during a group recollection, Tim was informed that the fräuleins were not, as he believed, legendary German sirens of the woods that lured intrepid explorers to their doom or some collective dream they'd shared on the tour bus—they were just insane fans on a mission. At first, Tim argued the point. And after he heard the facts, after a bit of consideration he decided that his version of the story was still the truth, because, truth be told, it is a much better tale to tell.

Guam, 1987

The band played a show for the American armed forces stationed on Guam and discovered that the spirit of Lieutenant Colonel Bill Kilgore, Robert Duvall's napalm-and-surf-loving character from *Apocalpyse Now,* lived on. The surreal tour of duty surrounding that gig started on the flight over for Andrew Farriss. So many things can go wrong traveling—and Andrew's thought of all of them.

His flight to Guam rattled the poor man to the core. Over a nine-hour flight from Los Angeles, across the aisle of a DC-10, Andrew watched a tiny, middle-aged Asian man swill enough scotch to sideline Charles Bukowski. "He kept ordering more and he couldn't take it," Andrew says. "He'd drink a bottle and drop it at his feet until he had a little island of about twenty of them there. And he kept sending the stewardess for more. Eventually she told him—and I believed her—that he'd drunk all the scotch on the plane."

In-flight service at the time still included metal silverware, and the drunk threatened the stewardess with his serrated knife when she returned empty-handed. She promptly procured two more bottles emphasizing that these were the last she had. The red-faced man nodded at her, downed them, and some ten minutes later, demanded more. He was in no shape to make use of that modified butter knife, so when she refused to serve him, he took his intimidation over the top. "He went over to the emergency exit door and put his hand on the handle," Andrew says. "He was shouting, saying that he'd open it if he wasn't given more scotch."

As Andrew and the rest of the passengers kneaded their seat cushions, the captain calmly strode down the aisle and approached the man. He made it clear that the scotch was gone, but that a wide variety of alcoholic beverages was available in the galley; and should he choose to accompany his captain there, he might choose his poison and indulge as much as he liked.

The captain knew that offering a drunk more drink was a foolproof plan: the belligerent fool willingly followed him to the back of the plane. "And when he got him there, boom! The captain knocked him out with one punch," Andrew says. "Then he dragged him back to his seat across from me. The man was completely unconscious, so the captain strapped him in, and said to him 'There you go, sir, that should do you fine for the rest of the flight. If you need anything else, be sure to let me know.'"

FROM KIRK'S DIARY: *Landed in Guam. Army man in a white 50s Ford Thunderbird convertible took Andrew and me on a tour, bypassing a scheduled interview at the island's only radio station. Garry and Tim did interview instead, poolside at the hotel, while watching a bikini contest. How terrible for them. Our driver got us stoned on weed that blew our heads off. Two hits and the palm trees swayed. He drove like a maniac—hit 80 miles an hour on one-lane roads through small towns of shacks—completely insane.*

Upon landing in Guam, Kirk and Andrew's guide chauffeured them to the top of a mountain and stopped outside a simple hut. "There was a zebra-striped leather couch inside, which was bizarre," Andrew says. "He brought us there to meet his son, who had a huge open wound on his leg. He wanted to show us a bit of the local culture . . . and, he certainly did."

Unbeknownst to the band, their gig was sponsored by Budweiser. They strictly avoided corporate sponsorship—in fact, years later when "New Sensation" was licensed by Atlantic for a Sea World commercial, they threatened litigation. That night, when they spied a ten-foot-high inflatable Bud can at the front of the stage, the band dispatched their managers to have it removed. The promoters refused and no compromise was reached come stage-time, with a full house waiting for the show.

"Hey, don't worry about it, let's just play," Michael announced to everyone in their dressing room. Their team was shocked, because he hated corporate branding more than any of them.

They should have guessed that Michael had a plan. He'd found a broom down the hall, broken the handle, and concealed it in his sleeve. The band followed him to the stage, still miffed at the looming beer can, and applauded when their singer lanced that eyesore until it drooped into lifelessness.

FROM KIRK'S DIARY: ***Flight crew joined us backstage and partied all night. Once the booze was gone, the crew fetched mini bottles from the plane! All went down to the beach. Fun!***

More than a few revelers awoke prostrate on the sand the next day. Tim Farriss will tell you all about it because he remembers it well—he awoke with a lobster flambé for a backside.

In Flight: Cancun, Mexico, to Miami, Florida, 1993

On a ragged Mexican runway, INXS endured a nightmare: their pilot stood on the brakes and halted their takeoff seconds before the point at which the jet's speed and distance from the end of the runway allowed no turning back. They screamed to a stop because the pilot detected an engine problem so severe that they might have combusted upon liftoff. Their near-miss didn't worry the ground crew; however, the rusty remains of past crashed planes decorated the outlying terrain like morbid sculpture.

Peering out the window, the band watched the local mechanics tend to INXS's plane as quizzically as humans would a UFO. "I got worried when I got a good look at the pilot," Andrew Farriss says. "He was looking from the plane to these little guys on the runway and back to the plane. Then I saw him get on the radio to contact his charter service back in California." Andrew thought that his fears would be alleviated if he talked to the mechanics. They weren't. "One guy was smoking a cigarette next to a vat of jet fuel, telling me how some diplomat's plane had landed incorrectly and burst into flames a few weeks before. I thought, 'Right. Okay . . . I want to go home now. Can I go home now?'"

FROM KIRK'S DIARY: *Remained overnight in Cancun. Local promoter threw us a party. Much festivities, much of everything. No sleep at all—night turned to day too soon.*

Garry Beers and Michael Hutchence ended up in Garry's hotel room that night—well, morning—where they continued to enjoy mountains of local snow. The band's minders chronically called to remind them of their departure, but it was no use. "It was a blur. We'd get a call, 'Baggage in six hours,'" Garry says. "Then it was two hours, one hour, half an hour, at which point I began stuffing my bag. And Michael just looked at me and said, 'Why are you packing *my* bag?' He thought we'd been in his room the whole time! 'No, Michael, this is my room,' I said. And he just stared at me for a full minute, then said, '*Right.* Well, where's my room then?' Michael had this romantic notion that he'd stay in Cancun one day longer than the rest of us, to absorb the culture on his day off. He stayed there, all right, but all he absorbed was his bed."

Mexico City, 1991

When the band played Mexico City, they were the first international act to do so in more than twenty years. Following the death of four people outside of a concert by the band Chicago in 1975, global acts had stayed away. INXS filled the Sports Palace, playing to fifty thousand, among them the president's son. The show made history and reopened Mexico as a tour stop for other bands, just as INXS had done through most of South America. In the next two years alone, everyone from Michael Jackson to Metallica to U2 to Paul McCartney followed INXS's lead and booked shows in Mexico City.

FROM KIRK'S DIARY: *Andre kidnapped before show. Bought back for 400 dollars.*

Garry Beers's former bass tech, an African-American named Andre, known for his love of ganja, candy, and cakes, was grabbed by the Mexico City police mere hours after his arrival. The cops nabbed him scoring pot in the square outside of the hotel. He was promptly cuffed and stuffed and soon learned that Mexican police officers are dubious, subjective law-enforcers. Their guns and badges seemed to grant them the freedom to interpret the law on the fly: warrants and crimes were subjective and justice was relative in the presence of cold, hard cash.

Andre spent the rest of the day in the back of a police car, observing Mexico's version of *COPS,* wherein the officers raid the homes of known drug dealers and emerge with drugs and money instead of handcuffed perpetrators.

After a few hours of making their rounds the police called INXS's tour manager and demanded ten thousand dollars in cash in exchange for Andre's freedom. In 1991, one American dollar equaled about 3,000 pesos—ten thousand American dollars equaled 30,000,000 pesos, enough to buy a king's castle down there. INXS's managers didn't flinch—they offered the cops four hundred bucks and the deal was done. Andre was deposited at the hotel, the cash was exchanged, and their bass tech was free—and indignant.

"Man, my people were born into slavery," he said. "My people were freed in 1865. I never thought, after all of that, that I'd be abducted by, of all people, *Mexicans* and sold back to *Australians* like a slave?! You kidding me? What the hell is that? And for only four hundred American dollars? Damn!" The moral of this story? Watch your back in Mexico and remember that a dollar goes a long way south of the border.

Majorca, 1985

Rick Sales called it "The Fag Bag," the case that held the band's makeup, which grew larger in direct proportion to the size of the venues they played. By the time they were selling out arenas, the Fag Bag was serious business. They'd learned the art of maquillage early: Michael Hutchence's mother was a makeup artist who showed them how well-applied foundation and a touch of eyeliner made them more gorgeous under stage lights.

In his former jobs, Rick Sales had witnessed metal bands apply makeup with the subtlety of a toddler wielding a crayon—they did it to shock. He'd *never* seen musicians take to it with delicacy in order to enhance their natural traits. Rick was confused—INXS didn't want to look extreme, they just wanted to look good to the fans in the nose-bleed seats. Rick ridiculed their understated heterosexual glam, and in return, they did all they could to make him all the more uncomfortable about it.

So when the band landed in Majorca, passed through customs, convened on their bus, and realized that no one had plucked the Fag Bag from the baggage carousel, naturally, en masse, they ordered road manager Rick to go back and fetch it.

"I couldn't believe that they were being so ridiculous," Rick says. "I called them all kinds of names." Nevertheless, off he went, and when he reappeared, Fag Bag in hand, the band cheered.

"Here's your Fag Bag," Rick snarled, slamming it down. "It's *scary* how much your makeup means to you."

"Yes it does, Rick and thanks very much," Kirk said smirking, as his band mates guffawed. "We *really* appreciate it. Um, you know that bag's got all the drugs in it, right, mate?"

Canada, 1988

INXS effortlessly sold out six thousand-seat theaters across Canada, and as a token of their esteem, the promoters gave them enough cocaine to reenact *Scarface*. They did as much of it as they could, but as they approached the border, preparing to cross back into the U.S., they still had so much white dust that deciding how to jettison it became the evening parlor game. Gary Grant did his part by offering everyone in sight a massive line. But there was a catch: the line had to be consumed midair; Grant would toss it above the recipient's head and laugh hysterically as they tried to catch it nasally.

INXS never thought they'd see the day when they'd happily turn cocaine into carpet freshener, but life had become so luxe that they knew more awaited them across the border. They'd left a hefty package of illegal goodies in a safety deposit box in a hotel in Buffalo. That night they were, however, behind schedule, and, as snow-blind as he was, Gary Grant realized that a decision must be made: they'd either catch their connecting flight to the Midwest or procure their Stateside stash and spend the night in northern New York.

"Guys, listen," Grant said. "Either we miss the plane, which is the last one out tonight, or we pick up our drugs, stay in Buffalo, and fly out tomorrow. What do you want to do?"

A cacophony of voices answered him instinctually, in unison, mocking the question.

"Drugs! Drugs! Drugs!"

“C’mon, mate, don’t be stupid.”

“To the hotel, Gary, have you gone *mad*?”

Gary rescheduled the flight, INXS made the next night’s show on time, and that particular evening, the boys, their crew, and every patron present in the bar at the Buffalo Hilton partied the crap out of that shack.

Spain, 1988

> FROM KIRK’S DIARY: ***All learned two lessons today. 1) Never,*** **ever** ***carry Michael’s luggage. Don’t even ask, touch, or think about what he’s got in there. 2) Trust Jeff Pope. It’s good to have an Aussie cop on board looking after us. And looking after Tim!***

Michael was never one to covet material possessions, but he’d kept a leather satchel at his side since his teens. He stowed lyrics scrawled on bits of paper in there, as well as other essential personal items—among them, (it’s been reported) a massive black dildo, handcuffs, X-rated Polaroids, and video cameras, which he constantly lost, that contained footage to put Paris Hilton to shame.

One morning in Spain, Michael nonchalantly asked Garry to tote his bag through customs, and onto the plane for him. Michael assured Garry that no drugs were inside, but nonetheless, Garry did a quick sight check. “The first thing I pulled out was a home pregnancy test covered in mud,” he says. “That was it for me.” He dropped the bag as if it were a hot pile of shit and told Michael to lug it aboard himself.

Meanwhile, Tim Farriss, drunk as Bacchus, was close to being arrested. He’d not slept off one bit of the night before, and had packed his passport in the luggage he’d checked—a common Tim occurrence. On line before the customs booths, Tim dumped the contents of his carry-on on the floor, in a woozy, well-intentioned effort to find his papers. When an armed guard approached him, however, he displayed as much eloquence and respect for foreign culture as George W. Bush on a European tour. “The Spanish guard didn’t speak English, thank God,” recalls security chief Jeff Pope, “because Timmy was telling him to fuck off something awful.”

Quietly, everyone else in the band queued up as far from Tim as humanly possible. Jeff Pope, an Australian police officer who never leaves home unprepared, acted fast. Before the Spanish guards could arrest Tim, Jeff did. He slapped his cuffs on him (to Tim's utter confusion), and flashed his Australian badge at the authorities.

"This man is in my custody," Pope said, cool as steel, while Tim swayed beside him. "This man is a fugitive we apprehended in Australia. I am delivering him to the Spanish police to stand trial for crimes committed here."

England-Ireland, 1991

FROM KIRK'S DIARY: *Saturday, July 13, 1991: Wembley. WHOOAAH!! Massive. So cloudy but didn't rain. Quite a bit of nervous tension in the change room but everyone in great moods. On stage at about 8:45. A few technical problems but overall a FANTASTIC show. It went very quickly. Audience was amazing. Bit of partying in the change room afterward until about 12:30 then back to the 9th floor of the hotel for more.*

X was a huge success, the tour was massive, and everyone in the band brought their significant others along for the best part of the ride—a landmark bunch of sold-out shows at Wembley Arena followed by more in Glasgow and Dublin. Andrew Farriss's wife of two years, Shelley, came along, Tim and Buffy Farriss's two beautiful sons were there, as was Kirk Pengilly's longtime girlfriend, Karen Hutchinson, and their baby daughter, April. Garry Beers's wife, Jodie, was there too, three months pregnant with their first child. Jon's fiancée, Leslie, also joined the party for those dates, as did Michael's girlfriend, supermodel Helena Christensen.

The culmination of the *X* tour did more than duly celebrate INXS—it caused a sudden exponential luggage expansion. The men of INXS compete constantly, as do brothers and most males—Australians in particular. At the time INXS's hottest competition revolved around shopping. If a man in the band showed up with a new gadget, rest assured that the next morning, each of them had one. Case in point: each guy has footage of his bandmates on the tour bus, shooting footage of one another with their freshly bought camcorders.

Factoring in the presence of family and the degree of success, it is easy to see how the spoils of their tour of England and Ireland in 1991 rivaled that of a caravan of British royals at the height of the empire. "There were six members in the band, plus three significant others, two children, my own baggage, and the tour manager's baggage. That adds up to twelve people," says Jeff Pope, the man responsible for getting all of it back to Australia. "How many bags do you think they had in tow? Take a guess. Exactly one hundred and five." Six porters manning three four-wheeled trolleys hauled it all to the first-class desk. And despite the regulations, somehow, some way, Mr. Pope got them all on the plane without paying excess charges.

Competitive shopping in Paris.

"Want to know how I did it?" he says. "Talk, talk, talk, talk, talk. You'd be surprised how effective talk can be."

Texas, 1986

At one point in the mid- to late eighties, modern pompadours—antigravity, highly-permed mullets really—ran rampant in the INXS family. Michael sported a modified version, while Tim Farriss, Jon Farriss, Garry Beers, and tour manager Gary Grant donned 'dos that were nearly the same. Back then Grant looked quite like Tim, which paid off one night in Texas.

Gary was the perfect tour manager—disciplined enough that he balanced the books each night before he indulged in any post-show festivities. On the night in question, he planned to meet the band at an after-party once he had calculated the day's profits. A knock on the door of his room disturbed him, and he found a gorgeous six-foot blonde on the other side.

"I had a great time tonight," she said. "And I *really* want to party with you."

She was stunning, determined, and packing a bottle of champagne, a gram of cocaine, a boom box, and a fist full of joints. What else could he do but put his bookkeeping aside? Grant reports that she was a fast machine, she kept her motor clean, and was the best damn woman he had ever seen. It seemed that she had the sightless eyes, tellin' him no lies, and proceeded to light him up with those American thighs. Furthermore, he recalls that before too long, the walls were quakin', the earth was shakin', his mind was achin', and they were makin' it. It's safe to say that she shook him all night long. She really shook him—yeah, she shook him. All. Night. Long.

Tim Farriss returned around dawn wondering why Gary never showed up at the party. He sauntered over to Grant's door, but opted not to knock due to the sounds he heard. The next morning, as the band loaded into the bus and Gary's conquest made her way to her car, his peers openly gawked at her beauty.

"Thank you for last night," Ms. Texas said to Gary. "That was amazing. You know, I really loved those red and black pants you wore onstage last night."

Gary Grant didn't own red and black pants and he wasn't onstage the night before—in fact he wasn't even at the side of the stage. As it dawned on him that he'd just enjoyed the greatest case of mistaken identity, Tim Farriss stepped in.

"Oh, thanks! That was me in the red and black pants," Tim said, smirking. "Glad you liked them."

Ms. Texas smiled awkwardly, and as it all sank in, Grant kissed her good-bye, leapt onto the tour bus, and told the driver to beat it.

Phoenix, Arizona, 1990

Michael spotted her right away, an athletic Arizona blonde, in the front row in a short pink skirt and tight white tank top. She moved to the music so seductively that he brought her onstage during "What You Need," and put her on a riser so that her crotch was at eye-level. In the pit between the stage and the crowd, Jeff Pope noticed right away that the lady was riding sans culottes.

Michael danced with her, serenaded her, and slid his hand up her thigh, into her skirt, ecstatic to find no panties in there. She gyrated to the music and adoring Michael's caress, no one but she, Jeff, and Hutch were the wiser. As the song climaxed, so did she.

"I couldn't believe it," Pope says. "While it was happening Michael kept looking at me like, 'Are you *seeing this*?' I didn't believe something like that was possible. Afterward, backstage, I said to him, 'You're a sick fuck, aren't you?'"

"Yes I am," Hutchence said, laughing. "Yes, Jeff, I am."

Guns N' Roses, Texas, 1988

FROM KIRK'S DIARY: *September 17th, 1988. Dallas, "Texas Stadium," 55,000 capacity—Smithereens, Ziggy Marley, Iggy Pop, Guns n' Roses, INXS. Leisurely day for most. Most down to the show at different times. Some rain in the afternoon, due to hurricane Gilbert. Lots of friends down for the show. In the end about 40,000 in the audience. Guns n' Roses finished early (sounded terrible). Fantastic gig—we finished with "Don't Change." Bit of a party backstage and then some back to the bar at the hotel and eventually most off to the M.H. suite for party till very late, along with Iggy Pop, our L.A. friends, Duff (from Guns n' Roses), etc. etc. etc.*

INXS headlined an MTV-sponsored gig at the Texas Stadium—the home of the Dallas Cowboys—that was arranged and promoted by Chris Murphy. Dubbed "Calling All Nations," it boasted a diverse line-up from Ziggy Marley to Iggy Pop to the Smithereens, which entertained fifty thousand fans. Murphy also enlisted Guns N' Roses months before the show: he loved their music, knew they were bound for glory, and hoped to be the first to let them shine on a major stage. They jumped at the opportunity, but in the half a year that followed, Guns had become the hottest band in America—and could barely deal with it.

Guns had never played a stadium, weren't known as the kind of band to share a bill with the Smithereens, so as the show drew near, they did what they could to get out of it. They asked to be coheadliners (Murphy laughed), they asked to be let out of their contract (Murphy refused), and so in the end they did all they could to fuck up the show. Minutes before their scheduled stage time, their manager demanded that the set be cut short because Axl Rose, apparently in the throes of drug withdrawal, couldn't deliver. Whether it was a ruse or not, Axl told a crowd of forty thousand that he wasn't sure where he was that night because he'd done too much cocaine for too many days.

Michael and Andrew met Axl and Slash backstage earlier that night and found them highly amusing: Hutch and Farriss were eating dinner in the artists' cafeteria when Guns' dynamic duo popped in, circled their table, and nervously sat down nearby. Michael called them over and asked them how it all was going. Axl did most of the talking, saying that their sudden success was tough to bear and how worried they were to play to such a huge crowd that night.

"What's the problem with that?" Michael asked. "What's the matter? Just play. Just do what you do."

"It's just a lot of pressure, you know," Axl said, shifting in his seat. "There's a lot of pressure on us to be our best. It's your dream to always want this . . . and then you get it and you *have* to be your best. Your have to be your very best every fucking night."

Michael had every right to be haughty, having spent the better part of his life on the road, but he wasn't: instead, he was wise, compassionate, and elegant. "Lighten up, man," Michael said warmly. "You have to *dream.* That's how you got here. And you have to keep on dreaming. There is always going to be someone greater than you—*always.* And you know what? So what, man. That doesn't matter. Just do fine work and enjoy yourself. Believe me, that's what it's all about."

INXS was midway through a three-month tour of the States. Before that they'd toured Europe and elsewhere for eight months. And before that, they'd toured for over a year. And before that they'd toured for the better part of their lives. They were veterans, they were tired, they'd achieved their goal and worked hard for it. And they knew that this next level of success meant that the work wouldn't stop any time soon.

Andrew fixed his eyes on Axl. "So how long have you been on tour?" he asked.

"Five weeks," Axl said. "It's been fucking rough, man."

"Yeah," Andrew said. "I bet it has."

Onstage High Jinks, All Years, All Times

During the *Kick* and *X* tours, behind-the-scenes activities took place that the audience knew nothing of. A staple of the set was an acoustic version of "Shine Like It Does," performed by Kirk and Michael, which the other band members looked forward to—it was their recess to urinate and take drugs. Kirk's potty break (and, if he was quick enough, drug interlude) was "Never Tear Us Apart." But he couldn't dally—his transcendent sax solo in the coda made the song. He usually cut it close though. Kirk is famous for getting lost, particularly in the bowels of arenas.

Here's another fun fact: Kirk and Andrew mixed margaritas on stage, between songs. Kirk's tech stashed tequila, margarita mix, a bucket of ice, and a blender behind Kirk's guitar amp. He and Andrew would nod at each other midsong when they were thirsty, and meet in the dark once the tune was done.

"We had a very efficient system," Andrew says. "I'd toss in the ice, Kirk would pour in the liquor, and I'd run the blender during the audience's applause so no one would hear it. I'd pour out the drinks, we'd salute each other, slam them back, get back to our instruments, and start the next song."

Spinal Tap, 1984

On tour, every band watches movies on loop. The films on the bus become surrogate friends, and it doesn't take long for film dialogue to replace everyday conversation. The longer the tour, the more those films foster in-jokes alien to the outside world.

In their heyday INXS made *Caddyshack, ¡Three Amigos!,* and others their own, but *This Is Spinal Tap* stopped them in their tracks. Rob Reiner's rock mockumentary satirized a music world far from INXS, but Kirk Pengilly took it to heart.

"It affected my performance. I'd never thought about what I looked like onstage before then," he says. "After I saw *Spinal Tap,* I'd be playing a solo, wondering if I looked like David St. Hubbins." His humility is endearing—there isn't a lead guitarist further in style from Kirk than David St. Hubbins. Kirk is an understated technician, an able player in command of his instrument who emotes flawlessly with soul to spare—he's like an engineer with a Ph.D. in rock.

The wise words of tour manager Rick Sales set Kirk straight. In case you forgot, Rick had toured exclusively with metal bands, pre-INXS. Rick told Kirk what he needed to hear: his darkest nights on the metal circuit weren't spent witnessing gross depravity. They were spent watching *Spinal Tap* with hair-metal bands that didn't get the joke; bands who thought *Spinal Tap* was real. Rick is never at a loss for words, but what could he say to a band that was furious because they'd never opened for Spinal Tap?

The Rolling Stones 1987 and 1991

After the band's 1987 Madison Square Garden show, Andrew Farriss and a friend shared a quiet celebratory beer alone backstage in the green room. And then Keith Richards walked in and freaked Andrew the fuck out.

Keith, one of Andrew's idols, strolled over, started chatting to him about music and INXS's set. Andrew is a multi-instrumentalist and has always been a core songwriter in the band—but for all of his artistic expression, he is without a doubt the shy one in INXS. Most of the famous folk who came backstage at gigs by then weren't hankering to meet him—they were in search of Michael—and Andrew was convinced that Keith would be no different. To make matters more uncomfortable, Andrew's friend suddenly realized it was "Keef" and dropped her beer, which smashed loudly onto the cold, concrete floor. Too embarrassed to stay, she jumped up and dashed out of the room.

Andrew fished around in his pockets for his cigarettes, suddenly realizing he had left them in the dressing room. He spied the familiar, red box of Marlboros in Keith's shirt pocket and asked for one. Keith handed over a new packet and when Andrew tried to pull one out, he fumbled over the tightly wrapped package, and spilled its entire contents out onto both of them.

As he tried to pick them off the floor and stuff them back in the box, Andrew said, "Keith, you know, thanks, it's great to meet you, but if you're looking for Michael, he's down the hall in the dressing room."

"What?" Keith barked.

"Well, you know, if you want to say hi to Michael, he's down the hall," Andrew said again.

"Why would I want to do that?" Keith grumbled. "He's just a singer. You and me, *we* play the *music*, man."

Four years later, in 1991, following INXS's sold-out concert at London's Wembley Stadium, Andrew, Michael, and Jon entertained Stones bassist Bill Wyman at the after-party. Bill sipped champagne, while the room of VIP revelers grew more rambunctious. There were two visibly drunk girls opposite them, and suddenly one threw herself backward with such force that she got stuck inside a hole of her own making in the plaster wall.

"She fell through the wall," Bill Wyman said, flatly.

Andrew walked over to help the girl back on her feet.

"I realized in that moment just how much that man had seen," Andrew says. "That was nothing to him. He didn't react in any way. He didn't even blink. He just held his champagne and said, 'She fell through the wall.' It was amazing."

Rocking with the Royals, Melbourne, Australia, 1985

INXS and a select group of Aussie bands entertained Prince Charles and Princess Diana during Australia's 150th anniversary. VIPs filled the Melbourne Arts Center, but massive screens erected outside allowed forty thousand others to enjoy the show as well. Prince Charles snapped his fingers in time, and Di rocked out in her seat as intensely as princess protocol allowed.

The performers were granted a meeting with the Royals and there were bets in the INXS camp as to how Princess Di would react to Michael's infallible sex appeal. The man moved like a cat—he was sex in motion—and women of all types fell to pieces in his presence. But not Di—she virtually ignored him. Charles greeted him thusly, proclaiming, in reference to the show: "You must be right *shagged* after that."

If Di showed anyone favor, it was Kirk. Several eyewitnesses claim that Di stared at him, very obviously, as he made his way along the receiving line. "It made sense to me that she'd be more interested in Kirk than Michael," Gary Grant says. "I'd always taken her for the type who'd like intellectual guys with glasses."

"We had a moment, Di and I," Kirk says proudly. "It's true. And you know, if Charles hadn't been around that night, I'd have been there."

The History of Ralph Pounder

TIM FARRISS was INXS's first fan; he was their original cheerleader, ringleader, manager, and overseer—positions he's never relinquished as the years have gone by. Tim, the eldest Farriss son, had rock in his blood straightaway: he sectioned off a portion of their basement and declared it his bedroom, compromising comfort for the freedom to spin Beatles and Stones records whenever he liked. Tim is the most fearless Farriss, the one who never bothers to read the directions. "I never really worried about any of my boys," says father Dennis Farriss. "But there was that one time that Tim nearly blew himself up with his chemistry set. He was twelve, I think, and experimenting up in their tree house one Christmas. I don't know what he did, but he caused an awful eruption that blew nearly every blossom off that tree, yet somehow Tim wasn't hurt. Our lawn contractor was very surprised to see bare branches and a lawn full of flowers when he came round. There was no easy explanation for how that had happened."

Tim and Kirk Pengilly are great friends, and have been ever since the day they met at the Forest High School. Both played guitar and soon formed a duo called Tim and Kirk, and then their first band, Guinness, which they advertised as a group that played psychedelic country jazz. When that

Alias: Tim Farriss

Born: August 16, 1957

Instruments: guitar, bongos

Married: February 6, 1981, to Bethany Anne Reefman

Children: James and Jake

First Band: Guinness

Sports: deep-sea fishing (catch and release), cricket, swimming, tennis, speed shopping, skin diving, golf, snowboarding, anything else humans might do

Alternate Aliases: Hugh Jardon (pronounced, en français, *'Uge Ard-on*), Captain Flange

band fizzled, it was Tim who thought to enlist his little brothers, Jon and Andrew, as well as their bandmates Michael Hutchence and Garry Beers into a neighborhood supergroup they called the Farriss Brothers. Tim was also the man who talked Kirk into joining their musical adventure in spite of his friend's insistence that he had no interest in doing so. "We always used to call Tim the shoe salesman back then," Kirk says. "If he really liked something he was so convincing about how great it was that you'd just want to say, 'Okay, I'm sold—I'll take ten!'" Dad Dennis Farriss agrees: "If Tim weren't in the band he would have been a top-drawer car salesman. He's got the salesman's charm and the motivation to do anything. He always manages to get his way in his own way—and that is something you can't teach."

Tim was the first Farriss, or member of INXS, to be married; he wed his high school sweetheart, Bethany (better known by her nickname, Buffy), on February 6, 1981; she was twenty-two, he was twenty-three. They met in biology class during their last year of school, and Tim exhibited every ounce of his trademark suave demeanor that day. "He shared the desk with me and told me right then what he was going to do with his life. He had no doubt about it," Buffy says. "He had an energy and drive and outlook on life unlike anyone I'd ever met. After all of these years, I still haven't met anyone else like him. He was beyond optimistic. I'm quite sure the other guys wouldn't have made it without him."

Buffy was immediately smitten with Tim, the charismatic, "funny-looking little guy with lots of fluffy hair," who wooed her in Bio. But she saw little of him in the hallways for the rest of the year; Tim left school before taking his final exams, choosing to spend his days landing gigs for the Farriss Brothers. It wasn't until the men of INXS returned from their sojourn in Perth that Buffy and Tim got seriously involved, and once they were, they married a few years later. "We'd both come from families of long marriages, which is why we were able to survive through all of the pressures of raising a family while Tim was constantly touring," Buffy says. "It was tough in the beginning, but I never worried about what I was getting into. I'm not someone who particularly cares about money, though my parents were very worried. I liked having to work because I've always liked having my own life. If I hadn't, I don't think we'd still be together."

For their wedding present the band pooled their resources and gave them a communal one hundred bucks. "That was huge for us," Kirk says. "And it looked like a huge wad of cash because it was almost all one dollar bills!" At the time, the band's weekly wages, as a group, was about $250.

Kirk was Tim's best man and he nearly missed out on delivering the obligatory reception toast. Kirk was, according to his diary from that year, "being social in the men's room" with a friend at the time who was known for the particularly potent pot he dealt. It took thirty minutes for the others to find Kirk, and thirty more for Kirk to regain his composure. In the end, Andrew Farriss stepped in to set off the night's speeches, and Kirk brought up the rear. "It took me a full half hour in a cubicle alone to gain any kind of coherent composure," Kirk says. "When I did return I said all that I was capable of saying—I proposed a toast to the bride and groom. Hey, they're still married after twenty-five years, so, I ask you, what's the problem?"

Tim and Buffy's first son, James, was born in 1982, just as INXS began its endless tours of the States and Europe. "That was Tim's first big trip away," Buffy says. "It was the first time I wasn't so sure I wanted to be a part of all that was coming our way. It was very hard. All of the guys were so consumed with what they were doing, plus my parents had moved to Indonesia. I was tending to our son by myself and it was very lonely. Tim would call me, having the greatest time and, I tell you, he'd get an earful. He'd be on a terrace overlooking some beautiful sunset somewhere and I'd have a crying baby on my shoulder. It wasn't easy for us to connect." Tim, for his part, felt horribly guilty, particularly as the band's schedule did nothing but grow busier. "I missed a lot of my older son's life," Tim says. "He took his first steps in an airport with his mother when they were coming to visit me. And I was away more and more in the years that followed. It was getting ridiculous for a long time and it caused a lot of problems between us. But I think that now my oldest boy at least understands why I was away, and that if I could have, I'd have been with him every day."

When time and money afforded Tim the option of flying Buffy and his son out to accompany him on tour, his wife soon discovered that it wasn't her cup of tea. "I found myself wondering why the hell I was there," she says. "I'd be living in a bus and a hotel. We'd go to beautiful cities, but I'd have very little time to see anything and when I did, it was usually not with my husband. I preferred to stay home and have my own life."

Though their bond has never been broken, Tim and Buffy were tested by the dizzying success that consumed INXS. Six-month tours turned into two-year tours, and when the band finally got time off, like deep-sea divers there was a necessary, uncomfortable decompression session. "There was a time that I was worried about an excessive usage of substances going on out

on the road," Buffy says. "Tim has such an energy that he gets carried away with whatever his passion is. But when he came home, he'd become normal again pretty quickly. And if he didn't, we'd just give him a hard time until he snapped out of it. Apart from his career in the band, he's a very normal guy. He's a dad, he loves to fish and golf. He had us to keep him grounded, but Michael worried me as they grew up. Michael had to be a certain person on stage, but whereas Tim could turn that part of himself off when he came home, Michael couldn't."

After Jake was born, Tim was tortured by his time away from Buffy and his children, yet found that he spent the band's longer breaks in 1989 and 1992 pursuing hobbies that took up just as much of his time. "It's still hard for me to think about, but back then I'd be so upset to be away from home for seven months at a stretch, I'd cry all the time because I missed them so much. But then when I did get home, and was set to be there for a while, I went in search of things that took me away from my family. I don't know what it was all about. I should have gone to an analyst to figure it out. But instead, I went fishing."

When Tim Farriss does anything, he does it big—actually, he does it bigger than big: Tim goes colossal. He bought a 36-foot, three-station, game-fishing boat, named it *King Kong,* and complete with a captain, first mate, full wet bar, and an arsenal of rods got so into tackling rough seas in search of marlin that he even hired a film crew to shoot a documentary of his exploits. He called it *Fish in Space,* in honor of and as a piss take on his bandmate Michael Hutchence's acting debut in the film *Dogs in Space.* His adventures with *King Kong,* however, are tame, as a result of a lesson at sea learned earlier that nearly cost Tim his life.

Tim had always loved to fish and had begun to do so competitively long before he bought *King Kong.* His zeal first drove him and his dear friend Bryan Lynch to purchase together a smaller boat called *Watchaneed,* and then Tim bought a beach house at Port Stephens that included a mooring for the boat. Port Stephens was appealing not just for the beautiful seaside solitude, but because the town hosted one of the biggest fishing tournaments in Australia. Tim and Bryan entered the four-day, two-weekend contest hungry, armed only with their skimpy twenty-one-foot outboard *Watchaneed,* joining nearly three hundred other boats who piloted to sea that day determined to win. On the final day, they left at 5 a.m. and motored thirty-two miles into the deep blue, far beyond the sight of land, to a spot where they knew the big fish fed. They'd brought along a ton of burley—Australian for chum (a.k.a. chopped-up, bloody fish)—and laboriously dumped it in the water. In addition, they set a series of thirty-pound (ten kilo) test game fishing outfits baited with four to five pound tunas on thick hooks. And like Hemingway's old man at sea, they waited. And waited.

With the boat tossed by forty-knot (forty-six miles an hour) winds and twelve-foot swells, Tim noticed a reel slowly winding out and took it in hand. After ten minutes, it was clear to him and the others on the boat that there was a massive fish on the line. The boat captain fired up the engine and put the throttle down, as Tim struck the fish with the reel engaged. Tim wrestled his Moby Dick for three and a half hours, repeatedly drawing it close to the surface and watching hopelessly as it dove again. "I thought my back was going to give out, and I thought about cutting the line many times," Tim says. "This thing was huge and it was driving us around in circles, using up all of our fuel." When they finally caught a glimpse of it, Tim and his compatriots were awed: he'd been fighting a terrifying sixteen-foot tiger shark. They'd used up more than half of their fuel tiring it out. Tim reined it in, and his crew gaffed it, then tied it alongside the boat, and it was far too long and far too heavy to be hoisted aboard. They secured the shark to their ship, but the monster wasn't dead. The shark began to strain against its bindings, and the boat groaned as its fiberglass hull began to bend in two. "One guy cut one of the ropes so the boat wouldn't crack in half," Tim says.

The shark was then lassoed by the tail and they let it drag a few feet behind their motor as they started to wonder if they had enough fuel to traverse the thirty-odd miles home. It was late afternoon, the tides had grown rougher, and it was very clear as their boat's engine strained to tow the load of the giant fish that they'd see the bottom of their gas tank long before they'd see land.

Tim radioed a friend he knew was nearby on a much larger sport-fishing boat and asked for help. The two competing crafts rendezvoused and good sportsmanship ruled the day: the opposing crew agreed to haul Tim's fish back to shore, because it was obvious that he'd caught the winning fish. But all wasn't well: the sea was far too rough for either boat to draw close to the other, so the onus was on Tim to earn his catch. "They said if I swam over to them with the rope tied to my shark, they'd bring me and my fish back to shore," he says. "Without the extra weight, the other guys could make it back. The waves were huge, but that wasn't the real danger: they'd been dumping burley in the water for hours to lure sharks. The water around their boat was so thick with blood that it wasn't even water anymore. And there were shark fins cutting the water every direction you looked."

There is a crossroad where bravery, insanity, fate, and stupidity meet. Tim Farriss swam through that crossroad and didn't even flinch: he tied the rope bound to his shark around his waist and made like hell for the other boat. When he got there, the surge was so huge that the back landing of the vessel smashed his shoulder making his right arm numb, and when it did, he thought he'd been bitten. "They hauled me onto the boat, and all of them kept telling me that I was fucking out of my mind," Tim says. "They were right, I was out of my mind. Completely out of my mind."

Tim took home the trophy for the tournament's champion angler, and his boat, as a unit, came in as the runners-up of the entire competition. Looking at his prize-winning catch, Tim felt remorse for killing such a beautiful creature. "I told my fish I was sorry, actually," Tim says. "I felt horrible. That experience was one of those moments where you've been sent out to become a man. And I did." Afterward, Tim stopped fishing for sharks and devoted himself to marlin, which he catches and releases, cherishing the sport of the chase, not the spoils.

Fishing isn't Tim's only favorite sport—he's just as crazy for cricket. Tim lives in Manly Beach and he is currently president of his local team, the Manly Cricket Club. He once even parachuted from an airplane onto a cricket field to raise money for a charity sponsored by Simplicity Funerals, a local funeral home. Let it be known that Tim would have sooner swum with sharks again: he *hates* to fly and is afraid of heights. "By the time I got up there, I hated being in the plane so much that I would have jumped without a parachute," he says. "It was worth doing though to see the look on my sons' faces when I landed. But I'll never do it again."

Tim and his "mini-me mullet" son James

Tim follows his sporting muse where it takes him, be it skin diving, snowboarding, golf, or surfing, and he has mastered them all to the best of his ability. But he's proven himself a master at one sport above all, a sport that can be enjoyed indoors or out, year-round: shopping. He took it up in his youth, when INXS's travels provided an opportunity to net exotic treats unseen in Australia. "I could always tell when Tim had gone shopping with Michael in Paris," Buffy says. "He'd bring me these rubber or leather outfits and all sorts of weird, sexy things. He's a bit of a devil like that." But that was just the beginning: when Tim built his former studio, The Chaps Club, where a heap of local talent recorded over the years, Tim indulged a spontaneous passion for exotic fish with a huge wall-sized aquarium in the studio.

Tim's zeal for his hobbies, as hot as they might be at first, cools quickly when he's on to something new—and that is the beauty of Tim Farriss. For example, Tim once bought a Rolls-Royce during a tour of England and shipped it back to Sydney where he had it fully customized by a company owned by Tony Woodhall, the man who later became Michael Hutchence's bodyguard. "Timmy had us put everything in it, huge subwoofers packed into every inch of this car. It was out of control. He loved it. And then the next time I saw him, he'd sold it. He was over it. And that's just Tim."

There's one purchase and one passion that Tim Farriss never reneged on—his farm. It is as much a cherished constant in his life as Buffy and his boys; in fact it is an extension of his love for them. It is a lush 130-acre property in Kangaroo Valley that he purchased from his brother Andrew. The land includes ancient rain forest and is also a hidden valley where Tim has spent recent years with his family, making up for all of the times he'd missed them on the road. Their land has rolling hills reminiscent of England, a full-time staff to tend to the cows and sheep, a rushing river, ponds, creeks, geese, ducks, chickens, turkeys, guinea fowl, alpacas, donkeys, horses, a huge fruit orchard, fields where the family border collie can roam free, and a swimming hole with a sandy beach. The property is Tim's heart—his parents lived there in the years before his mother's passing, and it is where he retreated the day that Michael Hutchence died. Tim is a multifaceted man, a ringleader who loves to conquer the world when he steps out with INXS, but in his mind, he's always at home. As he's grown older, he's found it ever harder to be away from his family. "I don't know what I would do without my farm," Tim says. "Sometimes my whole family comes together there. I spend time with my sons, I work on the land with the staff, bailing hay and inspecting the livestock. I like to get my hands dirty and work on the land. Sometimes I forget that it's mine, a beautiful place I will pass on to my boys. No one should own anything as beautiful as this. And that has made everything I've done—the good, the bad, the gifts, and the sacrifices—worth it."

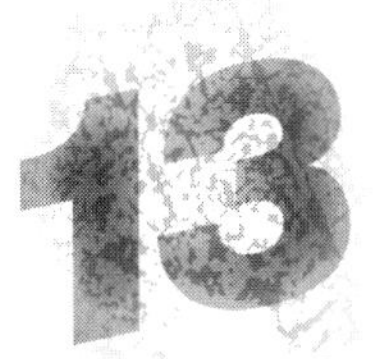

When the Love Around Begins to Suffer

JOANNE PETERSEN, INXS'S LONGTIME FRIEND and representative at Warner Bros. Australia, recalls how much sudden success changed INXS by the time the *Kick* tour reached Australia. She'd seen them grow up on the road and knew them when they were so poor that Chris Murphy stocked their van with bags of oranges to fend off scurvy (to this day, Kirk can't eat an orange). "When they came home after the *Kick* tour, suddenly all of them were buying really expensive clothes and living the high life," Petersen says. "Michael in particular really got a bit out there. He was completely flipping out during their Australian tour of that record. He'd taken to wearing a white suit and calling himself Fabien Sparkle. That's simply who he was if that suit was on. He'd be on stage in that suit, completely inhabiting this character he'd invented. I kept thinking that he was becoming a bit too Elvis." Luckily his band of brothers kept him in orbit. "The other guys were always so great at reining Michael in when he'd get too far out," Petersen says. "They'd let him go as far as he wanted, but they'd put him right back in his place at the end of the day."

Michael wasn't the only one showing signs of wear: in the last half of the eighties, everyone in the band began to unravel from the exertion and

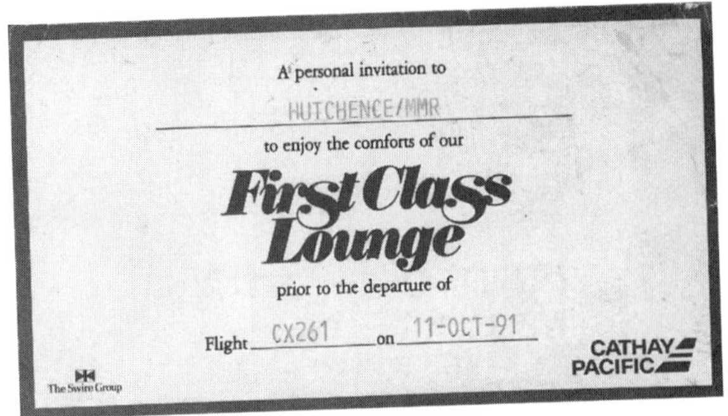
A personal invitation to
HUTCHENCE/MMR
to enjoy the comforts of our
First Class Lounge
prior to the departure of
Flight CX261 on 11-OCT-91
CATHAY PACIFIC
The Swire Group

pressure. The first wake-up call was Jon Farriss's health. Like his brother Tim, Jon has Exostoses, which afflicts the bones and joints, primarily of Caucasian males. For years, Jon's doctors had routinely drained hundreds of cc's of fluid from his knees and prescribed him a steady diet of cortisone.

Jon shared an apartment—a seven-story walk-up—in Hong Kong with Michael during the *Kick* years, and as he walked down those stairs to catch a flight to America to begin the next phase of the tour, he knew something was very wrong with his knee; then midway through the flight, the pain became intolerable. "There was a tremendous amount of fluid built up on my knee and the cabin pressure in the plane made it much, much worse. I couldn't bend it at all for the entire flight. It blew up like a balloon," he says.

For a week, Jon fulfilled his duties as best he could. He knew that time was of the essence—the album had just begun to move up the U.S. charts. He refused to quit to the point of insanity: at his worst, Jon couldn't walk. He'd be chauffered onstage in a wheelchair and relied on a drum machine to provide the sound of the bass drum he was unable to play. It was obvious to everyone that Jon needed help and that the tour must be postponed. "I was so disappointed because I've loved every minute of this career so much that I didn't want to ruin anything," he says. "But I had to rest. We lost revenue that was already spent, there were tens of thousands of tickets sold, and I was letting everyone down on our payroll. It was a horrible time." Jon recuperated over six weeks at a hot springs resort in Calgary, Canada, where anti-inflammatory drugs, detoxifying herbal tea, and self-hypnosis healing tapes sorted him out. He'd like to take a moment to thank the resort staff and his doctor. He couldn't have done it without you.

Following the massive global success of *Kick,* INXS finally had the money, the prestige, and the freedom to take a crucially necessary, well-deserved break. In 1989, the band agreed to a year's respite, much to their manager's chagrin. "I did not want to lose the momentum we'd built up," Chris Murphy says. "I was convinced that if we let up, we'd lose it all. In my mind, if we stopped, we'd lose our footing. But I was voted out, so we took a year off. In the end it all worked out . . . I guess."

That year was the first time since adolescence that the men of INXS could devote themselves to life outside of the band. Andrew Farriss married the love of his life, Shelley Blanks, in April, after two years of courtship. He also wrote music with Jenny Morris, a gifted Australian singer-songwriter and longtime friend of the band whose backing vocals can be heard on *The Swing* and *Listen Like Thieves.* That year, Andrew produced, cowrote, and played guitar and keyboards on Jenny's album *Shiver,* which yielded a string of hit singles in Australia.

Garry Beers spent the year getting serious with his girlfriend Jodie Crampton, whom he married two years later. He also recorded and played with Absent Friends, a band of well-known Sydney and Melbourne musicians—Wendy Matthews, Sean Kelly, and James Valentine. The outfit released an album, *Here's Looking Up Your Address,* and charted a single with "I Don't Want to Be with Nobody But You."

Tim Farriss spent his year fishing. Tim being Tim, he made fishing his calling, won a few professional trophies, and made a film of his exploits.

Kirk Pengilly spent 1989 coproducing a couple of tracks with Tim for a Sydney band called Crash Politics. On the personal front, Kirk's partner, Karen Hutchinson, gave birth to their daughter, April, in 1988 and he was glad to have the time to be with them both.

Jon Farriss spent most of 1989 in Hong Kong, recovering from his knee problems and suffering through the end of his nearly seven-year relationship with a Texan girl named Lisa. Hong Kong allowed Jon the peace he needed—it was disconnected from everything he knew, and it allowed him anonymity. That year, he and Michael moved into a house on the water in Tai Tam, overlooking the junks and fishing boats on the South China Sea. They turned the house's third bedroom into a home recording studio, filling it with cutting-edge equipment, including a Macintosh SE (the beige box with the tiny black-and-white screen) loaded with sequencing and composition software that, by today's standards, was as modern as an abacus.

In 1989, though, that Mac allowed Jon to grow as a songwriter; it enabled him to compose songs from a rhythmic point of view. A globetrotter by nature, Michael usually wasn't around, but when he was, he and Jon wrote together. One of their best collaborations, "Disappear," ended up on the band's next album, *X*, and was one of the biggest singles in INXS's career.

Jon also spent some time in Australia, to play and write music. He recorded with Richard Clapton, Jimmy Barnes (he appeared on "Seven Days" off Barnes's *Freight Train Heart*), and singer/songwriter Sharon O'Neil (on the song "Physical Favors" from *Danced in the Fire*).

Michael Hutchence didn't really take time off in the conventional sense. He spent his hiatus globetrotting, simultaneously courting and shirking the jet-set life he'd stumbled into. His house was in Hong Kong but his home was wherever he set his hat in 1989: he hopped from Australia to L.A., through Europe and back again all year long. Michael had no reason to stay in one place; he and Michele Bennett, his only true love according to those who knew him best, had ended their seven-year relationship. It was a seismic shift in his life, though Michele and Michael remained close until his death. He needed Michele, and in the years to come always called her to seek advice and comfort. He called Michele the night he died; she was the very last person he spoke to.

By the end of 1989, however, Michael had a new girlfriend, Kylie Minogue, a popular Australian soap-opera star who was then launching a career as a pop singer. Kylie was beloved in Australia: for years she'd been on *Neighbors* (which also spawned actress-turned-singer Natalie Imbruglia) and was poised to be Oz's Tiffany. Just like that eighties American mall maven from Long Island, New York, Minogue came to fame by covering a sixties classic; Tiffany's golden ticket was Tommy James and the Shondells' "I Think We're Alone Now" and Kylie's was Little Eva's "Locomotion."

Michael and Kylie thrilled Australia's tabloids: he was a notorious party-hound sex-god and Kylie was Australia's sweetheart. Suffice it to say that they learned from each other: Kylie grounded Michael and Michael made Kylie a sex symbol. She was a reason for him to cut back on his clubbing (from nightly to every other night), and he allowed her to go where she'd never gone before.

Michael forged another relationship during INXS's time off: he formed a band with Melbourne punker Ollie Olsen, with whom he'd collaborated on the score to Richard Lowenstein's film *Dogs in Space.* Olsen was what Michael was not: loud, rude, contrarian, unemployed, and unknown outside of Melbourne—he was exactly what Michael was after, in light of his increasingly pop persona. The duo wrote songs, enlisted mutual friends, and recorded *Max Q,* an album that is worlds away from INXS. *Max Q* is what Michael yearned to be: openly political and extremely alternative. The music wonderfully combines industrial rock, futuristic disco, radical lyrics, and Michael's beautiful tenor. It was the singer's pet project, and on his dime, the art and ambition ran wild. The singles "Sometimes," and "Way of the World" cracked the Australian charts and the album was critically praised everywhere, though it sold poorly.

Michael insisted in the press that *Max Q* was devised to explore musical ambitions that did not suit INXS and was not at all an indication that he intended to leave the band.

Nevertheless, *Max Q* made the others very nervous. "Chris Murphy had always played a big part in making sure Michael remained grounded and close to the camp," Kirk says. "But this is when everyone started to lose their ability to control Michael—even Chris. We'd all been affected by our success, but Michael changed the most. He became this great star at that point. It definitely went to his head through that period. I believe that is why he and Michele grew apart. He was now very suddenly, officially a true rock star."

If *Max Q* had been a huge commercial success, it might have spelled the end of INXS. Chris Murphy knew this, and though he helped Michael market the album, he didn't quite give it his all. "One of the changes we saw in Michael was that he suddenly felt that he was being held back by us at that time," Kirk says. "If *Max Q* had been successful outside of Australia, he would have thought that he could go it alone. But even if he had, I know he would have come back to us after a while. He needed our support. We were always his family, really."

Andrew Farriss first learned of *Max Q* at a dinner party, when the band's video came on MTV, and every guest present turned his way. He acted like he knew all about it and told them all that he'd heard the album and that it was great. "I do think the recordings are great, but I was very upset," Andrew says. "I was upset because instead of spending time writing music with me, Michael chose to spend time writing with them. But, you know, that was Michael. He'd gone and done what he did best: he was a true bohemian, who flew, like a butterfly, from one thing to another."

If *Max Q* had broken up the band, some members were so spent that they would have welcomed it. All of them had discovered that they could find musical satisfaction through production work and other collaborations. Those members with families relished the chance to make up for lost time—and were reluctant to lose more. The break also allowed the band members time to reflect on all they'd just been through, and latent tensions boiled to the surface. *Kick* generated a tremendous amount of money but for the first time in the band's history, it wasn't distributed equally. "We'd set up a very fair publishing arrangement among ourselves early on," Kirk says. "Fifty percent went to each song's songwriters and the other fifty went to the whole band. It was fair because no matter who had written the song, when we were in the studio, everyone contributed to the music. But when it came time to do *Kick* our producer, Chris Thomas, pushed us to do an entire album of singles and looked to Andrew and Michael, the pair who'd written our biggest singles at that point, to write them."

The success of *Kick* cemented Hutchence-Farriss's status as the Lennon-McCartney of INXS. "The formula really worked, but it also really fucked things up, because it granted Andrew and Michael a stranglehold on the writing and publishing," Kirk says. In the music world, a band makes its money through touring, merchandise, and publishing. The publishing rights to the music are a band's most valuable asset; it's a certificate of ownership that grants the owner a royalty every time the song is played or otherwise licensed. Tour and merchandise profits make money in the short term, but publishing is an artist's 401k—the rights to just one huge hit can fund early retirement.

Previously, Kirk, Tim, Garry, and Jon contributed at least a song per album, and there had never been rules as to who might write with each other or whose songs would make the final cut. The old arrangement fostered constructive competition and free collaboration. The new arrangement shut the others out of the creative process, and by extension, established an unequal division of the profits—somehow an aristocracy had displaced a democracy. On *Kick* and forever after, Andrew and Michael split 50 percent of the publishing, leaving 50 to be split evenly among all six band members. Jon Farriss, because he lived, and sometimes wrote, with Michael was the only one to easily, though infrequently, penetrate the Andrew-Michael think tank.

Jon and Michael's Hong Kong residence was another thorn in the others' side. It didn't go unnoticed that the two bachelors in the band, those with the least financial and familial responsibility were enjoying the world's best tax shelter. But to legally maintain their residency, there were restrictions that affected the band. Citizens of Hong Kong could work in the United States for just four months per year, which negated the option to record with America's top producers, as the best of them would not travel and those four months were best spent on touring. As Cyndi Lauper once said, money changes everything.

Bands that survive for decades, even the best of them, endure major low points. The Rolling Stones and David Bowie are two of our mightiest living rock icons, and both completely lost it in the late eighties. They started the decade off right, the Stones with *Tattoo You* and Bowie with *Let's Dance*—but a few years later they were serving up aimless funk and wearing neon blazers. Maybe they were trying too hard to stay abreast of the times, to fit in with INXS's funk-rock revolution, but neither did it well and it took each of them years to rediscover their strengths.

The year 1991 marked INXS's fourteenth anniversary and they had never hit a low point. They'd climbed to the top slowly and surely, and entered the nineties on top of the world. They scaled the highest of the many peaks they'd climbed and once they reached the top, they found, for the first time, a steep stark valley below.

This Ain't the Good Life

INXS ENTERED THE NINETIES IN TOP FORM—they followed up *Kick*'s multimillion-selling international success with *X*. They had found a formula on *Kick*, and on *X* built upon it very well. Producer Chris Thomas urged Michael and Andrew to condense their strengths, from the full-bore onslaught of "Suicide Blonde" to the reflective sway of "By My Side" (written for Andrew's wife, Shelley) to the progressive ode to societal alienation captured in "The Stairs"—*X* has some of INXS's best. One of the album's most successful singles is "Disappear," a slice of rock and pop led by Michael's angelic falsetto over four on-the-floor choruses.

INXS's music has swung from the edge to the middle, from alternative to classically gorgeous pop, and each incarnation has incorporated at least a sense of the other. But "Disappear" was something else—it was the one song that tipped the scales. It was as pop as INXS ever got—and it worked. The song was the only one on the album not written by Michael and Andrew—it was a Jon Farriss–Michael Hutchence production the pair had written while living together in Hong Kong.

"Disappear" broke an American record—it became the seventh consecutive single by one non-American band to break the Top 10. The last band who'd done so was Culture Club in 1983. *X* earned INXS two Top 10 singles in America, as well as in England and several throughout Europe. The album went multi-platinum in the States and sold solidly throughout the world. And for the first time, the only country who'd held out on INXS finally joined the party. They'd toured there for half a decade, sold out shows, charted singles, sold records, yet remained ignored or hated by the press—in jolly old England INXS were still a down-under donkey show. Maybe they rubbed the "right" people the wrong way, or maybe it was just a case of cultural collusion.

Australia was claimed for England when the explorer Captain James Cook crashed into it in 1770. In 1888, England's Parliament ruled that it should be a penal colony—an enormous, desolate, isolated penitentiary for their society's hardest criminals. Disease ran rampant in London's prisons given that sanitation and nutrition were nonexistent, so a term served in Australia—a land theoretically worse off than England—was considered a de facto death sentence. Convicts journeyed there by sea in the bowels of slave ships, and if malnutrition didn't kill them, the hard labor and violent environs that awaited them usually did.

Exiling prisoners to Australia made sense on paper, but in truth it was stupid. The British turned their empire's richest untapped resource into a cage with great weather. "I don't know why the English didn't lock up their prisoners in London and move the entire country to Australia," Garry Beers says. "They should have left the convicts there to rot. And moved here, where there's sun and ocean. The English made a mistake and I think they've always held it against us—they sent their prisoners to Club Med. But it's not our fault. If I'd have been imprisoned in Australia in those days and survived my sentence and was shipped back to England, I'd steal the first loaf of bread I saw, I'd punch a cop—anything to be sent back to Australia straightaway."

Of all of England's former colonies, Australia is closest in spirit and tradition to the motherland. Their government is a constitutional monarchy and a parliamentary democracy, and they cherish tea, cricket, and regulated public school uniforms. But the Anglo-Aussie competition runs deep; many an Englishman has dismissed Australians as convict stock. There's been a long-standing conception in English culture of Australians as "wild colonials": brave, brash, unruly, and uncivilized, which both intrigues and repulses the English sense of sensibility. Britain was literally the last territory on earth to endorse INXS, in spite of the fact that, since 1984, the band had consistently sold out venues larger than their record sales reflected.

The English music press was nothing but hostile toward INXS throughout the eighties, but nonetheless, the band packed legendary theaters like London's Hammersmith Odeon (capacity 3,700) and Brixton Academy (capacity 5,000) with each passing year. The critics insisted that the band had no English fans and that their U.K. shows were full of Australian expatriates. If the press was to be believed, INXS was an Australian band that traveled the world with a 747 full of rowdy Aussies to pack every venue they played.

"The English press were vicious to them," says Joanne Petersen, the band's English-born representative at Warner Bros. in Australia.*

"Murphy was right in ignoring England and touring elsewhere. The English are very snobby about Australians. I'm English and was married to an Australian so I've seen both sides of it. Really it's just because the English are still pissed off that they sent their convicts to get a suntan while they wasted away in the cold and rain."

So it went in England, even when *Kick* hit Number 9 on the album charts, and both "New Sensation" and "Devil Inside" reached Number 1 and Number 3, respectively. The press remained tepid, when *X* fared equally well, peaking at Number 2.

INXS were a wild outback anomaly to the English press—their popularity was accepted with a smirk. "Let's face it, there is a terrible tabloid culture in Australia, but it's nothing compared to England," Tim Farriss says. "The tabloid media there is shit. And the critical press love to put people on pedestals one week just so they can tear them down the next. In their daily papers, any blond girl who's willing to show the world her tits can get a full-page feature—it's a viable way for someone who otherwise couldn't get arrested to launch a career."

The English condescension toward Aussies even extended as far as the record company's boardroom. "I'd go in for meetings with the entire label's staff, ready to plan the launch of an album," Chris Murphy recalls,

*** Joanne is married to Colin Petersen, drummer for the Bee Gees, and spent her first years in the music business as the personal assistant to legendary Beatles' manager Brian Epstein. She was the unfortunate soul who found Epstein dead of a drug overdose on August 27, 1967.**

"and all they wanted to talk about was cricket. I'd be full of ideas, ready to get started, and they'd keep saying, 'So, Chris, how's the Australian cricket team going? You *do* follow cricket, don't you, Chris?' I wasn't going to give any of them the satisfaction of knowing how much they were bothering me. It took every fiber of my being to be cool and not throw everyone in that room out of the window."

Australia, a land of convicts' kin, turns out the top cricketers in the world and has won the World Cup of Cricket in 1987, 1999, and 2003. It's glorious karma that Australia—the badly behaved colony England tried to forget—routinely beats them at the stuffiest game they've got. INXS's victory in England was much the same: they defied the flack, beat the odds, and persevered until they took home the prize.

"When we first started touring internationally," Gary Grant says, "the plan was simple. We went where we were wanted. We knew that England was going to be tough for an Australian band; we'd need a real press coup to make it there. So in the beginning we just didn't go. When we had hits in France, starting with 'Original Sin,' we made the English record company fly English journalists over to France to see the shows rather than trying to woo them on their own turf. The English writers came out because it was a free trip. But inevitably they'd meet the band, realize that they're a wonderful bunch of guys, and see the music for what it was—a powerful, energetic experience. And they'd go back to England and spread the word even if they didn't write about it as much as we'd have liked. It spread slowly, but every time we showed up in England to tour, we blew everyone away. It was just a matter of time."

There is one moment that proves, unequivocally, that INXS had taken England, the final frontier. On July 13, 1991, they played to a capacity crowd of 72,000 in London's Wembley Stadium, earning a place among the icons who've done the same: the Rolling Stones (a record fourteen times), the Who (with the Clash opening), Queen, David Bowie, the Beatles, and Led Zeppelin. INXS and AC/DC are the only Australian acts to have done so.

That monumental day, INXS was supported by five opening bands: Deborah Harry, Hot House Flowers, Roachford, Jellyfish, and Jesus Jones. INXS's two-and-a-half-hour set that night was incredible—the band unanimously agrees that it is one of the best shows (out of over three thousand) that they've ever played. It's a damn good thing that they filmed it.

It was Chris Murphy's idea. He thought that *X* was good, but in his mind, the band had grown lazy. He thought the new songs were too slick and too much like *Kick*. "I was worried. I knew I had to do something to bring it back to the basics, back to the strengths of the band," Murphy says. "Doing the film and releasing a live record accomplished that. It was a way to remind the public of how powerful INXS was live, in case they'd written them off as a band who only released pop singles."

They spent half a million on filming the Wembley concert; Murphy spent $250,000 of the band's money and coaxed the other half out of PolyGram, their European record label. Murphy hired David Mallet,* who utilized sixteen 35mm cameras, two of them mounted on roving helicopters, to capture the scale of the show and the massive stadium: it cost more to shoot it all on film, but it was well worth it—video wouldn't have done the spectacle justice.

"At the time, everyone in the band was pissed at me," Chris Murphy says. "I remember Andrew coming up to me and saying something like, 'We must be making a lot of money tonight, we sold this place out.' As I explained how much the production of recording the film and the live album cost us, he began to look very unhappy. And when he realized that, basically, we were coming out even, he looked miserable. But I knew that we needed to do this and I was right—the film and the live album is one of INXS's greatest feats of credibility. I told Andrew that he might hate me now, but when he was forty, looking back on this night, watching the film, he'd understand why we had to do this."

Chris was right. "I *am* so glad we did it," Andrew says. "Thank God we did. That same band is not here anymore. Michael is not here anymore. But we have that beautiful snapshot of that moment, forever. And that is worth all of the money we spent and more."

INXS's guest list that day topped off at about three thousand and their backstage greeting room was stocked with mountains of sushi, buckets of champagne, and—moments before they went on—filled with 250 people, among them Debbie Harry and the Stones. "I'd always thought of sushi as a delicacy," Andrew Farriss says. "I was so nervous—all of us were

*** David Mallet was an up-and-coming talent at the time who has made a name for himself skillfully capturing live concerts. He'd been tapped by David Bowie to film his Glass Spider tour in 1988, then Madonna during her 1990 Blond Ambition tour. But INXS's *Live Baby Live* made Mallet's career: he went on to shoot the Rolling Stones' *Voodoo Lounge*, U2's *Zooropa*, Bon Jovi, Tina Turner, and many more immediately afterward.**

so nervous, and the last thing you want to do at a time like that is look at a table full of sushi. I remember thinking how it was all going to go to waste while people were starving in the world. Then I thought about how terribly unhygienic it was to have all of that raw fish lying around."

Chris Murphy and the others worked the room, but Andrew couldn't deal with the scene: he escaped to a bathroom down the hall where he spent ten minutes alone, enjoying a beer and a cigarette. "A few years ago I told that story to Mark Rankin who sang for a band called Gun. He's Scottish and I'll never forget his reaction. In his thick Scottish brogue he said, 'So you mean to tell me that you chose ta spend tha minutes before the height of yer fucking career alone in a toilet?' 'Yes, I did,' I told him. 'You know what?' he said. 'The fucking truth is, what else do you get at the top? A fucking beer and a cigarette.' He's right. It was exactly what I needed to appreciate that moment."

Meanwhile, Michael—even for Michael—was in top form. He minced about the band's party suite like the belle of the ball. It should be clear by now that Michael loved mischief, and this night was no exception; armed with a formidable stash of grade-A Ecstasy, he dispersed pills to a select few of the inner circle, instructing them not to pop them until the band played "The Stairs."

"Michael was in such good spirits, I'll never forget it," *Live Baby Live* producer Mark Opitz says. "He was the best host. You'd never know he was about to take the stage to entertain nearly eighty thousand people. He was walking around that room with a portable disc player and headphones, making certain people—and I was one of them—listen to Massive Attack's first album, *Blue Lines.* It was important to him that a select group of his friends heard some of it before the show. He'd put the headphones on you and watch you as you listened. I was listening to those tracks as he pushed that pill into my hand."

Michael was, according to Kirk, most likely a few pills deep before the show even began—his stellar performance is a testament to his poise and vocal gifts. Nonetheless, he joined Kirk, Tim, Mark Opitz, and others in another dose of Ecstasy four songs into the set as he announced, "This is 'The Stairs.'" It was all captured on film, and a careful viewing of the *Live Baby Live* DVD will reveal Kirk very obviously chewing on something other than his tongue as he settles into the song's smooth locomotive

Love Baby Love: playing a sold-out Wembley.

groove. The indulgence didn't hurt the band's performance at all, but it does explain their cuddly behavior: at one point in the show, Michael and Kirk pow-wow on Jon's drum riser, and later on Michael bear hugs Andrew into near paralysis.

All the sedatives in the world wouldn't have effected INXS's energy that night. Even Andrew, the man perennially stuck behind the keyboards (aside from his turns on rhythm guitar), strutted his stuff and truly went for broke during "Who Pays the Price." During his harmonica solo, he slid on his knees to the front of the stage, wailing those distorted blues with uncharacteristic abandon.

"Even though I was off my face, I was well aware that the show was fucking great," Mark Opitz says. Opitz took in the proceedings from the soundboard, because he was producing the live album. "It is a treasure that we recorded that night. Anyone who doubts INXS cannot deny what that footage recorded that night. They were at the top of their game. They were just incredible."

That night, Garry Beers's wife, Jodie, three months pregnant with their first child, was safely situated in a VIP box beside Princess Di and Carly Simon. Jodie had a grand time until she realized that she'd begun to bleed profusely. Terrified that she was miscarrying in a massive arena in the midst of a rock show, Jodie was ferried to the first-aid tents.

"We'd spent every day for the last few months shopping for baby clothes and planning how we were going to rearrange our house for the baby," Garry says. "It was everything we talked about and everything that mattered to us. It was so unreal for me to walk offstage, at one of the high points of my career, feeling like I'd conquered the world, only to learn that something was wrong with Jodie. It was so loud that it took a few minutes for me to even understand what the security guards were telling me. All that I could hear was that Jodie was bleeding. And I fell to pieces." The infirmary was as far from the stage as physically possible, so a phalanx of four guards surrounded Garry and escorted him there. "We went directly through the audience," Garry says. "People are recognizing me, thinking it's part of the show. They're shouting and grabbing at me. It took half an hour to get across the stadium to Jodie. And when we found her, she was sitting there on a gurney talking to some kid who was having a bad acid trip, helping him calm down. In that moment, I saw everything I love about her: she is the most giving, strongest woman I know. She'd almost lost our baby that night, but her instinct to help someone else took over and she did what she could for that kid, thinking nothing of herself." Jodie did not lose the baby: Lucy Mae is very much alive, healthy, and beautiful. As is her little sister, the equally gorgeous Matilda Bonnie.

The History of Basil Leaves

GARRY BEERS was born in Manly, a town on the Northern Beaches of Sydney, to Bill and Lola Beers. His dad drove a front-end loader (that would be sort of like a dump truck in America) for a living, and his mother worked odd jobs to make ends meet. Garry has one sister, Kerry, who is four years his senior. Garry's mother was a champion swimmer, and his father, by everyone's account, was a champion man—a truly charming fellow who died of lung cancer in 1989, just as his son's career hit its apex.

Garry was born with one name, but he adopted his moniker in high school for no discernible reason: someone started calling him Garry Gary and clearly it caught on. He wasn't a musician by birth—no, Garry was born to be a "meat pie," which in Aussie slang means a jock. Garry played rugby for Belrose, where the Farriss boys lived, and played for Rugby Union while attending both Forest Primary and High School, where he made the acquaintance of Kirk Pengilly and Tim Farriss. A Beers family fun fact: Garry's grandparents, Gwen and Vic, were the first family to settle in French's Forest, the suburb next to the Farriss household.

Garry was a lifesaver (lifeguard) down at Queenscliff Beach and an avid surfer, but the waves-and-babes scene down there left him a bit hollow. After he graduated from high school, he enrolled in a technical college, but dropped out after

Alias: Garry "Gary" Beers

Born: June 22, 1957

Instruments: bass, guitar, keyboards

Married: February 1991, to Jodie Crampton

Children: Lucy Mae, Matilda Bonnie

First Bands: Legolas Elvin Warrior, Dr. Dolphin

Sports: surfing, rugby league, Rugby Union

just one year—clearly Garry was "finding himself." It was 1975, and he opted to make the most of his avid love of rock bands like Yes, Pink Floyd, Deep Purple, and Led Zeppelin. Garry started to play guitar religiously, as the ax-wielder in a fellowship of three named Legolas Elvin Warrior, which included his best mates, Bill Hucker and Glen Fender. The trio threw down a gauntlet among their ranks: the worst guitar player among them must learn to play bass, and Garry was unanimously declared the winner/loser in the Who's Most Crap contest. "Yes, it was me," he says. "I was the worst of the bunch on guitar. We didn't even debate it."

At the time Garry worked at the local Esso gas station, as he did all through high school and his brief tenure at Technical College, and when he'd saved enough cash, bought a Toyota Hi-Ace Van. Those wheels were quite the asset once Garry joined forces with Andrew Farriss and Michael Hutchence and formed Dr. Dolphin.

But before that, when he was only halfway through high school, Garry's parents bought a mobile home and took off to tour the massive expanse of Australia, leaving Garry and their homestead to be minded by his recently married older sister and her husband, Ray. Garry's sister was only twenty-two years old and her little brother took full advantage of his suddenly longer leash. Garry's friends did too; they now had a place to play records and practice as loud as they liked.

Garry's dad, Bill, was a bird lover and had built an aviary in a wide metal shed at the back of the family property. Bill's collection was impressive—everything from cockatoos to lorikeets to rosellas, peacocks, and other native birds. He'd made a paradise for them to inhabit, complete with a waterfall and a rock garden. The birds' heavenly songs, however, were often too much for the community to bear; a very religious neighbor took to shooting .22 gauge bullets at the walls and windows of the aviary. "We kept finding broken windows, and then noticed shattered windows in the old Pontiac we had parked in our yard," Garry says. "We couldn't work out what was going on, until one day we saw this guy openly shooting at our house. My dad caught him doing it and when he approached him, the guy just smashed him across the face. I was playing in the backyard and all of a sudden there was my dad with the trail of red stuff streaming from his head. Every day after that, my friends and I threw rocks at that neighbor's windows. And a year or so later, he moved away."

It's a good thing the man of Christ did move, because once Garry's parents took off on their retirement tour, the racket grew much louder and

less melodic. Bill sold his bird collection, leaving the large metal shed ready for his son and friends to rock in. "Nobody in the neighborhood played music, and nobody wanted to hear ours," Garry says. But Garry's musical education didn't just take place in the bird house. He took aural studies in his friend Dean Cooper's room, who was a slightly anarchistic sonic whiz-kid. "Dean was building speakers and amplifiers back then that blew everyone away," Garry says. "We used to sit in his room, listening to Pink Floyd and Yes on these speakers he'd built, and it blew my fucking mind. This guy was so ahead of everything. He built me bass cabinets that sounded better than anything you could buy. He used to steal the computer chips from traffic lights to make soundboards that were more sophisticated than anything you could imagine at the time. Actually he got in trouble for that."

Garry and his boys used to head down to the Horden Pavilion, where he saw, at a very impressionable age, Black Sabbath, Queen (whom he'd later tour with), Rainbow, Supertramp, Staus Quo, the Eagles, AC/DC (who were just a local Aussie bar band at the time), Billy Thorpe (a truly bombastic Australian rocker), and local acts like Ariel and the excellently named Sherbert. He spent his days surfing and his nights at the local "bop," a rough all-ages venue in Forestville where bands played to teenagers who wanted to rock as much as they wanted to fight.

Garry attended Forest High School, the same institution as Tim Farriss and Kirk Pengilly, though they hardly knew one another. He did, though, know their band, Guinness. One night, at the Bilgola Surf Club,

Garry approached a guy who looked a lot like Tim, but wasn't—it was his younger brother Andrew. He introduced himself and learned that Andrew had a band called Krauss, with his other brother Jon, who was just thirteen at the time. Andrew invited Garry to come by for a jam. "Jon was already amazing," Garry says. "And once I joined them, Andrew and I began to write some very melodic stuff, leaving Jon and their guitarist, Martin Tool, to rock out amongst themselves."

Garry and Andrew found musical common ground, but more important, both lost their virginity to "the beautiful girls who went to Andrew's school" according to Garry. And just when their creative escapades plateaued, Michael Hutchence returned to Sydney after a year of living in Los Angeles with his mother and fired up the proceedings quite nicely.

Garry Beers is Mr. Reliable, as his matter-of-fact retelling of this next story shows. When INXS, still known at the time as the Farriss Brothers, relocated to Perth, they crossed those thousands of miles, as naive youth would, in the rickety vans they owned at the time. And when they moved back to Sydney eight months later, they drove again, but being young, adventurous, and stupid, Tim, Kirk, and Garry opted to motor straight through the desert in two and a half days tripping on acid. "Tim drove for an hour and he couldn't handle it," Garry says. "So Kirk and I did it all. We sat, all three across the front seat, taking in the Nullabor Desert, which is dead straight as far as you can see. Suddenly on the horizon, a dark shape appeared in the middle of the road, and as we got closer we saw that it was a dead kangaroo, all bloated and rotting in the heat, which was some 110 degrees. Kirk was driving and I assumed, as did Tim, that he'd seen it too. None of us said anything, because it was in our vision, growing larger for twenty minutes or so. But Kirk drove over it, and it exploded underneath the van, filling it with an unbelievable smell that lasted forever."

When they arrived back on the Northern Beaches, Garry tried to cleanse himself of the smell by surfing. His board had been on top of the van, so the wax had long since melted, which made the first wave he caught a zinger. "I got smashed," he says. "The board went one way and I went the other, and I was wearing dodgy old shorts with dead Velcro, so they came clean off, leaving me naked treading water. I had to cross a four-lane highway with nothing but my board for cover."

Garry met his wife when he was still a kid and she was even more so. She was, literally, the girl next door; she was his sister- and brother-in-law's neighbor's daughter. Following their parents' retirement road trip, Garry and his sister had shared the family home until Garry and the band moved to Perth, at which time his sister and her husband bought a house of their own. When Garry returned to Sydney, he had nowhere else to crash but with his sister until he got on his feet again. And that's how he met Jodie, who was only ten years old at the time. She used to sit outside and watch the weird older boys (Garry and Andrew) in the yard next door, barbecuing sausage and playing guitars. Years later, when Jodie was eighteen and her brother was twenty-nine, Garry's sister formally introduced them. "My sister was the matchmaker," Garry says. "And she was right, to do so. We were married for twelve years and never once raised our voices, never argued, and I think that is something to be proud of."

Jodie came on tour through the band's wildest days, and her fondest recollections aren't of the celebrities she met or the cities she saw, but of the unsung heroes who make rock tours happen, day in and day out: the crew. "They really are the people who make the tour," Jodie says. "In the INXS family, people like Bernie Bernil, Rob Kern, Rick Salazaar, Andre O'Neil, Collin Ellis, Judit Heidenrich, and so many more made it all such a wonderful experience, not just for me, but for every audience that saw the band play. I'll never forget the last night of the *X* tour at the Sydney Entertainment Center. Michael used to end the show by picking up Kirk's guitar after the final encore and he'd play it terribly, just making noise. But that night, Tim's guitar tech, Rick Salazaar, who is an incredible player, hid offstage and played an amazing solo while Michael just slammed away. It was hilarious, because Michael thought he was doing it! He couldn't believe how amazing he sounded and the look on his face was priceless!"

Garry Beers has always taken pride in setting up his own equipment. He is the man who loves sound check, the dependable guy who remembers the song arrangements after they haven't played together in months. He's never wanted to do anything but be in a rock band. He loves the music and the lifestyle and all it has given him, but has never wanted to be a superstar. "Garry never cared to be on the cover of a magazine," says former road manager Bruce Patron. "He used to tell me that he hoped he was never even mentioned in the articles. He didn't care, because he was making the same money as the other guys, and was still able to go to shop at a mall before the gig without anyone bothering him. It meant more to him that he could walk through the audience and buy a hot dog in the stadium if he wanted to without being recognized."

Garry has always been a bit bass-head obsessed with his equipment and the sound of his instrument. He is a perennial student of the bass guitar and grew up studying the techniques of players such as James Jamerson, John Paul Jones, Paul McCartney, Chris Squire, Bernard Edwards, and many other talented pioneers. His knowledge and experience have led sound companies such as Ampeg and G&L guitars to seek his design advice.

Garry built two world-class recording studios on his farm in Australia. Mangrove Studios became a popular haven where Australian and international bands could record in the serenity of the Australian bush. Garry made his guitar and amplifier collection available to all, even "old faithful"–the 1958 Fender Precision bass that had provided the INXS sound for years. The studios are now gone, but Garry continues to produce up-and-coming artists in Australia.

Garry's bass lines are the pulse of INXS; intertwined with Jon Farriss's kinetic drums, Garry anchors the rhythm section and Tim Farriss's bombastic chord-play. Garry was always steady and stalwart, but he surprised everyone—including himself—on the band's final tour: he had an affair with one of the backup singers that cost him his marriage. He and Jodie had been married for seven years and had two children Lucy Mae and Matilda; they were having some marital problems that no one expected Garry to sort out in the arms of another. "If I can give advice to anyone who is even thinking of having an affair, I'd like to say that you should work out what's going on at home before you do anything stupid, like I did," he says. "Take a look at what you might lose before you do anything. If there's a problem at home,

try to sort it out first. Because the cliché is true: you don't know what you've got until it's gone."

Jodie divorced Garry after he confessed the details of his affair, but they've been working toward reconciliation in the years since. They've never let his mistake affect their children and have been doing their best to heal. They're not remarried, but they work together to properly raise their daughters. "Jodie and I have been divorced now for three years," Garry says. "We love each other dearly and all I can say is that I live in hope that we can get through this and one day we will be married again. She is my best friend."

The Tallest Poppy Must Be Shorn

INXS'S TRIUMPHANT WEMBLEY SHOW was captured forever and released in 1992 on CD and video as *Live Baby Live* and went Gold in both formats. Sales aside, the video and album document a glorious pinnacle and a perfect moment that ended an era.

Live Baby Live was unjustly and unexpectedly panned in Australia. A critical snowball effect ran wild back home thanks to Ian "Molly" Meldrum, a one-man Australian institution known as the "guru" of pop music.* Molly, who'd been an INXS supporter, declared war on the band in 1992. "He went on national television and said that our live album was a crock of shit," Chris Murphy says. "On a program broadcast into every Australian household he said that there were so many remixes and overdubs on the record that it should not be considered a live album. He said that INXS had cheated and that they were not at all the great live band that everyone thought they were."

The Australian press followed Meldrum's lead, echoing his take in nearly every review of

*Meldrum's been an influential personality in Australia since the sixties, first as a music journalist, then as the host of *Countdown,* Australia's version of England's *Top of the Pops* or America's *American Bandstand.* Meldrum, in short, is Australia's Casey Kasem. Meldrum is still around, via his shows on cable and his radio program, and he's still considered one of Australia's most respected pop-music critics.

the album. "I was fucking flabbergasted because ninety-five percent of the Australian music industry had no idea what took place at that show," Chris Murphy says. "Most of the people who claimed they'd seen the concert and that it was terrible weren't even there. I should know, because I controlled the guest list. But fuck all that—anyone who has seen the film can tell you that it's goddamned obvious that the whole thing is live."

For the record, Chris isn't lying; the film and record are all the way live. Mark Opitz produced it, and considering the fact that some of the band was flying high on Ecstasy that night, he arrived at the studio expecting many mistakes. "To be honest, I was blown away at how perfect their performance was that night," he says. "Really, truly, I didn't think it would be so good when I listened to the recording. But it was—their playing was amazing. I did nearly *nothing* to that recording. There were exactly two overdubs: Kirk rerecorded two saxophone notes in the studio—not a solo, just two notes—because his wireless unit had cut out for a moment. The original recording was altered because of a technical malfunction, not because of the band's playing."

Unfortunately, the Australian media's attack of *Live Baby Live* was the start of a backlash. It is shameful that even today, most Australian music fans aren't fully aware of INXS's legacy. "I was listening to a radio show just last year in 2004, where an Australian band, Baby Animals, was being interviewed, by phone from London, and they were so excited to be playing Wembley," Garry Beers says with a laugh. "I'm not even sure that they knew they weren't *really* playing *Wembley.* They were playing Wembley Arena, the theater that holds ten thousand people, and they were opening up for Bon Jovi or someone like that. I wanted to phone in and tell them to ask some old usher to walk them out the back of the building and point out the stadium—*that's* Wembley. It held nearly eighty thousand when we played, and now that they remodeled it, it holds ninety thousand. Australians listening to that interview on the radio have no idea. We played in a very historic stadium that isn't even there anymore. I'm so proud that we were able to be a part of the musical history of that place. It's something no one can take away from us."

They Come from the Land Down Under: INXS wrap themselves in the Australian flag.

There is an innate cultural anomaly in the Australian national character that's well known to Aussies, but must be explained to the rest of us. It's a condition known as "The Tall Poppy Syndrome," a weird indigenous brand of quality control. It seems to be born of integrity, yet it comes off more like an inexplicable *Lord of the Flies* survival instinct: generally, whenever local talent succeeds beyond Australia, they're penalized. When a public figure is perceived as a singular individual who has branched out beyond the homeland, they're treated like a wild poppy, one that has grown taller than the others in the field. And when they do, Australians come together, and like a dutiful farmer, hack the wayward plant down to size and back into line with the rest of the nation. In the U.K., the tabloids pass moral judgment; in the U.S., they're parasitic voyeurs.

In Australia they're a bit of both, with a hefty dose of small-town pride. But there's no true rhyme or reason to the Tall Poppy Syndrome: Australian society's love and hate of their celebrities is too hypocritical and inconsistent to predict.

It's odd that Aussies would criticize their cultural figures at all; it defies their overt national pride. Generally Australians love being Australian—as they should. They inhabit some of the most beautiful and least habitable terrain on earth. The population of Australia is roughly 20 million—more or less the equivalent of the combined populations of New York City and Los Angeles—but Australia, the sixth-largest country in the world, is nearly as large as the United States. With so much space, for so few people, on an island so removed from the highways of global culture, one would expect Australians to consistently champion their own.

"It is strange, the Tall Poppy thing," says longtime rock promoter Harry Della. "If someone gets to the top in a lot of countries, Australians have respect for them, but they criticize them more than ever. Take Greg Norman; he's an incredible success, he's won so many golf titles, he's taken in probably a hundred million in earnings. But all that people want to write about or talk about is when he doesn't win."

It is easy to understand why Americans don't have a distinct national identity—the country is so large and diverse that its citizens' references are regional: they align with their home state and city more than with the country as a whole. But Australians, though they are certainly diversified by region, are first and foremost Australian. Shouldn't they celebrate any of their countrymen's achievements abroad? And shouldn't they hold them up as heroes when they come home? "Australians will brag when a band or a team of theirs is winning overseas," former Cold Chisel front man Jimmy Barnes says. "They'll be proud of them while they're away. But when they return, if they're perceived to be too confident or proud, they'll be punished for it. INXS was never like that, but they got it anyway."

Humility is more than a virtue in Australia, it is an unstated moral code that must be upheld—and when it isn't, society is quick to punish the offender. Australia prides itself on its middle-class virtues, where hard work, integrity, and credibility mean more than commercial, monetary rewards. On paper, the U.S.A. is of the same mind, though a cursory perusal of American media—print and otherwise—proves that celebrity and wealth, however they are achieved, in and of itself equal success. Integrity is an accessory to American public figures; it's something to be bought, styled, or otherwise acquired and if it isn't, that's okay: to make it in America these days, celebrity can be had with a sex tape, a reality show, and a bad reputation. To be beloved in Australia, an artist must be credible and put in the work—and if they ever get precious, they'll hear about it.

Kylie Minogue, for example, has remained a darling in Australia, most likely because it took her nearly ten years to achieve international success as a pop singer. It didn't hurt that Australia grew up with her, since she was once a regular on *Neighbours,* a soap-opera institution down under. And when Kylie comes home, she's portrayed as the girl next door: the tabloids never catch her clubbing, they snap her having lunch with her mum. Until recently, the press portrayed Nicole Kidman the same way—as a down-to-earth Aussie girl done good. Yet both conceptions are ridiculous: super-rich Kylie Minogue and Nicole Kidman have little in common with the average Australian lass.

"Australians have always been that way," Jon Farriss says. "It's just how it is. I don't know what it's about, but I do know that for us, when we got really successful, we felt like we had to sneak back into Australia. We'd play to eighty thousand people in South America every night and I thought of that as good news for Australia. We never expected a hero's welcome when we got home, but we did hope to get some type of acknowledgment for what we'd done. And we discovered that no one really knew what we were up to and no one really cared. And the feeling I got was that if I was going to inform anyone about it, I'd be labeled a horrible braggart."

INXS got such a Tall Poppy weed wacking in the nineties that the syndrome might as well be renamed the X-Factor. "The thing about Australians," says rock legend Jimmy Barnes, "is that they dislike celebrity. They like underdogs. As long as you're fighting for your existence, they're on your side. Once it seems like it's too easy for you, they'll knock you down so you've got to struggle again. So many Australian bands had gone abroad and never made it, and they were almost loved more for it. That didn't happen to INXS. But there was nothing that people could hate them for. They were making it abroad and Australians said they couldn't care less, but they'd also come home and tour and put on such great shows that no one could argue about why they were so big abroad. Their audiences in

Australia were never disappointed, but still, people were waiting for them to fall on their face. And because INXS never did, Australia finally just knocked 'em down."

"We learned very quickly that in America if you looked like a rock star and acted like a rock star and arrived at parties in a limo like a rock star, you must be a rock star," Kirk says. "In Australia if people saw you getting in and out of limos they'd get right in your face and say, 'Why don't you take a fucking taxi, mate? You only live around the corner.' That's the Australian reality check."

Reports of their big tours of America and Europe, the band's jet, and the rock-star parties, and limousines that were nothing but de rigueur artist transportation filtered back home and festered into an ominous boil in the press. "I'm not going to cry about it, but I do feel that we got hit hard by the Tall Poppy thing and were one of the first Australian artists to experience that," Jon Farriss says. "We worked really fucking hard to get where we did. It felt like we were supported at home to a certain point. Once we'd gotten too popular to play two thousand-capacity theaters and were doing tours of football stadiums, it felt like the hometown support disappeared. Once we went beyond what anyone else had done, suddenly we became this group who thought they were superior to everyone else." INXS as a band and a family were always humble. Sometimes Jon wonders whether they should have been. "Maybe we're to blame," he says. "We never came home beating our chests after a great tour abroad. Maybe we should have. We'd come home to all our mates, and if we were anything but the guys they'd always known, they'd quickly bring us back down to earth. If I'd say, 'We just played Madison Square Garden.' They'd say, 'Yeah? Who fucking cares?' It's a good thing we're a band who never went in for commercials and endorsements. If any of our mates saw us on a poster with a Pepsi can in our hand, in those days we'd never hear the end of it. It's a bit different now—just about everyone is endorsing something and no one minds at all."

It is particularly unjust and Tall Poppylike that INXS paved the way for so many other Australian bands and still gets no credit for it. In 2003, a government-sponsored Australian television station (their equivalent of Britain's BBC) aired a four-hour documentary on the history of Australian rock. INXS's 35 million albums sold, multiple Number 1 records and singles, and their heap of ARIAS (the Australian equivalent of the Grammy Awards) were smashed into less than five minutes of airtime.

The series' segments were divided by decade and somehow, INXS wasn't even mentioned in the eighties installment, the decade they helped define. They popped up as a requisite footnote in the nineties episode, where they were characterized as a lucky pack of wannabes who cashed in by copying the sounds of the day. They were even satirized in a dramatic re-creation. "They had actors dressed like us—one of them with big glasses like Kirk, sitting around a hotel room doing lines of coke and being ridiculous," Garry says. "I was offended because they got it all wrong: we did *much* bigger lines of coke than those. But all jokes aside, it was insulting. The series concentrated on bands that were big in Sydney and Melbourne and never made it anywhere else, while we had conquered everything. It's terrible because that will probably be the only definitive documentary of Australian music ever made—and we virtually aren't even in it."

"The media in Australia can be very fickle," says Peter Garrett of Midnight Oil, who was elected into the Australian Parliament in 2005. "The media and the music industry are the only people aware of what an Australian band achieves overseas. And I think they get confused as to whether they should be genuinely proud or whether they should distance themselves from it. Outside of the industry, people have no idea how much success a band has abroad."

Andrew Farriss agrees. "We always meet people in Australia who tell us how our music was a huge part of their life growing up and tell us that they're so proud that we're Australian. But we've always had a weird relationship with the media. They like to acknowledge us—because they have to—but they never celebrate us, either for our achievements or on a critical level."

The media's disdain for INXS may be due to a deeper confusion, caused by their (pun intended) inaccessibility. Chris Murphy's management style perhaps protected them too well. To Murphy, their job was to perform and create; his job was to take care of business, and buffer them from the music industry and the press. He didn't tell them when the executives at Atlantic hated *Kick* and he didn't tell them how broke they'd be if that tour didn't succeed. He made many a move that the band never knew about, because in the worst of times, the truth might have ruined their focus.

“Chris never wanted the band to be readily accessible,” says Richard Clapton. “He kept them, as time went on, in an artificial bubble and people got erroneous impressions of the band. They were signed to Warner Bros. Records in Australia for years and they rarely went to the label offices. By the time the band members realized how they were perceived, they were nine years into a successful career and it was far too late. To this day, they’ve never gotten the acknowledgment they deserve because of it.”

The business side of the music community, and the media as well, still regards INXS as a bit elitist. Murphy rarely allowed press in the studio, and granted few interviews at all. “We were isolated from the Australian music business,” Andrew Farriss says. “Sometimes we couldn’t figure out why or where we stood in the industry. We’d go away a lot and each time we came back, it seemed to be worse than before. We realized that we were regarded as people who thought they were too great for everyone else—just too arrogant and too big for everyone else. We’d painted ourselves into a corner. And how the fuck did we get there? Because we’re not like that at all.”

It helped nothing that the top dogs in the Australian music business hated Chris Murphy. He was internationally known, wildly successful, respected, influential, and rich. And Murphy made no effort to be nice; he’s the kind of visionary that managed to get what he wanted on his own terms. The fact that he didn’t rely on the local scene to succeed wasn’t his worst offense; it was the fact that he’d succeeded so far beyond the scope of almost any Aussie manager in history that was unacceptable.

It all came to a head in 1992, when INXS agreed to headline a benefit show in Sydney’s Centennial Park. That year, the band was in the midst of recording their next album, *Welcome to Wherever You Are,* in their Sydney studio, with Mark Opitz producing. They’d taken a year off again after *X*, and returned to the studio determined to broaden their horizons; the new songs were an amazing departure, particularly “Baby Don’t Cry,” a track that featured the Australian Concert Orchestra.

INXS was approached to headline the Concert for Life, a benefit for St. Vincent’s Hospital in Sydney, and AIDS research. They wanted their appearance to be special, so they decided to reproduce, at their own expense, the same elaborate stageshow they had toured abroad—a spectacle befitting an exclusive preview of songs from the new album. “Our shows had always been simpler affairs in Australia,” Kirk says. “It was too much trouble to ship all of the lighting and stage ramps back home. But this time, we said 'Bugger it!' and spent the money to step it up." They hired the orchestra to join them for their encore, to re-create "Baby Don't Cry" and "Never Tear Us Apart" in all their glory.

The event was to be held in Centennial Park, a 500-acre oasis of mangrove trees, pines, gardens, ponds, fields, and walking trails just three miles from central Sydney, that had never hosted anything larger than outdoor film screenings and classical music concerts at that time. To accommodate the scope of what the benefit was shaping up to be, the area needed major reorganization. INXS and the hospital organizers split the cost to beef up the stage, cart in porto-toilets, hire adequate crowd control, and ensure that the one hundred thousand people who showed up would be well cared for.

The band also took it upon itself to convince public officials to allow the concert to procure the manpower to run the show, and enlist more talent. The city handed them a hefty list of restrictions and fines they would pay should anything be damaged. "It was a mess from the start," tour manager Gary Grant recalls. "The very first semi truck of gear that rolled in to Centennial Park was too tall to clear this huge branch on a tree way too far from the stage to even think about unloading it there. I was very aware that damage of any kind to a tree in the park would cost us a thousand dollars, per the contract, no questions asked. I stood there with our crew guys, trying to figure out a way around that branch, when all of a sudden this park ranger leaps on top of our truck, fires up a chain saw, and just slices the branch clean off. The whole time, he's shouting at us over his shoulder, 'No worries, mate! I'll sort you out!' It wasn't a good sign. I watched him thinking to myself, Right, there goes a thousand dollars."

The bands on the bill that day included local talents Def FX, the celebrated Aboriginal outfit Yothu Yindi, Crowded House, and Johnny Diesel. The event was an all-day festival that began at 10 a.m. By 11:30, there were fifty thousand people gathered on the lawn, and by the time INXS took the stage at sunset, fifty thousand people were bouncing in time. When the orchestra appeared for the encore, the crowd was blown away. "We wanted to do something really special," Grant says. "And we did." It only cost twenty-one dollars a ticket, all of which went to two very worthy causes.

INXS sorted the logistics of producing the event and inadvertently drew the blueprint for what has become a mainstay of Sydney summertime culture: it was such a success that the Parks Department immediately set about rebuilding the performance structure to industry standards. INXS led by example, and the city reaped the rewards: it's become one of Sydney's premier outdoor venues.

After all was said and done, $250,000 was raised. Not so in the media—nearly every critic blasted INXS for treating the charity as if it were their party. The reported fact that INXS arrived at the show in limousines and enjoyed a private dressing room apart from the other acts commanded more ink than any honest reportage of the day's events. INXS was accused of squandering money on the orchestra and their complex stage production that might otherwise have been donated to the cause. Most of the hoopla was pure, unadulterated garbage: the concert raised a quarter of a million dollars, and the band paid for their production values—they donated nearly $200,000 to make the concert possible. INXS still refers to it as the Concert for Strife.

Australian music insiders saw the show as a chance to finally crap on Chris Murphy, and by extension, INXS, and they truly dropped bombs. Several prominent local promoters fed journalists facts and figures about the cost of the show versus the ticket sales, claiming they'd seen the accounting reports. It was pure hearsay, but a few journalists ran with it, declaring the concert a failure weeks before the ticket sales and promised corporate pledges were even tallied. They did irreparable damage.

The true death blow was a surprising stab in the back. The band allowed a prominent journalist and well-known fund-raising advocate, whose wife was stricken with AIDS, into their inner circle. He approached them under the guise of writing an article on the event and asked them to allow a group of HIV-positive children to attend the show as the band's special guests. INXS agreed and granted the writer and his young charges complete access; they watched the show from the side of the stage and they spent the evening in INXS's dressing room. Everyone seemed to be happy, but the resulting article indicated otherwise. The journalist took offense at INXS's arrival by limo and said they were pretentious to demand a larger dressing room than the other acts on the bill. The reporter used his access to skew the facts and portray INXS as spoiled, bloated stars who'd greedily swindled a charity. He also insinuated that INXS had actually turned a profit from the event. The slander was devastating. And didn't stop there:

the writer showed his true colors when he published an unauthorized bio of Michael Hutchence mere months after his death.

"We got killed on that concert in every way," Murphy says. "And it all had to do with the little shitheads in the music industry in Australia—the little, tiny, weaselly, unsuccessful people who took a dislike to INXS being international rock stars. Our stage show wasn't extravagant—the album had strings, so we brought in the orchestra. We had a bigger dressing room because we were headlining. So fucking what?"

The event's organizers were furious that INXS and the event had been so misrepresented, and decided that a media blitz was necessary to correct the misinformation. Chris Murphy was one step ahead of them; he'd prepared a statement the morning after the show, just after he read the first bogus review. "It was all a crock of shit," Murphy says. "The press claimed that the stage show was so extravagant that it exceeded the money earned through ticket sales. The charity took home two hundred fifty grand and INXS didn't make anything. The band was offered twenty-thousand to perform at that show, and instead of pocketing it, we chose to spend it—and a hell of a lot more of *our* money—to improve the quality of the show. I wanted to take out an ad, asking, very simply, every journalist who had claimed that the concert made no money whether they'd had actually seen the accounting. It seemed to me that they should peruse it before they suggested that we'd taken a profit or that the event lost money for the charity. I also wanted to ask them if they'd ever seen accounting statements of large charity events elsewhere in the world, or whether this one was their first experience. I wanted to caution these people about passing judgments before they'd done proper reporting."

Murphy's statement didn't make it to print. A prominent member of the St. Vincent's fund-raising committee was an executive at one of Australia's largest advertising agencies, and insisted that Chris let him handle it. The man was just as furious as Chris; actually he insisted that the journalists who'd slandered the event should be ashamed to call themselves Australians. But the statement he released didn't really work. "It was the one and only time I let someone else speak for us," Murphy says. "And God bless him, because he had the right intentions, but he got it wrong." The disclaimer declared the concert a success and advertised the money made, but it was vague and lacked the necessary bite to silence the critics. "The whole situation snowballed and carried on in the paper for weeks," Murphy says. "I could have stopped it with one little statement telling everyone to shut up and be careful about what they were saying. I'd have issued my statement, fielded as many phone calls as it took, and the whole thing would have been managed."

Instead, it dragged on. Michael let it go because he didn't live in Australia. Same with Murphy and Jon Farriss, but Andrew, Tim, Garry, and Kirk couldn't—and most of them had kids in school, who endured jibes and questions about their daddies' band for months. Those who hated Murphy and hated the band for their success had won. INXS's image in Australia was tainted, and there was nothing they could easily do to change public opinion.

The band finished recording *Welcome to Wherever You Are* less joyously than they'd begun it. After the Concert for Strife, they scrapped a plan to debut the new songs on an exclusive tour of Australia. "At that point I said to them, 'You've got to make me a promise,'" Chris Murphy says. " 'Even if I'm not managing you anymore, you've got to promise me one thing: that you won't tour Australia again until the year 2000.'" They nodded at him, unsure if he was joking or not.

"Listen to me," Murphy said. "*You must stay away from Australia.* You can make twice as much money in Europe, America, and Canada. You can go to South America and make a ton of fucking money. You don't *need* to play here. If you stay away for eight years, trust me, when you return in 2000, you'll be fucking *heroes.* But if you come back a moment before then, you'll be fucked. If you're ever so desperate for money that you need to tour Australia, you're in serious shit. I'd advise you to get a day job instead."

16 Kiss the Dirt

THE BAND RETURNED TO THE STUDIO to finish the album but opted not to tour. Instead, they decided they would record another album a few months later, then tour both of them. They had the cash and leeway to make studio recordings with no time constraints, and had begun to enjoy their time off—perhaps a bit too much. "I was very worried at that point," Chris Murphy says. "To me *X* was a *Kick* replica. It didn't outsell *Kick* because it wasn't a big step forward. The band was very blasé about that. Going forward, I felt it was very necessary to do something different. The band already had their popularity, now it was time for them to have fun and experiment. Their audience gravitated to them because they were different, so they needed to lead them to a new place."

Welcome to Wherever You Are was produced by Mark Opitz, rehearsed in the Sydney Opera House, and recorded at Rhinoceros Studios. Though it was criminally overlooked in America, it is arguably INXS's finest work. It's a true departure: it's neither sly funk nor straight-ahead rock and roll—it's a nuanced return to the sinewy sensuality of the band's earliest work, couched in a more complex musical landscape. There is a sixty-piece orchestra on the epic "Baby Don't Cry," while a Far Eastern horn—played by Kirk—opens "Questions," the first song on the album. The smoldering six-string sex of "Taste It" is balanced by the lush, moody meditation of "Wishing Well," the melancholy pop of "Beautiful Girl," and the timeless romance of "Not Enough Time."

"The album is very much Andrew, Michael, and myself," Mark Opitz says. "We didn't have everyone's minds on the job because some of them were going through significant things in their personal lives." Jon Farriss was preparing to marry Leslie Bega, an aspiring actress he'd met in L.A. the year before. Garry and his wife were awaiting the birth of their second child. Tim Farriss suffered the worst onset of Exostoses he'd ever experienced. He was bedridden through most of the recording, so Kirk filled his shoes. Kirk, for his own part, was recovering from the end of his ten-year relationship with Karen, the mother of his child.

The album is nearly every member of the band's favorite and it was critically lauded everywhere. It debuted at Number 1 in England, but in the U.S., only "Not Enough Time" cracked the Top 30. The video for "Beautiful Girl," a single that did not even chart, garnered more attention in the States than anything else. Andrew wrote the track for his daughter, Grace, who was just five months old, inspired by her beauty.

The video was a different affair: it tackled the issue of anorexia and bulimia with images of the devastation the diseases caused the bodies of young women striving to be what society deemed beautiful. It is powerful, and sad, and drew attention to a worthy cause. It was nominated for a Grammy that year—INXS's third nomination.

The album was a commercial failure in the States, for two reasons: the American musical climate had changed, and the album was virtually shunned by Atlantic Records.

The band's relationship with the label had deteriorated since the departure (just before *Kick*) of Reen Nalli, the woman responsible for signing INXS in the mid-eighties. The label's corporate push, or lack thereof, had never hindered them before—Chris Murphy always found a way to work around it. But he couldn't rely on his secret weapon this time: INXS wasn't going to tour.

Without a tour, only the marketing and advertising muscle of the label could sell the album, and Atlantic didn't get it at all: they thought the album was too great of a departure. INXS was one thing to them—a pop-rock hit factory and they weren't interested in promoting them as anything else. When the band needed Atlantic most, the label turned their back, and let the band's best album go virtually unnoticed.

With proper support, *Welcome to Wherever You Are* would have been a successful record in America. In 1992, grunge had begun to take hold, but the Seattle explosion was still a year away. The charts were packed with performers like Simply Red, Michael Jackson, and Cher, but interesting, experimental pop was making inroads into the mainstream. In 1992, R.E.M. crossed over with "Everybody Hurts," and bands like the Cure, Nine Inch Nails, and Sonic Youth were recognized as leaders of alternative rock. *Welcome to Wherever You Are* was completely attuned to the times—it's a shame that American fans more or less missed it. It's no surprise that English music fans adored it: the album is complex, guitar driven, melodic, and gorgeous—just like the best British rock.

Since the band didn't tour the album, American fans lost touch with INXS in the early nineties. Those who hadn't heard their new music remembered them for what they were in the eighties—a sexy, stylish, hit-making powerhouse. But the times had changed, and in America, the eighties were out for the moment. Grunge was the new black, and the new rock stars were anti-rock stars: they looked just like the kids in the front row, and they swore up and down that they didn't want to be famous. Truth be told, all of those "anti" rock stars are bigger divas than Michael on his worst day. They act the part; Hutchence lived it. "I've always said that Michael was the real thing," U2's Bono says. "I would go onstage and *play* a rock star, but Michael, he was different. He was, honestly, a rock star through and through, every minute of every day."

In the eighties and nineties, Michael's string of high-profile relationships—with Kylie Minogue, then supermodel Helena Christensen—made tabloid headlines and did little to convince American music fans that he, and by association, INXS, were anything but bratty rock peacocks. But why would he care? He was dating Helena Christensen, arguably the most beautiful woman on earth at the time. They spent five years together, living in Hutchence's four-bedroom villa in the South of France or in Christensen's home in Copenhagen, Denmark.

Helena introduced Michael to the fashion world, where he indulged the jet-setting nightclub lifestyle to the fullest. At the same time, Michael enjoyed the peace and quiet he found in France; for the first time in years, he could be anonymous.

One night in Denmark everything changed forever. Michael and Helena rode their bikes—the preferred mode of transport in Copenhagen—to a club. At the end of the night, Michael headed outside ahead of Helena to fetch them and he sat astride his bicycle, waiting for her.

Suddenly a taxi sped around the corner, so close to Michael that he fell over. He got up, pissed off, and punched the hood of the cab. The driver got out, walked toward Michael, and without a word, cracked him in the jaw. Michael's knees buckled as the man hit him again and again until he fell to the ground, his head smacking the pavement, rendering him unconscious. He awoke in a hospital bed, where he remained, recovering for two weeks.

Whether it was the blow or the fall, a nerve in his neck had been destroyed; his sense of smell was lost for the rest of his life, which virtually eliminated his ability to taste. He had also suffered a severe concussion that bruised his brain. Andrew paid him a visit at his home in the South of France, and was alarmed by what he saw. "He was badly injured and I could see that he was very shaken by the incident," Andrew says. "Michael wasn't one to let anyone know when something was wrong, but he couldn't hide it then."

A bruised brain can cause massive mood swings and behavioral problems until the swelling goes down. Michael's condition turned his otherwise sweet soul sour; he became inexplicably irrational, violent, and confrontational, as his bandmates learned when they reconvened to begin work on their next album.

They'd decided to christen a studio that had just reopened on the island of Capri, Italy. Michael and Mark Opitz had insisted on it during the recording of *Welcome to Wherever You Are* after they had seen an ad for the studio in a trade magazine. Opitz was overjoyed—he'd been to Capri as a boy, and pledged that one day, he'd make it his home. And he did—shortly after recording there with INXS, Opitz moved his family to the island, where they lived for three years.

The band was worried about Michael, and thought they should postpone the recording sessions. But Michael insisted that he was fine and that his injuries should not delay the proceedings.

In theory, the Capri plan was genius—a small, inaccessible island; a brand-new, cutting edge studio; an in-house chef; a villa for each band member, large enough to accommodate their families if they chose to visit—and it was in Italy. What could be better? It sounded like a creative paradise; the island was only accessible by boat, there were no main roads, and no cars were allowed. The studio compound sat atop a breathtaking cliff, surrounded by lush trees above the deep blue ocean. There was nothing to do but eat, sleep, and make music.

The reality was a bit different. "We flew something like forty hours to Rome, then took a bus to Naples, then a ferry to the isle of Capri, and then it was a long walk to the studio," Kirk says. "It was horrendous. There were no cars on the island, so you had to walk up a huge flight of steep steps. Terrible trip. But an amazing place once you got there."*

INXS thought that isolation would force them to focus; it would keep Michael from nightclubbing and negate the others' excuses for arriving late and leaving early. "We also just wanted to have a bit of fun now that we had money," Kirk says.

Unfortunately they'd overdone it on the solitude: they'd booked the studio during the off-season, and Capri is a vacation destination with few full-time residents. It was the rainy season, and when the sea was rough, which it often was, no boats journeyed to the mainland. The degree of convenience they were used to was impossible, which they learned within hours of their arrival. Everyone had run out of cigarettes, and when they asked where they could get more, they were told that someone would fetch them from the mainland tomorrow—if the tide wasn't too strong. "It was like a five-star Alcatraz," Kirk says.

The setting did nothing to soothe Michael's bruised brain. The isolation agitated him, and his behavior became increasingly unpredictable and

*** Capri was more or less man-made. It was nothing but a jagged rock with an amazing view until Roman Emperor Tiberius fell in love with it. He shipped soil and trees to the island and retreated there toward the end of his reign and made throwing lush parties and orgies first on his agenda. Rome and the Empire was in dire straits, but Tiberius didn't care—he'd made Capri his home. He stayed in touch with the capital by mirror: the information was communicated in a series of flashes passed from outpost to outpost until it reached Capri, where Tiberius routinely ignored them.**

bizarre. He took to heavy drinking, which turned him into an utter terror. "I shared a villa with Michael; he lived upstairs, and I lived downstairs," Mark Opitz recalls. "The night we arrived, I went to bed at about three a.m. At four a.m. I awoke to the sound of furniture being smashed upstairs. At four-thirty my phone rang. It was Michael, completely distraught, telling me that he was leaving in the morning because he couldn't stand to be with the guys anymore and couldn't stand being stuck on this fucking island." Opitz went upstairs and talked with him until Michael calmed down. It wasn't the last time he did so—in fact, he got used to the routine.

The band jammed and wrote music in the afternoon, then broke for dinner, where they enjoyed lush Italian feasts. They'd do their best to return to the studio in the evening, but it wasn't easy. Generally Michael had swilled enough wine and champagne over dinner that he was completely intolerable before the end of the meal. He grew very fond of Limoncello, a potent aperitif of fermented lemons and alcohol that was dubbed "Michael's firewater." The local custom is to sip the liqueur in small glasses after dinner. Michael took to toting a bottle of it around and swigging from it freely.

"Michael had very violent moments," Kirk says. "He threw equipment off the cliffs outside the studio. He threw his microphone stand around inside the studio, and he threw violent tantrums all the time. Our very first night in the studio he sprayed a full bottle of champagne all over the brand-new mixing board. The engineers were devastated. And it halted the proceedings for several days until it could be repaired." Over those six weeks, Michael threatened or physically confronted nearly every member of the band. They did their best to get through to him, but nothing seemed to help.

One night, Garry sat with Michael, trying to understand what his friend was going through. Hutch just sat there, repeatedly dropping a knife into the wooden floor of the studio.

"Michael, why are you destroying this beautiful floor?" Garry asked.

Michael snatched the knife out of the floor and turned on Garry. "I'll fucking stab you instead," he yelled.

Garry could tell by the look in Michael's eyes that he meant it.

"I was able to wrestle the knife away from him but it wasn't easy," Garry says. "It was not a good night."

"I don't think Michael even realized how he was behaving. It was the brain bruising, which is a very serious condition," Kirk says. "He was very frustrated at the time and all he could do was act it out."

Michael had always been the member of the band most on top of changing trends in music, film, and art; he was the savvy creative director they turned to for inspiration. Michael always knew what was coming next. He introduced the band to dance music, and pushed them to release club mixes of their songs.

During the recording sessions on Capri, it was clear that Michael, for the first time, had lost his edge, which baffled his bandmates more than his erratic behavior. Day after day, Michael emphatically insisted that the band reinvent itself as a grunge rock outfit. More than once, he sat everyone down in the studio and forced them to listen to Nirvana's *Nevermind* from start to finish. He'd play the album at such a high volume that he eventually destroyed a few speakers. "We were like, 'Yeah, it's great, Michael, but what has it got to do with us?'" Kirk says. "I had huge arguments with him about it. I told him that we've always ignored what was going on and in that way we've often led the way musically. I kept pointing out that Nirvana and every band that came from Seattle were already out there. Anyone who does a version of a sound that is already out is destined to fail, because by the time they record and release their version of it, that sound is either long gone or so well established that they look ridiculous. He just didn't understand that trying to be grunge was altogether against everything we'd ever done."

Michael's condition made recording a trying process, to say the least, but the band managed to get half the album completed before they broke for the Christmas holidays. Michael returned to France, then joined Andrew in London to write more songs. His brain bruising had begun to diminish and though his sense of smell never returned and his sense of taste was forever a fraction of what it had been, his behavior slowly returned to normal. He didn't openly apologize and didn't choose to discuss it with the band, but when Michael returned to Capri, he took to the work at hand with ambition and drive.

The resulting album, *Full Moon, Dirty Hearts,* is an oddity in the INXS canon. It is stripped-down, soulful rock and roll—a clear effort to shun the band's eighties image. But Michael did not fully relinquish his grunge obsession—it was manifested in the album cover, where the band is arranged in the back of a dusty van wearing flannel shirts and baseball caps. That wasn't the original plan for the album art. Chris Murphy commissioned iconic fashion photographer Helmut Newton to shoot the band's cover for a cool $100,000. "For that money, you got five photos, but they were worth it," Murphy says. "I knew that we needed a very strong image for this album—stronger than any we'd ever had." The resulting shots are arresting, and the one Murphy favored for the cover is amazing. It is black and white, picturing two busty leather-clad dominatrix/hookers in an alley under a billboard bearing the image of a scruffy, morning-after Michael Hutchence. "I thought it was perfect," Murphy says. "It was classic—black and white, sexy. Anyone who saw it would pick it up and say, 'Wow. What the fuck is that?' It would arouse the interest we needed to get people to dive into the album."

Unfortunately, Michael hated it. Really hated it—and disagreed that it should be the cover to the point that he would not sign any contract obliging him to tour or support the album in any way if the cover was not changed. In essence, it was a threat to quit the band over the album art. "I just couldn't believe that this guy who'd always been so cutting edge had become someone who was insisting on grunge covers in 1993," Murphy says.

Full Moon, Dirty Hearts is by far the least cohesive INXS album—it is the sound of a band in flux that has lost its center. It isn't a bad set of songs—it just isn't quite INXS, falling somewhere between a new direction and an odd disconnection. The album might have been very, very different, according to Chris Murphy. It was the last album the band was contractually bound to deliver to Atlantic, and since the label had made it quite clear that they would do little to promote it, the band considered it an opportunity to do whatever the hell they pleased musically. "The label had done nothing to help the last album, so I thought we were better off doing something really creative to get the best out of the situation," Chris Murphy says. "I also saw U2 basically trying to replicate us. It's a big statement to say that, but it's true. I saw them pursuing the fusion between being cool and dancey and groovy in leather and cowboy hats with *Zooropa.* It was getting all too interwoven. Michael was close with Bono by then and we kept telling him to stop talking to Bono about what we were planning creatively. In any case, I felt we needed to take a big fucking left turn—a really big one."

In 1988, Murphy had taken a trip to Jamaica, where he witnessed the burgeoning evolution in the dancehall and reggae music scenes, where synthesizers, early samplers, and new-school rapping had started a fire in Jamaican music.*

At the outset of planning the album, the time, he thought, was now: INXS should go to Jamaica, hang out, smoke pot, meet the bright lights of the Kingston music scene, and take half a year to make the most experimental album they could. In the early days on the beaches of Sydney and Perth, INXS was, in essence, a proto-ska band: Specials covers and stuff like Elvis Costello's "Watching the Detectives" were a mainstay of the Farriss Brothers' set. Jamaica, he thought, would bring out those roots, and inspire an album unlike anything their musical peers could conceive of.

*** Dancehall is a genre of Jamaican music that emerged in the eighties. It was initially called "ragamuffin," a style that featured a DJ half-singing, half-rapping about bawdy goings-on. The musical structure is rooted in reggae rhythm, though the tempo is stepped up, driven by drum machines and synthesizers. Dancehall's influence has become a staple of millennial hip-hop and pop, from Sean Paul to Missy Elliot to Gwen Stefani.**

It wasn't meant to be, because as Murphy discovered, he'd lost his co-visionary. "We had all decided to pursue the Jamaica thing—the band was all for it and I'd begun to research who we should meet and where we should work. Then one day Michael told me that he was dead against it and wanted to record in Capri, and so we spent those disastrous weeks there," Murphy says. "I guess Mark Opitz had a thing for Capri, because he moved there afterward, so that's probably how that all started. He's the fucker I should kill." It was the first time Murphy and Michael did not see eye-to-eye as far as the band's direction went. "He and I were dangerously out of sync at the time," Murphy says. "We were always the ones listening to music from all over. He'd ring me and we'd talk about bands and DJs, and during this period, for the first time, I felt that I was more in the know than he was. He'd gotten very caught up in dance and grunge music and was a bit too isolated by the celebrity circles he ran in. I was flabbergasted when he didn't want to go to Jamaica. I'd thought that if anyone would understand why we should do it, Michael would."

Murphy's vision might have been the glue INXS needed: reggae rhythms and dancehall beats came into vogue in pop music just a few years later. It certainly would have destroyed preconceived perceptions of INXS as a band who'd fallen behind the times. "Everyone would have freaked.

Michael could easily have proto-rapped. I just knew his vocal style would evolve if he were immersed in the Kingston music scene," Chris Murphy says. "I still believe in my heart that if INXS had made a Jamaican-influenced album in 1993 they would have been the heroes of the music industry."

Once the plan was vetoed, Murphy entered into damage control mode, wherein he did what he could to make an album he had little faith in a more interesting package. He commissioned a series of remixes and arranged to shoot a video for every song on the album, each on a small budget by a different up-and-coming Australian director.

He also enlisted Chrissie Hynde and the legendary Ray Charles to duet with Michael on "Full Moon, Dirty Hearts" and "Please . . . (You Got That)," respectively. Those tracks are the highlights of the record, and the experience of working with the legendary Mr. Charles was an honor the band will never forget.

Ray Charles's studio was built to his specifications forty years ago, inside a small, square building located at 2107 West Washington Boulevard in Los Angeles, which has been declared a landmark and turned into a museum since his death. The studio was an antiquated affair overseen by Mr. Charles's engineer, a quiet, dapper man named Mr. T. Mr. Charles had a few rules in his house, the most important of which was that everyone call him Mr. Charles, including the boys in INXS.

The studio room contained a small vocal booth where Mr. Charles would sing just a few feet away from the entire Ray Charles Orchestra, who sat in silence between takes. "When Michael and I walked in, we were instructed to call him Mr. Charles, which I almost forgot to do a few times," Mark Opitz recalls. "When he came in from the recording room he was carrying a huge porcelain beer stein, the type you see at Octoberfest. I later found out that it was filled with one half Bols gin and one half very strong black coffee—that was what kept Ray Charles going. When I shook his hand I noticed that he had a massive coffee stain all over the front of his white shirt. This guy held the people who worked for him in so much fear that no one had told him that he'd soiled his shirt."

Michael played Mr. Charles the song and the legend took to the vocal booth to sing.

"Stop the music," he said, just after it had begun. "I only hear it on one side."

INXS and Mr. Charles.

Mr. T made adjustments, but could not quickly figure out what was wrong.

"Damn it," Mr. Charles said, "I'll fix it myself."

As Mark and Michael watched, amazed, Mr. Charles threw off his headphones, walked, unassisted, out of the vocal booth, down a few stairs, through a door, up a few stairs, and into the control room. He strode past everyone, brushed Mr. T aside, and, without hesitation, reached for one switch among hundreds on the mixing-board control panel. And don't you know, it was the right switch, too.

I Thought I Was Doing No Wrong

TRUE TO THEIR PLAN, INXS embarked on a tour following the release of *Full Moon, Dirty Hearts.* They were set on getting back to basics and shedding their eighties arena-rock reputation: they dubbed the tour "Get Out of the House" and booked themselves into clubs and pubs as small as those they'd played years before when they had no choice. They did their best to include as many of their original haunts as they could, though many had been torn down, renovated, or no longer hosted live music. They did manage to book a few rooms they knew too well, including the Manly Vale Hotel and the Avalon Beach RSL. It was 1994, two years after the Concert for Life, and the Tall Poppy syndrome still plagued INXS. The media and public still regarded the band as prattish rock stars, but in true Tall Poppy form, it didn't stop anyone from snapping up the tickets to the tour with record-breaking speed. It sold out across the entire country in mere minutes.

To their accountant's disgust, the band booked a tour of similarly sized venues—average capacity about five hundred—around the world. Their intention was to bill the tour as an exclusive, intimate evening with a band that had not played stages that small in years. They wanted it to be a hot ticket, and a chance for fans to experience the new music, close-up. They intended to follow up the tour with a major arena tour the following year.

In America, the band's stripped-down tour sold out as quickly as it did everywhere else but it was hardly a money-making venture. The cost of transporting the band and their equipment overseas was roughly one hundred thousand dollars—a figure that rendered the tour a financial loss before they even began. Profit was never the point—they wanted to generate excitement for their new music and their return to the road. To the band's shock and dismay, they endured more than financial loss—in America, the tour seriously damaged their reputation. The media did not portray it as a rare chance to see a major rock band in an intimate setting; most critics characterized it as a major rock band's fall from grace. They did not report that INXS had sold out the entire tour in several hours; instead they declared that INXS was so out of fashion in the grunge era that the former arena rockers could do no better than fill the nation's smallest rock clubs. It didn't help that *Welcome to Wherever You Are* had gone vastly unnoticed in the States and that the pub tour was the first the Yanks had seen of the band in nearly three years.

"Our intention was to make it a hot ticket, to penetrate with our new music and then return for a big tour," Andrew says. "Coming off of the Wembley period, I guess it wasn't the best idea. Instead of seeing it as our desire to blow people's minds in a small setting, the perception was that we weren't big anymore, that we'd gone from huge stages to small pubs out of necessity."

The tour sold out so quickly that the band and management believed that their intentions were clear and understood. They didn't think it necessary for the first time, do everything they could to publicize their tour—and paid the price. "That tour was fun for us," Kirk says, "but unfortunately it didn't help anything. In fact, it didn't *do* anything. Most of the time people didn't even know we were touring because the pub or club had sold out in five minutes so the local promoter had no need to spend money on advertising. It left a lot of the media scratching their heads about why we were doing this."

Around the world, the band's intention was lost in translation: the shows received top marks by the critics who reviewed it, but mostly it was regarded as a sad exercise. It didn't help that *Full Moon, Dirty Hearts* was the least accessible, commercially successful, critically lauded, or corporately supported album in INXS's career. Even when the band played live with Ray Charles on *Late Night with David Letterman,* the wonderful performance did little to shift the perception of the band as out-of-time eighties pop stars. "The problem moving forward was that the band didn't stand for anything and that was important in the early nineties," says former road manager Bruce Patron. "Michael tried to change that—he tried to be political with songs like 'Guns in the Sky,' which I don't think really accomplished his goal. I think the problem became that Michael, unlike the rest of the band, was unwilling to accept who they were. They were an incredibly sexual dance-rock band. And that alone is something to stand for. Michael got caught up, I think, in trying to compete with Bono, when he didn't need to, anymore than Bono and U2 needed to compete with INXS. As time went on, Michael wasn't happy with INXS being this rhythm-and-blues band. That's who they were, and what they should have done in the nineties was gotten experimental and progressive. They should have worked with producers like Nellie Hooper instead of trying to continue to be an arena rock band. Michael wanted to be 'Guns in the Sky,' when he should have been happy to be 'Cock in My Pants.' He seemed to want to be Van Halen with a mission rather than being what they are: the sexiest, most unusual funk band on the planet."

In the nineties, the band lost sight of the qualities that made them superstars. They'd been a cutting-edge group who'd taken the mainstream by storm, because they'd consistently innovated. "They're not a band like Van Halen, whose audience wants them to put out the same album over and over," Patron says. "INXS's audience wants them to be original—that's why they'd loved them in the first place. And an audience like that will be the first to move on to the next group of innovators."

The year 1994 was a critical low point for INXS, both commercially and internally. Over seventeen years, they'd never experienced an ebb in their career, and were unsure of how to handle it. It didn't help that the members spent less time with one another than they ever had when they weren't working. Everyone's lives outside of INXS became their priority; they'd spent years climbing to the top and all of the long miles had finally caught up to them. They were ~~were~~ disillusioned, disinterested, and disjointed.

The pub tour was followed by another long hiatus—this one three years—that was less a creative strategy than an instinctual salve. This break wasn't a vacation, it was the calm before the storm; it took three years for the band to even consider making music collectively again. And when they did regroup everything had changed: they had a new record label, had lost the only manager they'd ever really known, and were doing everything they could to save the man among them whose life had spun out of control.

It seemed, to everyone who knew him well, that Michael Hutchence had found a fitting partner in supermodel Helena Christensen when the couple took up with each other in 1989: both were gorgeous sex symbols who lived equally surreal realities, yet were made of stuff strong enough to maintain a grip on reality. They were good for each other, and the time they spent on Michael's idyllic five-acre refuge in the South of France allowed them to live in peace. Michael had bought his French property in 1987, just after the commercial success of *Kick,* but Helena was his muse for renovating the house to make it a home. They regularly entertained their friends there: everyone from Bono and Adam Clayton from U2, to models Claudia Schiffer and Elle Macpherson, to Prince Albert of Monaco and Johnny Depp.

"It was wonderful spending time there with them," U2 front-man Bono says. "Helena was Lauren Bacall and he was her Clark Gable. I know that the metaphor is slightly off, but anyone who knew Michael would say that he was definitely more of a Clark Gable than a Humphrey Bogart." Bono and his wife, Ali, spent five consecutive summers in France at the couple's homestead in the early nineties and remember those times as very precious ones indeed. "The South of France is a great place to hang out if you're a rock star because the French are so into themselves that they don't even notice you," Bono says. "We had such wonderful times. Most of the time we spent just cooking and talking and relaxing. I had children and it wasn't all going out at night to parties. Not at all—it was about really cherishing our time off, and being allowed to do so. But of course, sometimes we'd dress up and go into Cannes to the casino or to a club to hang out."

One night, Michael and Bono, full of drink, decided that they'd walk all the way home on the beach from Cannes to Michael's house, a journey of several miles. "We ended up at the stretch of beach we had been to that afternoon, and went to sleep in front of this restaurant owned by these beautiful hippies who had been there since the sixties," Bono recalls. "As they were serving breakfast in the morning, here comes Michael and Bono, walking through the door, fresh off a night sleeping on the sand."

The South of France was the type of place where men of their profile were able to stop and smell the copious roses. "We were able, in those summers, to really appreciate the life we'd been given," Bono says. "We were very appreciative of it and let no moments pass us by. We knew that what we had was special, not just because we were in talented bands, but that we were lucky that our careers as musicians were also so special. We'd not only succeeded, but we'd both found a route out of preciousness. And in the South of France we'd found a place where we had the freedom to be ourselves and live a normal life, regardless of all that—and believe me, that is rare, indeed." The pair used to hoard new music to share with each other over their summer vacation. "Yeah, Michael was always onto what was next, usually before me," Bono says. "I remember that he beat me to it on the Black Grape album *It's Great When You're Straight . . . Yeah.* He was the first one to play me so many things. But I think I was the one who turned him on to Massive Attack."

Helena was an asset to Michael, a connection that would boost any man's ego. And Michael needed that, because regardless of what the world thought of him, he was riddled with insecurity. "I loved him with Helena," Tim Farriss says. "She is one of the most beautiful women in the world, but she's also one of the most grounded. It had to do with her family—her mother and father are wonderful. I've never felt more comfortable around someone so beautiful in my entire life, and that was because of how she was raised. I think Helena grounded Michael and brought him back to the way he was before he became a rock star. And I think that as time went on, that scared him."

Others saw Helena as a very different influence in Michael's life. They say that she was the type of partner who dug at his weaknesses and treated him as if he were a handbag. By their accounts, Helena was more likely to do things like tell Michael to cut his hair and once he had done so, tell him that he looked terrible, and ask him why he'd done it.

The relationship wasn't always easy. Michael's personal security guard for six years, Tony Woodhall, reports that they fought often and that Helena was prone to fits of jealousy. In a few instances, their arguments nearly became physical. As the couple's relationship deteriorated, Woodhall returned home one day to find a disheveled miscreant camped out on his stoop. He left his children in the car and approached the rumpled man and discovered that he was Michael.

"I just wanted to get away from it all," Michael told him. "They all know where I live, but no one will find me here. Can I stay for a few days?"

The "they" he spoke of was the Australian tabloid press, who was in a frenzy over the fact that he and Helena were on the rocks. He also wanted to hide from everyone else he knew, and during the week that Michael spent at the Woodhalls', Tony told many a white lie to management, band members, and everyone else who called him looking for Hutch. Michael's escape act didn't worry them too much: he was infamous for his disappearances, which usually preceded a phone call from him a few days later, made from a destination half a world away.

Michael escaped to the Woodhalls' because he needed to see, just for a moment, how life worked outside of the parameters that his had become. He wouldn't receive any rock-star treatment there—and didn't want to. "The rules were simple," Woodhall says. "I told him, 'You sleep on the couch, you make your own breakfast, and no staying up late because my kids are in school.'" Michael also arrived with some definitive, attainable goals: he wanted to mow the lawn and he wanted to order dinner, himself, at a McDonald's drive-thru. "He had been living in apartments and hotels so long that those were the two things that he saw as normal, everyday acts that he never had a reason or a chance to do," Woodhall says. "I completely understood."

The Woodhalls' grass wasn't quite due for a trim, so Michael waited until the end of his stay to fire up the mower. Michael did a few laps around the lawn, and decided that he didn't need to do the entire lawn to duly soak up the experience. Next came McDonald's. The only problem was that Michael didn't have a driver's license. So Woodhall drove to the restaurant, switched places with Hutchence in the parking lot and let him motor through the drive-thru. "There was no way I was letting him drive my car there without a license," Woodhall says. "Fuck, no. I'd seen him drive too many times to know better than that."

After a week of hiding out, Woodhall dropped Michael at the airport, where Michael bought a ticket on the spot and flew off to his next adventure. "I think he would have stayed longer at our house if I'd let him," Woodhall says. "He got out the notepad a few times and wrote lyrics. I felt like it was the first time he'd been close to real life ever since they'd made it. He'd started out, as all artists do, writing about real life, but that perception changes with success. Michael's life had become like a fishbowl—hotel rooms, first-class tickets, and that was it. He was removed from the simple things, the everyday things that filled the lives of the people who bought his records, went to his concerts, and in reality, paid for his life. I think he was trying to get in touch with that again."

Michael Hutchence valued experience above all—certainly above money. Michael understood money in the abstract; material possessions were never important to him. He cherished the freedom that money brought him; as long as he could travel, afford a hotel, and buy himself clothes wherever he might be, Michael was happy. He was never aware or concerned, much to his disadvantage, with his wealth or possessions. "You have to understand, it wasn't the money that had changed him—it was the demands of his fame and his life," Woodhall says. "The money never really mattered to him. I've never seen anyone less aware of how much or how little money they had. He hardly ever had cash on him, and when he did it was usually currency from a different country. I watched countless times as his credit cards got rejected, and he had absolutely no idea why. Usually it wasn't that he didn't have it; it was because no one had paid the bill."

During the time he spent at Woodhall's house, Michael spoke often of the band's slip from the top and how the world had disliked both *Welcome to Wherever You Are* and *Full Moon, Dirty Hearts.* He wasn't apt to see it as due to a change in times or taste let alone consider the record label's lack of support; he felt that it was all his fault. His urgency to change their image during the *Full Moon* sessions weighed particularly on his mind. He felt that he'd lost touch with the fire that had fueled the band for so long—he felt like he'd snuffed it out.

He was just thirty-four—young by any estimation—but Michael was burdened by a feeling that he and the band weren't kids anymore. Furthermore, he felt that he and his brothers had grown apart: he and Jon, but one year his junior, were the only two without children, and he was the only who had never married. Michael had begun to examine his life, but Woodhall noticed something more troubling: Michael no longer loved what he did best.

"I was close with Michael for six years," Tony Woodhall says, "and I remember how his composure in the studio changed. He went from standing in the studio, singing his guts out, to lying on the couch, falling asleep, and not seeming to care much when he was needed to cut vocals. I remember asking Michael if he enjoyed singing anymore, and if he remembered how excited he used to be. He said he loved it, and he loved performing live. But he also said that he'd started to feel like he couldn't stand to be in a room with the band anymore," Tony Woodhall says. "And that was tough to hear."

Michael had become a star and as much as he enjoyed the spoils, he wasn't properly wired to handle the attention that came with it. Whether the eyes of the world on him cast his insecurities in harsh focus in his mind or his sensitive soul was simply overcome by the pressure of living a public life, Michael had begun to retreat inward, and unravel beyond the reach of his nearest and dearest. The accident in Denmark was the start of the slide, and the end of his relationship with Helena Christensen deepened a major depression. "The end of their relationship had much to do with the permanent damage caused by his accident," Garry Beers says. "He had lost almost all sense of taste and smell, which was devastating to him. He loved food, he loved life, he loved sex, and there he was, living in the South of France, with this beautiful girlfriend, unable to enjoy so many sensations that he'd always—that all of us—taken for granted. After it happened he started drinking more heavily than we'd ever seen him do. That was the start of a depression that never let up."

Michael slowly changed: he became increasingly negative, judgmental, argumentative, and cruelly sarcastic. He'd never been that way before—even at his most indulgent, selfish, and distant, Michael remained a compassionate soul who took time out to comfort those around him. He was the kind of man who made whoever he was talking to the center of his attention. He was always the one to give, the one who would never burden another soul with his problems. "Michael was always, until the end, the kind of man who did not talk to anyone about his problems as much as he should have—that is why he acted out in Capri," Andrew says. "I don't think he knew *how* to talk about them—at that point all he could do was act. And for him to do so he was obviously in a lot of emotional pain. He was the first to do everything he could for other people. To him, his problems were never as important as yours, mine, or anyone's."

Michael and Helena Christensen parted in 1995, allegedly due to the fact that he took up with Paula Yates, an English journalist turned television celebrity who was, at the time, married to Sir Bob Geldof, an Irishman who was knighted, not for fronting the shambling, bluesy Boomtown Rats, nor for his starring role in Pink Floyd's iconic film *The Wall,* but for his civil works on behalf of African famine relief as the nexus of *Live Aid,* the concert and album, in 1984. He was also nominated for the Nobel Peace Prize that year for his efforts, though the award was bestowed upon Bishop Desmond Tutu, for his work to abolish apartheid in South Africa.

Paula Yates and Bob Geldof met in the late seventies, just as his band, the Boomtown Rats, landed an international hit with "I Don't Like Mondays," an ode to the thirteen-year-old Californian girl who thusly justified her shooting spree at her school. Yates made a name for herself as a blond, brassy journalist, who was raised to believe that her father was Jess Yates, a famous British broadcaster and television producer. In 1997, the same year that Michael Hutchence died, Yates learned that her biological father was Hughie Green, a British TV game show host and a family friend she greatly disdained. The revelation was a trauma that Paula could not bear.

Paula was a witty, intelligent scenester, who, from the start, did her best to make a celebrity of herself: she posed nude in *Penthouse* in 1978 and published a book of photos titled *Rock Stars in Their Underwear,* which delivered on the promise of its title. Andy Warhol proclaimed it "the greatest work of the last decade."

In 1982, Paula became cohost of *The Tube,* an English television institution, where she and Jools Holland interviewed celebrities until the show left the air in 1997. In 1984, she gave birth to Fifi Trixabelle, the first of three children she shared with Geldof—the others, Peaches Honeyblossom and Pixie, were born in 1990 and 1994, respectively. Geldof and Yates married in 1986, after a decade together.

Yates first interviewed Michael Hutchence on *The Tube* in 1985, when the band appeared to promote *Listen Like Thieves.* Yates was known, both on- and off-camera, for her love of musicians, provocative dress, and overtly flirtatious banter with the day's pop stars. From their first meeting on, it was clear that the tall blonde was smitten with Hutchence. Road manager Bruce Patron recalls the moment all too well. "She came up to me, pointed at Michael, and said, 'I'm going to have that boy,'" Patron recalls.

"He was still dating Michele at the time. By the way, I'm a very big believer that rock stars should stay with their original girlfriends. The original girlfriend will keep a guy honest and Michele was so awesome for Michael. I loved them together. Anyway, I told Paula, 'Why don't you stay away from him? Please? He's got a good relationship, he's a good guy, he's not a player who fucks a different chick every night. Just leave him alone.' He wasn't a player then, but he certainly was later on." Paula was unmoved and began to show up at INXS gigs everywhere for the next few years. "She was in New York at the Radio City shows we did in 1986, she was at the Beacon Theater show in '87, she even brought her kid to that one," Patron recalls. "She popped up everywhere in England. It was very clear that she was there just trying to fuck Michael." Yates was obsessed with Michael—those who knew her say that she had a photo of him, torn from a magazine, taped to the family fridge for years, and openly joked to her friends that she would have him one day.

As the eighties slid into the nineties, professional and personal connections brought Hutchence and Yates into each other's orbit more frequently. Geldof hails from Dublin, Ireland, and the same new wave scene that birthed U2; he and Bono have been dear friends since their teens. It was only a matter of time—and Paula's insistence, so say many close to the band—before Michael began to spend more and more time with Paula, Bob, and their inner circle. As Michael grew closer with Bono, he grew closer with Bob, and as he drifted further and further from Helena, he drew too close to Paula.

The pair began an affair—she was married to Geldof and he was still with Helena—which became public in 1995, when the English tabloids reported that Michael and Paula had a four-day tryst in a two-thousand-dollar per night suite at London's Halkin Hotel. Soon afterward, Bob Geldof, via a handwritten note to the press, confirmed that he and Yates had separated, that she had taken charge of their three children, and that the couple loved each other and were committed to their family.

Michael and Helena still appeared together in public and refused to confirm or deny the allegations. The English tabloid press speculated about it on a daily basis, however. Michael was hounded wherever he went, and in March 1995, just after Paula and Bob's split was official, he assaulted a photographer who'd snapped a photo of him and Paula emerging from a luxury country hotel. Michael tried to kick him, kung-fu style, and allegedly never connected with the poor slob. Nonetheless, the man fell down, suffered a "bruised knee," and filed a hefty lawsuit against Hutchence. The incident was widely reported, as was the fact that Helena had dumped Michael. A slew of tabloid "reportage" ensued: Michael's ex-girlfriend, Virginia Hey, cashing in on the moment, informed England's *Herald Sun* that he had cheated on her with Paula as early as 1988. The same papers that had adored Michael's bad-boy ways changed their tune overnight. "After Michael had gone through the honeymoon period with the press where he was the funny Australian, he was done for," Garry Beers says. "He'd gone and pinched a knight's wife. That's a whole different thing. To his credit he stayed in England and faced it."

By July of that year, Michael and Paula were in the tabloids as often as Charles and Diana. Geldof and Yates filed for divorce and soon after, Yates filed for bankruptcy, all of which was documented in all of its glorious minutiae on a daily basis. Both Andrew Farriss and Chris Murphy lived in England during the years that Michael and Paula were publically together and witnessed the scope of the scandal firsthand. "The three people who were on and off of the cover of the tabloids, literally each day, were Princess Diana and Michael and Paula," Andrew says. "He went, in a very short amount of time, from this celebrated, adored, wild colonial boy misbehaving in London society to a criminal who was not 'their boy,' at all—he was an Australian who wasn't supposed to be there, at all."

Andrew spent a lot of time with Michael and supported him as best he could. Michael tried to turn his troubles into songs; he was busy writing lyrics, both for a solo album and for INXS's next effort. It was no help that the band was on hiatus—the papers regularly reported that Hutchence had not only broken up a marriage, but the band as well, in order to pursue a solo career. "I wasn't sure how to help him a lot of the time," Andrew says. "He wanted to write with me but he wanted to go solo as well. He said he wanted to get out of himself and to write songs that were nothing anyone would expect from him. But he also said that he had no intention of leaving the band." Andrew still wonders if he could have done more, because even when Michael assured him that he was okay, he knew that his friend was in over his head.

This Is What U Need: Co-songwriters Michael and Andrew.

At the time, Andrew and his family, like the other members of the band, were consumed with their own trials. He and Shelley had moved to London at Chris Murphy's urging, to be closer to Michael and to keep the nexus of INXS somewhat together. Shelley had just given birth to their second child, Josephine, and was in the throes of postnatal depression, in a city where the couple had few friends. It didn't help that everyone they met bombarded them, in the politest way possible, of course, with questions about Michael and Paula. "I still think that I should have paid more attention to certain things to do with him," Andrew says. "I don't know. I just don't know. For all of us, life outside of the band had become like the Stay Puft Marshmallow Man from *Ghostbusters.* We'd all avoided dealing with important issues in our personal lives for so long that they'd grown into large monsters. In simplest terms, we'd existed on the road so long, but tried to create normalcy outside of that. Yet, ever since we'd achieved a degree of success, all of us had played catch-up with our lives. And we did our best, but I don't think any of us were able to devote the time to Michael that we needed to at that point."

Even if they had, it wouldn't have been easy: their brother wasn't the type to seek assistance. "Michael was not the kind of man who let anyone tell him what to do with his life," Andrew says. "He was the type who told everyone what *they* should do with their lives. Usually he was right, but when it came to his own affairs, he didn't listen to anyone. For a long time, he would listen to Chris Murphy, but that changed. In those last years, not even Chris could get through to him."

Michele Bennett remained close with him after their breakup in 1988 until his death nearly a decade later. She spoke to him when their paths crossed, and whenever one of his subsequent relationships was on the rocks, Michele received calls from him, seeking her advice. Over the years, she noticed a drastic change in Michael, one she couldn't make sense of. "His accident definitely had a lasting effect on him chemically," Michele says. "He didn't handle drugs and alcohol the way he used to after that. Neurologically his brain had changed and I think those substances became a bad combination whereas they used to never be." Bennett says that when Hutchence started taking antidepressants in the years before his death, the change grew more drastic when the prescribed substances mixed with the illicit ones that Michael continued to ingest. "I think the combination was a significant factor in the very obvious change that took place in his behavior. There was just a weird ecosystem in his brain, which, combined with the unrelenting pressure from the English tabloid press, and the reality of what he'd gotten himself involved in with Paula, was very hard on him. It began around 1995. The easiest way I can communicate it is that Michael was always such an optimist; he never spoke a cross word about

Young Hearts: Michele Bennett and Michael Hutchence.

anyone. But suddenly he became cynical, judgmental, and negative about everything."

He was also unwilling to listen to criticism of any kind. He would call Michele to seek advice, but the moment she pointed out that perhaps he'd gotten himself into a situation that could not end well, and that his expectations were unrealistic, Michael wouldn't have it—he'd argue, insisting that she was wrong for hours. Then he'd catch himself, change the subject, and do his best to be the happy-go-lucky Michael he felt he was expected to be. "He was in a very difficult situation and I truly wanted to help him," Michele says. "I felt that he was only going to listen to me if I condoned what he was doing, which I did not. He began to spend most of his time with people who did tell him everything he wanted to hear, but I think, in his heart, he yearned for the familiarity of those who knew him best."

In 1996, Yates's divorce from Geldof was official, and the battle over the custody of their children began. In a bizarre legal arrangement, in May of that year, Paula and Michael took up residence in the home she had shared with Geldof, and Geldof bought and occupied Michael's mansion. In July, Yates gave birth to Heavenly Hiraani Tiger Lily, her fourth child, and her first with Hutchence. In September, while Yates, Michael, and Tiger were in Australia, the housekeeping staff at their new London home discovered a quantity of opium in a shoebox under the couple's bed and turned it over to the police. Though no charges were brought, the publicity was devastating. Once news of the drug bust reached Australia, Michael and Paula were besieged in their Sydney hotel, where the paparazzi continually set off the fire alarms in an attempt to force them outside where they might be photographed. "I went five days straight without sleep," Michael's security guard Tony Woodhall reports. "We couldn't trust anybody." They decided that Paula should get back to England to deal with the authorities, and that Michael would join her there. To get her safely and secretly on her flight back home, Woodhall talked the authorities into allowing her to enter the plane through the baggage hold. "We arranged for a decoy car to lead the press away, thinking that Paula was inside," Woodhall says. "Then we left by a different entrance and took her right onto the tarmac. She went up the baggage belt surrounded by her bags. Then we took Michael to a private airport and flew him up to Queensland in northeastern Australia to get away from all of that harassment."

Tiger remained in Australia with Michael, where his brother and sister helped him look after her in a remote hideaway on the beach along the country's beautiful Gold Coast. When he was ready to return to England to support Yates during the fallout from the drug bust, Michael realized that his baby daughter did not have a passport and therefore would not be allowed entry into England without her mother present. Michael was obliged to fly to Melbourne to get Tiger a passport, then back to Sydney and then to London—all with an infant who hated flying more than Tim Farriss.

Paula was arrested but never charged for possession of narcotics. But the damage was done; the highly publicized arrest ruined her shot at winning the battle over the custody of her children. In October 1996, the court awarded Geldof legal custody of all three daughters. And in the year that followed, until Michael's death in November of 1997, Paula and Michael descended into a miasma of drugs and drama.

Paula Yates was a heroin addict in her teens, one who was successfully rehabilitated. When she became a beloved journalist and television personality, she buried her past, with the help of her influential father. And she did so very well—even when she and Michael were busted for drug possession and her divorce was the day's favorite scandal, she still came off in the English press as an innocent who had lived a clean and sober life until Michael seduced her and ruined everything. Michael was definitely the one who knocked Paula off the wagon, but reports that she'd never done drugs or drank before meeting him are entirely false.

At the start of their relationship, Yates urged Hutchence to end his drug abuse, citing his younger brother, Rhett's, debilitating heroin and cocaine addiction as reason enough for Michael to clean up his act. But one night, as the couple enjoyed a cruise around Sydney Harbor with friends, she suddenly snatched a glass of champagne from a tray and swilled it like a parched sailor. "It was madness, to be honest," Tony Woodhall says. "She had one glass and she was off her face. She took her shirt up and was showing everyone her breasts. I was standing at the back of the boat and she came up to me and stuck them inches from my face. I closed my eyes because I didn't want to be rude, while she was telling me how good they were. Michael was standing there starting to get jealous, which is why she liked to do that kind of thing. It was crazy."

Paula Yates was a very intelligent, very ambitious, resourceful woman who knew how to get what she wanted. As her relationship with Michael became more serious, before it became public, Michael was the only one who didn't consider that Paula might be using her connections in the English press to expose them. In the early days of the affair, they'd rendezvous at the most exclusive hideaways in England, yet somehow, a few paparazzi were always lying in ambush. "I got a phone call from Michael one night during that time and he was screaming at the top of his lungs. 'Doesn't anyone control what's going on?' he asked me. 'The media is out of control. The media is everywhere I go!'" Chris Murphy recalls, "He accused me and the band and our PR people of tipping the media off as to where they were. I said, 'Michael, we don't know where you go with Paula. We're always the last to know about what you're doing.'"

"Are you insinuating that Paula's PR people are advising them as to where we are?" Michael asked.

"Michael, if anyone is advising them as to where you are, it's not fucking me," Murphy said. "I've got the fucking chairman of PolyGram breathing down my neck. You might lose your record deal over this."

All of his frustration at losing Michael's confidence in the last few years suddenly came to a boil. Murphy was pissed off and addressed Michael as he would a petulant child. "*You* listen to *me,* young man," he said. "I want you to be careful about this shit you've got yourself in. And don't you ever dare talk about my staff the way you just did. We've never done anything but support you. If you do that again, I'll leave—I'll leave right now."

Michael apologized and Murphy did what he could: he hired full-time private security for the couple the next morning. "Michael was grateful," Murphy says. "I hired this guy to stay with them wherever they went, but do you know what they did? They fucking lost him on purpose. And that was the night they got caught in that hotel, in some four-poster bed where the maids found restraints and all that. That ordeal was the beginning of the whole nightmare. They were found out and just after that Paula and Bob were separated."

The next morning, Murphy called Michael and told him that he wasn't going to add spin-doctoring to his résumé as manager. He was officially stepping away from whatever tabloid mess Michael and Paula had created for themselves. "You two lost my security team on purpose last night, Michael, and I'm not going to be involved because you are playing games. If that's what you want to do, it's your problem," Murphy said. "It was one of the last times I spoke to him. One thing was clear, Paula was not going to leave him alone. Once she'd set her sights on him, that was it—he was trapped. And as much as he loved her, I don't know if he intended everything that happened between them to happen. I've questioned myself a thousand times since about what I should have done. Should I have gone over and punched him in the mouth, or tied him to a bed in a house somewhere far away for a year? What should I have done? I still wonder . . . What do you do when an adult you've known for so long goes AWOL on you?"

The History of Gaetano Peroni

JON FARRISS is a rare breed, indeed—a man who realized his life's calling at just five years old. "I remember my first day of preschool and the teacher letting us pick up whatever instruments we wanted to play," he says. "There was a big drum there in the corner of the music room, and I was drawn to it." Over the next few years, Jon taught himself to play in the room he shared with his brother Andrew on a fifty-five dollar kit bought by his parents. "Once I learned about floor toms and hi-hats, I realized that I could do a lot more than I had ever thought possible," Jon says. "I remember the first time I learned how to play with my left foot on the kick drum. It was the first moment I began to understand how to play a beat."

Alias: Jon Farriss

Born: August 10, 1961

Instruments: drums, samplers, sequencers, all things percussive, bass, keyboards

Married: February, 1992, to Leslie Bega

Separated: 1997

Divorced: 1999

Engaged: June 2004, to Kerry Norris

First Bands: Blackwater, Top Kat, Fish, Guinness (for a few months, at age ten)

Sports: golf, fishing

Alternate Aliases: Jet Lag, Juan Louder, Mickey Dee

At ten years old, Jon was so proficient that he was tapped to play drums by several bands, whose members were much older than he. At fourteen years old, Jon earned money playing shows, for more cash than his older brothers got in their bands. It was the mid-seventies and Jon was in an aptly named rock act called Blackwater, but his biggest money-maker was Top Kat (formerly known as Taurus), an outfit that donned polyester trousers and striped shirts seemingly stolen from Cheap Trick's wardrobe case. Young Jon got an education playing with Top Kat, particularly when they spent a weekend entertaining a nudist colony. "The night we drove up there my brother Andrew had gotten me stoned for the first time, since our parents were away for the weekend," Jon says. "I smoked this ridiculously strong Thai stick that my brother had bought from some surfer he knew. After the Vietnam War, all of the Thai sticks that weren't smoked by U.S. soldiers began to be imported into Australia. It was strong. It was a new experience; it was an inevitable introduction and part of growing up. I remember laughing, being at home, and being so high that I completely forgot that I had to go play a gig with Top Kat that night."

To make matters more strange, the dapper dons in Top Kat hadn't told Jon that their gig was at a nudist camp until they arrived. Well, it was obvious by then; as the band's van tooled up the camp's driveway that evening, the headlights' beams revealed more than the local fauna. "There were flashes of white bottoms and other bits bobbling along there on the road," Jon says. "And once we were in the camp, I'm quite sure that we were the only ones who were ever fully clothed. I'm really shy and I freaked out when we got there because I had this horrible feeling that I was going to be required to take my clothes off and play drums."

That weekend featured all that one might expect from their friendly neighborhood nudist camp: lots of activities that induce bobbling, like volleyball and trampolines, and plenty of naked people who'd look better clothed. "There was just all sorts of jumping around," Jon recalls. "All this jingling and jangling and flopping about. It was not at all just a bunch of naked people swimming and lying in the sun." Top Kat played two gigs, both of them so hot that they charmed the pants off the audience. "I remember that the colonists arrived at our show with clothes on," Jon says. "Then as the set went on, you'd see a bra fly over the crowd, then a pair of shorts, then men's underpants. By the end, nearly everyone was nude. That weekend was eye-opening for me then. It was an introduction to what was going to end up being a very blasé situation; who knew that ten years later I wouldn't bat an eye at something like that. It was a quaint memory before I knew it."

* * *

Jon is a born rock star—playing drums is the only job he's ever had. He's the youngest member of the band and was well looked after by the others. Still, he literally grew up on the road, a place where strange situations turn boys into men very quickly. "Out of all of them, Jonny was probably the most professional," Chris Murphy says. "He was at every sound check and he wanted to be the best drummer in the world. I always admired that in him. He was always nice and respectful but we all kept an eye on him, because we worried that he'd fall into the wrong hands. He did a few times, of course."

Jon's friendships with Michael, as well as with Australian rocker Richard Clapton, were invaluable to the young musician. "I met Jonny when he was barely seventeen, when I produced *Underneath the Colours,*" Clapton recalls. "Truth be told, Jonny's a very, very shy human being. And as he got more famous, it was often hard for him. Shy people are often taken for aloof or arrogant because they keep to themselves. When the band took off and he got this reputation as the greatest rock drummer in the world, that perception of him as a bit elitist certainly kicked in. It couldn't have been further from the truth."

Moving to Hong Kong to live with Michael in the eighties offered Jon anonymity, and when Michael was jet-setting, time alone. Clearly he didn't move there for creature comforts. "Our first apartment was in central Hong Kong. It was always noisy, located in the center of constant construction," Jon says. "There were jackhammers banging away all the time. It was a seven-floor walk-up and it didn't even really have a kitchen. We had some kind of gas burner on top of a cardboard box for a stove. It was basically mattresses on the floor, odd bits of furniture we'd inherited from people who'd moved away, and our suitcases. We had an air conditioner in each bedroom and one in the living room, but if we had more than two on at a time, we'd blow the fuse."

Hong Kong was dirty chaos to Jon until he and Michael relocated to a three-story, three-bedroom house on the water in Tai Tam Bay. "Our first apartment was in the midst of all these markets, just wicker cages with snakes, frogs, dried skins, and dogs all over the place," Jon says. "But our house was nothing like that. It was a great refuge, and I truly appreciated Hong Kong once we moved there." It was the mid-eighties and INXS was huge in Australia (after *The Swing*) and coming up in the rest of the world. But in Hong Kong, Jon and Michael were Aussie expats soaking in the wonder of Asia, inspired by the unique souls that fueled the city. "Both of us really loved the culture," Jon says. "And I met some of the most amazing people there because it's a transient place that attracts incredible people. I met one of my closest, dearest friends to this day in the first week that I lived there."

The house in Tai Tam was a refuge for Michael and Jon, one where they became closer friends and wrote music together for the first time. After the momentous success of *Kick*, the band and management agreed that Andrew Farriss and Michael Hutchence would be INXS's songwriting team. But Jon and Michael's home in Hong Kong was a creative recess: it yielded "Disappear," one of the band's top-selling singles off *X*. "I was writing on this new breakthrough software for the first time, just learning to use a computer to compose and arrange songs, experimenting with samplers and synths," Jon says. "It was very natural. We turned our third bedroom into a home studio and I was doing my thing in there, and Michael might be in his room writing lyrics or reading a book. He'd be listening to what I was doing and writing words for it. Suddenly he'd pop in, we'd get the microphone ready, and roll the tape."

The life of a musician who logs years on the road is full of oddities, surrealities, and strange tales. Those who actually "make it" are rewarded by three times the fun, plus the pressure of endeavoring to make it last.

With that in mind, Jon's got a wonderfully weird moment to share. The year was 1988. The place was the Four Seasons Hotel in Los Angeles, poolside. Back in the seventies a guy named Dave Clement had let INXS rehearse in his warehouse in Brookvale, on the Northern Beaches of Sydney, Australia—he was one of their oldest, most salt-of-the-earth friends—and he came to L.A. that year to see their show. Dave isn't a subtle man; he likes his lager and he speaks his mind loudly. He and Jon were catching up that day, lounging around a pool four stories above the street, when suddenly men in suits, sunglasses, and earpieces vaulted over the walls around the pool to secure the area. Moments later, George Bush Sr., then a vice president campaigning for his party's nomination to run for president, held an informal meeting with men Jon Farriss could not identify. Jon did get a good look though because he and Dave were, literally, stuck in the middle of it. "I was having trouble with my knees at that time, so I was lying in a lounge chair, with this very high-tech black cane I used to get around on at my side. And I needed to get back to my room to take care of something. So I walk past George and it's very clear to me that there's one secret-service guy who's been assigned to keep an eye on me and my black cane." Jon and Dave went to Jon's room to grab a book, and when they returned, once again passed under the watchful gaze of the men in suits. "Dave was hilarious, he just did not understand that these were secret service and that they should not be toyed with," Jon says. "He thought he was in a pub back home. We sat down and he starts looking at this guy who has positioned himself right beside us. The guy's got no neck at all, and Dave looks at him a while, then he says, 'Hey, mate, can you grab us a couple of drinks? That would be great. Listen, we'll buy you a beer. All right? You hungry? Want a burger and fries, mate? It's on us.' The guy didn't flinch. He just kept watching us. I was terrified that we'd be killed." When Bush's meeting was over, the secret service dissipated over the wall just as they'd arrived, leaving the pool—and theoretically, the Western world—completely secure.

Jon Farriss learned life's lessons in the circus of rock and roll, and he learned about love there, too. His first girlfriend was a Texan named Lisa; they met during INXS's first U.S. tour and were together for eight years. Lisa moved to Australia and lived with Jon for nearly four years—she came to the Manor in England when INXS recorded *The Swing* and shared those few months he had off tour with him during that period. "When you're on tour the way we were, you're lucky to see your partner five months out of a year," Jon says. "Touring that much is a strange thing—it puts you in this head space where your feet are so seldom on the ground. It makes you require a relationship—some connection to keep you sane—yet it makes it almost impossible to sustain one."

Jon and Lisa broke up in 1989, during the *Kick* hysteria, around the same time that Reiter's Syndrome sidelined Jon's ability to play. To say the least, drumming exacerbated his condition: it demanded a diet of cortisone,

chronic removal of fluid from his knee caps, and six weeks of rehabilitation. Yet he went on, recovered physically and emotionally, and after the band took a much-needed hiatus, during the *X* tour in 1990 Jon met Leslie Bega, the woman he'd eventually marry, at a party in Los Angeles. She was an aspiring actress from Hollywood.

Within months, the two were engaged. "Everything was going a million miles an hour for me during those years, and honestly, I really wasn't thinking straight," he says. "It happened far too quickly. We were married in Australia in February 1992, and it was a very tumultuous marriage." The two hailed from different backgrounds—one of a few fundamental differences that spelled their undoing.

Throughout the nineties, Jon and Michael maintained their residency in Hong Kong, and between living there and touring with INXS, Jon and his wife were hardly together and drifted further apart. It ended legally some years later, but in all practical respects, their marriage ceased to be in 1997 the same year that Michael Hutchence and INXS did as well.

Jon's divorce was a bitter legal exercise that drained him in every sense. Overwhelmed by the pressure, for a time he turned to prescription antidepressants. "I tried them, but it was way too heavy for me," Jon says. "I couldn't cope with how they made me feel at all. I went off them and I felt better, even though it got too fucking insane."

Michael's death weighed very heavily on Jon—it was another in a series of devastating losses. After the funeral, he retreated to Thailand, where he spent time sorting it all out in a resort in Phuket, managed by a

dear friend. While he was there, he met a French-Canadian girl named Mélanie. After a few months, they embarked on a relationship that lasted two years, which both concentrated and obliterated Jon's duress.

Jon was in pain, and he numbed himself with several years of parties, drugs, and alcohol. He'd bought a mansion in the eastern suburbs of Sydney in 1991 that was to be his sanctuary after moving back from Hong Kong. In the years following his divorce and Michael's death, it became the castle where Jon indulged, hid himself away, grew depressed, and hosted too many gatherings for all the wrong reasons.

In the midst of his divorce proceedings, in the throes of his darkest times, Jon's relationship with Mélanie began to fray. "I was in a very dark space," Jon says. "My mother had died in 1995, and it was hell on our family. I was in bad shape. I was very close to Mum—she was my best friend. Then Chris Murphy left, which was a huge blow to INXS after fifteen years of successful partnership. Then my marriage came apart. And then Michael died. It was all too much. Mélanie was with me through most of that, but it was often such a trying experience for both of us. It was not healthy, and it eventually wore us both out."

★ ★ ★

Jon Farriss never feared the future: he was the first drummer of his stature to embrace samplers and loops, and to use technology to his benefit. He knew that machines could never replace him, they were one more accent in his arsenal. He also learned life's lessons on the fly: he glimpsed normality through the windows of a tour bus. And he did his best to live that life. And after a series of highs and lows, he found everything he's ever wanted.

Jon met the love of his life, Kerry, at the close of 1999, after a long, self-imposed period of solitude. He made a commitment to himself to change his life, to focus on the positive, and to clean up his act. He healed on his own terms and once he did, he realized that he was finally able to truly, truthfully, give himself to someone else. He wanted to share the beauty of life and he wished for a partner to do it with. "I began to meditate on what I wanted, which was a down-to-earth, beautiful person," Jon says. "And it turned out I already knew her. Kerry and I had been introduced when I wasn't at all ready to know her. But we stayed in touch and then step-by-step we naturally fell in love."

Jon sold his old house, bought a new one in a beach community a few hours outside of Sydney, and embarked upon the best chapter of his life. "I feel like I've been reborn," he says. "I feel like I've been given a new life. I feel young, I feel healthy, and I feel clear in my mind and heart. I've realized that love doesn't have to be dramatic peaks and valleys—it can be, and it should be, wonderful, cool, and easy. I love Kerry's family dearly; they're beautiful people who have come into my life, and I love the beautiful home she and I have made. I'm finally able to look back on all of my difficult times objectively, as if it were another lifetime." Since he met Kerry, Jon has discovered a slew of new interests: he's delved into songwriting and he's begun to paint, and taken to it nearly as naturally as the drums.

"I think Jonny would have been a race-car driver if he hadn't become a professional drummer. He's got that kind of nerve," says his father, Dennis Farriss. "He's more introverted than my other two boys, I think. He's fairly deep, but the thing is, Jonny can leave fear behind. It's a gift, that is."

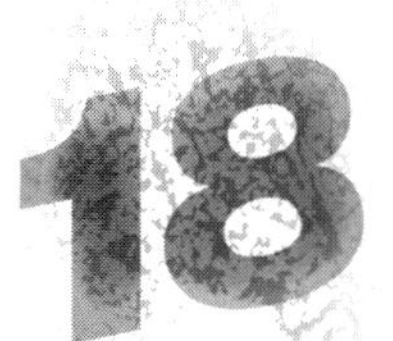

When Nothing Stays the Same

MICHAEL WAS IN TROUBLE—and within a year, he got much worse—but the rest of the band was too caught up or far away to grasp the extent of it. Tim Farriss's wife, Beth, had known all of the boys since high school, when she, Tim, and Kirk had first met. She'd watched them grow up, watched them work hard, and watched as time and the effect of the success they'd always wanted took hold. "They'd been together so long and knew each other's strengths and weaknesses so well that bickering was going to happen," says Beth. "I think they'd had enough of touring and of each other. But at the same time, every time they played they had a great time. It was natural; they'd all gotten older, they'd all gotten a bit jaded. I think a bit of therapy would have gone a long way at that point."

During the three-year hiatus that preceded the final INXS album, the other band members' lives were not as publicly trying as Michael's, but they were tumultuous, to say the least. "It was a very fractured time for us," Garry says. "Everyone was trying to get their lives together and we were so spread out over Australia, Hong Kong, and England that we lost our lines of communication." In 1993, Kirk Pengilly married Australian singer Deni Hines, with whom he shared an intense four-year relationship that ended in divorce in 1995. Garry Beers and his wife, Jodie, were more than busy raising their two children; Andrew Farriss and Shelley were expecting their third, Matthew.

Jon Farriss married in 1992 but the union was not destined to last, and by 1997, he was embroiled in a grueling divorce. "Of all of the Farriss brothers, I think fame and all that came with it took its toll hardest on Jon," Tim's wife, Beth, says. "He grew up on the road and he learned about life from such an intense, unrealistic perspective. He endured a lot of heartache and a lot of problems. Of any of them, I think life had its way with Jon."

As everyone in the band dealt with their ch-ch-ch-changes, their situation suffered a tremendous blow: their seventh member, manager Chris Murphy, resigned. Chris had become increasingly less interested in living and breathing nothing but INXS and relations between he and his charges grew strained. He'd moved to England in 1992, and put staffers like Sam Evans, Martha Troup, and tour manager Michael Long in charge of the band's daily affairs. Murphy was unmarried then, with two teenage daughters he'd hardly seen for their entire lives. They became his number-one priority, as did his other lifelong passion: polo. He was welcome in England's upper echelon through his skill for the game, and became as likely to play polo with Prince Charles as he was to show up backstage at a U2 or Oasis show. Murphy was by now in his forties, and the idea of running a record and publishing company and expanding his management roster appealed to him: it was a new challenge, one that required less time on the road. He began to pursue young Australian talent to sign to his management and publishing company, which was funded by the cash he'd earned by working with INXS. This did not go unnoticed by the band.

"We started to feel shafted by Chris as the nineties went on," Kirk says. "He started to manage other bands and he started a publishing company and then a record label, and soon we weren't getting the attention that we were used to receiving from him. We resented that his staff were the only ones tending to our affairs, because, let's face it, the only reason he had an office and fifty people working for him in the first place was because of us."

Chris Murphy had no intention of leaving INXS high and dry, however: after INXS fulfilled their contract with Atlantic Records, he secured them a deal for more money—yet less freedom—than they'd ever had. Murphy had favored licensing deals and representation by different record labels for different world territories. Much of that strategy's success was due to his boundless energy, tireless effort, and finessing of the various corporate players involved. The last deal he did for the band signed them to one label globally, ensuring that none of that juggling was necessary, because Murphy trusted no one but himself to pull it off.

Murphy's parting gift to INXS was a multi-album, international distribution deal with Mercury Records for a reported 40 million dollars. He then took the initial advance and did what he'd always done with their cash assets: invested it. He opened a very stable, conservative Merrill Lynch portfolio that would ensure steady, low-risk growth and guarantee them a consistent income. "Looking back on what he did, it's clear that he set up that deal for us because he wanted to leave us with a nest egg before he quit as our manager," Kirk says. "When it really came down to him quitting, he told us that he was ready to recommend a few great managers who could take care of us. He said he'd left everything completely in order so that whoever we chose would have an easy time of it taking up the reins."

Chris Murphy's departure was the equivalent of a band member leaving INXS. He'd stormed the corporate music castle, played labels against one another to the band's benefit, and handled the business end profitably without compromising their credibility. At his best, Murphy was as innovative in his management as the band was in their music. The band respected him, and while they'd not always agreed, they'd always compromised. "There were many times over the years when they staged a mutiny," Chris says. "They'd come to the office and make Michael or Kirk speak for them and say things like, 'We don't like your attitude. Can't you be a bit nicer?' And we'd talk and I'd explain that I had to have a bad attitude to get our business done, so it wasn't so easy to have a really nice attitude the very next day. But I always listened, and when they did ask me, I really did try to be a little bit nicer."

"Chris and I had a Robin Hood philosophy when putting the band's deals together," says their former lawyer, Bill Leibowitz, who now works for Sanctuary Records and Management. "We wanted to steal from the rich and give to the poor—the band were the poor and the rich were the record companies, and it really was a lot of fun. We were relentless strategy players. Timing was so important, as was setting up a competitive marketplace so that you never let your contractual partners feel comfortable. We always prided ourselves on acquiring something extra for the band." Leibowitz and Murphy paid attention to detail and took the time to ensure that their requirements were met in all of the band's deals—advantages that saved them. For example, Leibowitz labored ceaselessly to include a clause in the Mercury contract that stated, should any of the members die, that the band not be responsible for returning any of their advance. Good thing he had, otherwise they'd have be cutting checks made out to their employer before the end of Michael's funeral. "That extra bit of tactical thinking really can make all the difference in people's lives." Leibowitz says. "They were such nice guys that I loved delivering such results to them. Sometimes I look back at those old deals and think, Damn, that was good! I've dealt with just about every well-known manager over the years and Chris, when he was at his peak of being a manager, he was one of the smartest, most astute people I have ever met. He was also one of the great manipulators of business people that I have ever seen. He could take the top music executive in the world and wrap him around his little finger. He has an amazing ability to read people and figure out how to interact with them to get what he wanted. It is a truly great natural talent. If Chris had different goals, he could have ridden that to the nth degree."

That simpatico faded fast as the band's commercial success took a downturn in the nineties. Murphy's move to England did nothing to win points with several of the band members, those who blamed him for their slide in sales. The friction came to a head—as tensions often do in relationships—via arguments over money. "After we'd really enjoyed success, our lawyer, Bill Leibowitz, rang me one day and said that the band wanted to reduce my commission," Murphy says. "Michael said that they felt that my commission was excessive. It was just another mutiny. I told Bill to reduce it and to tell the band that I'd reduce the time I spent on their career accordingly. That was fine with me. INXS was getting one hundred percent of my life. I was living in England and I was working about eighteen hours a day: I'd get up at six a.m. to make calls to America and be up until two a.m. to speak to Australia. My children never saw me, I didn't have a wife or a girlfriend, and I didn't know any manager that worked as hard as I did."

The final straw was Murphy's handling of the Mercury money. It isn't clear if it was a unanimous motion, but a majority of the band demanded that Chris fork over their piece of the initial advance, his conservative investment plan be damned. Everything exploded when Murphy flew to Sydney to meet with everyone but Michael in order to plan the creative direction of the next album. "All I wanted to talk about was how to get the band back on track," Murphy says. "And all they wanted to talk about was how quickly they could get the money out of the investment fund. Some of them wanted to hand it over to Colin Diamond, who was the advisor handling Michael's funds at the time as well as a few of the other guys' as well." Diamond, a barrister and private investment broker based in Australia's posh Gold Coast, was a bit of a character known for his flashy dress and tremendous white Rolls-Royce. "I remember them telling me that Colin thought that the band's money was being wasted in the type of portfolio I'd set up," Chris Murphy recalls. "He'd convinced them that such a large sum of money should be doing more than earning interest—it should be generating tremendous capital. I told them that if they trusted a guy named Colin Diamond more than Merrill Lynch, one of the oldest investment firms on the planet, it was fine with me. They were welcome to do what they pleased with their money. And that really was it for me: I went home that night and I knew that I was through being their manager."

Murphy woke up the next day and phoned his eldest daughter, whose godfather was Michael Hutchence, to tell her that he didn't think he was going to manage INXS anymore. "Good," she said. "They got to have you for the first fifteen years of my life, now I'd like you back." Murphy's next call was to Michael. He told Michael that he was resigning as the band's manager to spend more time with his family. He offered to advise Paul Craig, the man who had become Hutchence's personal manager, on how to position the singer's upcoming solo album and help out in any other way he could. Michael laughed out loud—at first he thought Chris was joking.

Murphy then drove to his office at MMA Management and wrote a formal resignation letter. He didn't call his lawyer first, nor did he call his accountant, nor did he immediately inform his staff; he just scribbled his farewell notice, faxed it off to the members of the band, and drove home. And nearly every day for the next two years, Chris Murphy spent most of his morning shower talking himself through a list of what he needed to do for INXS that day. Sometimes it wasn't until he was nearly dry and ready to dress that he remembered that he'd left that life behind.

Michael told Chris that he understood why he wanted to move on. Not everyone in the band felt the same way. "It was the first time in my whole life in the band that I was ever really angry at Chris," Tim Farriss says. "After he left we had no manager and no control. He bailed at the right time; I guess he could see trouble coming. He had things going on in his life, but so did we. It felt like the captain of our ship had run off in the night. I'm still hostile toward him for leaving us when he did."

The band lost their manager, but they got what they wanted: they extracted their money from the Merrill Lynch portfolio and some of them handed their share over to Colin Diamond. Murphy, in part, understood what they were buying into; Diamond told them that the market share of their investments was flat, and that the capital could earn better in more dynamic markets. The band didn't realize that the portfolio wasn't designed for a quick profit; it was built to earn in the long-term. "Years later, when the market started to take off again in the last half of the nineties, I calculated that they would have nearly tripled their money if they'd left it where I'd put it," Murphy says. "And that would have been a very large sum, indeed."

It took the band some time to settle on a manager. They called upon those who had worked for them in various quasi-managerial capacities over the years, such as former tour manager Michael Long; former road manager Gary Grant; Sam Evans; as well as Martha Troup, the former wife of INXS's lawyer, Bill Leibowitz, and one-time assistant to Chris Murphy, who had run the New York office for many years. Eventually INXS, at Michael's insistence, signed up Paul Craig to oversee the band's international affairs and Martha Troup to represent their North and South American interests. Troup also managed Michael's projects outside of INXS, most notably the solo record that was unfinished at the time of his death.

"In my opinion, everything got worse at this point because everyone who stepped in to work with the band tried to elevate Michael to be more of a star than he ever wanted to be," former road manager Bruce Patron says. "They shouldn't have done it. I'm not saying that that is why Michael died, but I don't think those people knew him well enough to advise him on anything. He'd lived his life on the road, and only those people who spent time with him on the road really knew him. I don't think Chris Murphy even knew him that well as time went on."

When the band reconvened in 1996 to record *Elegantly Wasted,* their last album with Michael Hutchence, they were more creatively in tune than they'd been in years, but were, in every other respect, stretched to the breaking point.

"There was tension within the band," Martha Troup says. "Michael was getting into film and was really inspired by his prospects there. He was thinking of doing other things. And everybody was just getting tired. They'd been on such a high that was hard to resurrect. They were at a low point and weren't sure if they had the energy to see them through it."

Paula and Michael were settling into parenting, while Yates continued to fight with her ex-husband over her access to their three children. Paula portrayed Geldof as a terrible man and unfit father, which riled Michael to no end. Until the court awarded Geldof custody in October, Michael, convinced that Paula would win the legal battle, was intent on being a father to all of Paula's children. "All of a sudden, the world's greatest rock star, even though they weren't married, had a wife and four kids," Garry Beers says. "Her children were aged sixteen to nine, and then there was Tiger, and Paula wasn't handling the situation at all. She was taking happy pills every now and then, it was a circus. If you ask me, Bob did what he had to do to ensure that the courts ruled in his favor in the custody battle."

Michael's relationship with Paula was especially hard on Tim Farriss. Tim did not approve of his friend's affair with Yates when it began, nor did he see a happy ending for the couple, even when they announced that they'd marry sometime in 1997. Tim, who'd been happily betrothed since 1981, had always believed that Michael should be a father, not only because he loved children, but because Hutch needed a grounding influence and to experience the pure, selfless love that comes with parenthood. "It got really hard for me to feel that we could be friends again in a really full way because we'd lost touch with each other tremendously," Tim says. "I thought that Tiger would help him, and help everything he was struggling with internally. I thought that once he was a father, he'd gain perspective. But I don't think he did. His relationship with Paula was such a fucking freakshow, that it was impossible for me to relate to them, especially as parents."

Michael wasn't the only one dealing with dark times and emotional duress; Jon's divorce was destroying him. "It was totally horrible," he says. "We could not communicate, at all, even though I tried. Throughout the recording of the album and the tour that followed, I spent every spare moment dealing with it, from the legal issues, to the pain I was in."

In addition, the Farriss boys lost their mother, Jill, to cancer in 1995. *Elegantly Wasted* is dedicated to her memory. She'd been diagnosed with the disease in 1991 and her battle with the illness weighed heavily upon them. She'd been a caretaker, a selfless supporter of all of their endeavors, and a nurturing soul that taught each of them the meaning of compassion.

For his part, Kirk had survived a divorce from Australian singer Deni Hines and rebounded with a period of debauchery that gained momentum when he began a relationship with Louise Hegarty, a reknowned Sydney DJ. They shared a love for dance music and each other, but their chemistry was intense, manic, and overwhelming. They'd fight fiercely, party hearty, and the drama that ensued distracted Kirk tremendously.

It makes sense that the band members recall little of recording *Elegantly Wasted.* They worked at the Armory Studio, in Vancouver, B.C., with Bruce Fairburn and Andrew Farriss producing, and felt good about their new material. There is, however, one noteworthy story to be had. First, a bit of background: in 1996 at England's Brit Awards (the U.K. equivalent of the Grammys), Michael presented Oasis with Best Album, which they won for *(What's the Story) Morning Glory?* When the notorious brats arrived at the podium, Noel Gallagher looked at Michael and said that a has-been shouldn't be presenting awards to "gonna-bes."

Months later, in Dublin, while Andrew and Michael were visiting with their friends U2 and putting the finishing touches on the album demos, Michael met Bono one night at a pub, where Oasis singer Liam Gallagher showed up. The three front men sat down, drank freely, and as the night wore on, young master Gallagher became quite intolerable. As he's wont to do, Liam grew incomprehensible, belligerent, and very, very loud. Finally Michael had had enough.

“Hey, man, why don’t you shut up and sit down, you’re being a fucking asshole,” he said. “We’re just trying to have a good time, what the fuck are *you* doing?”

Liam garbled a threat, stood up, and got in Michael’s face. And Bono got between them keeping the peace as only he could, until Liam calmed down. The next day, photos of Liam and Bono nose-to-nose appeared in tabloids everywhere and mistakenly reported that the two nearly came to blows. No punches were thrown, but the incident put an end to the night.

Michael left the pub and returned to the studio, where he ran into Andrew Farriss, who was off to bed. “He said, ‘Man, don’t worry, you don’t need to stay, I just want to rerecord some background vocals. I don’t think I did a very good job of them today,’ ” Andrew recalls. Michael and the engineer spent the next hour or so doing just that, adding layers to the chorus of the album’s title track, “Elegantly Wasted.” No one realized exactly what Michael had done until six months later in Chicago, while Andrew and Michael were doing press at a radio station.

“I’ve been listening to this chorus over and over—great song, by the way, guys—but I’ve got to ask you, are you saying ‘I’m better than Oasis’? I swear I hear that on the backing vocals,” the DJ said. Andrew’s face flushed while Michael sat in silence, smirking like the cat who’d swallowed the canary. Andrew stuttered the best response he could: “Well, no, the chorus, as far as I know, is ‘I am elegantly wasted.’ I’m not sure what you’re hearing but that’s what we’re singing . . . Right, Michael?”

Elegantly Wasted is a deft mix of rock infused with dance beats that was, in 1997, ahead of the pack. The band’s new sound preceded U2’s similarly styled *Pop* and bridged the gap between the public’s taste for post-grunge rock anthems, and the slinky mechanical seduction of electronica.

The tour to support *Elegantly Wasted* started in South Africa, INXS’s first and only tour of the country. They booked a mixture of arenas and theaters around the world, with the emphasis on large venues. In the past, thanks to Chris Murphy and INXS’s agents, the band sold out nearly every tour they’d ever done. This time was different—only some of the venues sold out, which shook band morale.

To make matters worse, in addition to the responsibility of parenthood and the pressure of the very public circus that their lives had become, Michael and Paula were using heroin. And if his vocal performance never suffered, his behavior certainly did. He was clearly depressed, and the drugs made everything worse. "Michael was always a very exciting performer who did impromptu things every night. But he got very strange and erratic on stage during that tour," Jon Farriss says. "We would be playing a festival in Europe to forty or fifty thousand people, and he would climb up the scaffold and make a scene. Or he might jump into the audience and instead of walking out into the crowd, or crowd surfing above them, he would disappear *under* the stage. He'd be on the microphone, in the middle of a song, saying things like, 'Whoa, hey, man, it's *really* big down here,' while we were up there still playing, trying to figure out if we should keep the same song going until he came back or just end it early."

Paula came on the tour as often as possible, always with Tiger and one or more of her other daughters in tow. "I really liked Paula," Kirk recalls. "I thought she was intelligent and grounded and in many ways good for Michael, even though the situation outside of their relationship was as difficult as anything could ever be. But once she started drinking again, she was a different person, instantly. On that tour she was often sloppy and out of it. Tiger would be there on the bus and Paula would be falling over. It was horrible."

Michael wasn't the only band member who was unraveling. Garry Beers, who had been married for seven years to his childhood sweetheart, Jodie, and with whom he shared two daughters, struck up an affair with one of the band's backup singers. But, he wasn't the only man sleeping with a hired singer; Michael was, as well, whenever Paula was not on tour. Michael's paramour was a lesbian whom he'd seduced into heterosexuality—which, according to Beers, was the root of the thrill for Hutchence.

To say the least, the *Elegantly Wasted* tour was appropriately named. It was a far cry from the early days, and it weighed on Tim Farriss tremendously. "Those were the saddest days of my life with the band," he says. "I just didn't want to be there. I drank a lot more than I should have and didn't want to know about anything. What we needed to do was get off tour and lock ourselves in a house way out in the outback of Australia. We needed to get back to basics, and I really wish we did. We could have brought our fam-

On the set of the *Elegantly Wasted* shoot, 1996.

ilies and just hung out in a compound of our own making for a while . . . it would have changed everything."

Instead, the band returned to Sydney in November 1997 to rehearse for a week before setting off on the Australian leg of the tour—it was meant to be a triumphant big comeback. They set themselves up in the ABC Television Studios, where they'd rehearsed on and off in the past, in a room large enough to accommodate their full stage set up. The backup singers they'd hired, for better and for worse, had added new depth to the live show. "We'd never sat around and done vocal rehearsals and worked out all the timing; we were always too lazy," Kirk says. "Normally we'd just get it together while we were touring. But this time we were rehearsing really hard and Michael was in really good spirits. A few times I picked him up and we'd drive over to rehearsal together."

In fact, in the weeks and months leading up to Michael Hutchence's death, within INXS many things were better than ever. The band was more inspired than they'd been in years. They'd not found a manager on par with Chris Murphy, but they had settled on a team and written an album that were the crucial first steps into the next era of INXS.

Everyone in the band had their problems, but everyone knew that Michael really needed help. But they were hopeful because in those final months, Michael opened up to his brothers more than he ever had, and it seemed to be working. His bandmates were more a family to him than his kin, and to them those last days were full of promise. They saw a glimpse, through the dark clouds, of the Michael they knew and loved. The old Michael reached out to them, and though they did what they could, as much as he'd allow, that Michael slipped away in an instant, trailing questions and recollections that won't fade with time.

The History of Mr. Chardonnay

MICHAEL HUTCHENCE was the last rock star of the twentieth century, one whose millennial incarnation has yet to arrive. Born in Sydney, Australia, he was raised in Hong Kong—his father was an importer—and Michael attended British private schools. His family returned to Sydney when Michael was a teen and he attended Davidson High School, where Andrew Farriss and a few of his friends saved Michael from a beating by the local bullies on the first day of school. When Michael's parents divorced during his second year of high school, he moved to Los Angeles with his mother, a makeup artist, and attended Beverly Hills High. That year in L.A. changed Michael, and when he returned to Sydney, he was more confident, worldly, and well read. He had more of a swagger, and was consumed with writing poetry, but inside he was still the shy, sweet, skinny boy who'd gone off to the States. Michael grew into a sexy, silky, prowling performer as a young adult, but that boy remained inside him until the end.

Alias: Michael Hutchence

Born: January 22, 1960

Instruments: Voice

Children: Heavenly Hiraani Tiger Lily Hutchence, born 1996

Sports: jet-setting, reading, writing, seduction

First Band: Dr. Dolphin

Alternate Aliases: Dick Strangelove, Murray River, Fabien Sparkle

Died: November 22, 1997

Educated in Asia, schooled in British etiquette, Michael Hutchence was a born gentleman. While his Australian schoolmates sought intimate knowledge of nothing but surfing, girls, and cars, Michael occupied himself with girls, Asian culture, and philosophy, as well as liberal Western thinkers, like Hermann Hesse. He kept journals by then—lyrical sketch pads, really—and did so for the rest of his life. Michael cared deeply for his family, though his relationship with them was never easy; he once told a friend that the American sitcom *Married with Children* was exactly like life in his family, and that it was one of his all-time favorite shows. If Michael's funeral is any indication, he was right: his mother allegedly punched his father in the nose in the limo on the way to the ceremony. Disagreements over who should possess Michael's remains grew so heated that his ashes were split three ways.

Following his parents' divorce, Michael was close with his mother, though as an adult, their relationship fell apart; at the time of his death, they were estranged. In the months and years afterward, she and Michael's sister launched a lengthy legal battle over the distribution of Michael's estate, briefly attempted to gain custody of Michael's daughter, and wrote a tell-all chronicling their experiences and their life with Michael. Michael's father, Kell, was absent during Michael's adolescence, but they grew close in Michael's adulthood, making up for lost time. His younger brother, Rhett Hutchence, was very dear to Michael; Rhett battled with drug addiction for most of his adult life and Michael always played the savior. Rhett is rehabilitated now and chronicled his struggle and his life with his brother in a tell-all published shortly after Michael's death.

Michael's family was complicated, a union where love, obligation, trial, and tribulation met. He found a more consistent family in the Farriss brothers and INXS; he knew he could count on them. Andrew was the one who encouraged Michael to sing, coaxing him from the sidelines of the Farriss garage. He started as a backup vocalist, then took the lead, and when the Farriss Brothers got together, took on all the lead vocal parts. "When Michael got back from L.A. he was just hanging around doing some backup singing," Garry Beers recalls. "But he had something. He had something with the girls, even then. I think he knew it, but he kept it in check, until later, when he really abandoned himself to it. I think he realized that it was his job to do so and he'd best learn to officiate it."

Tim was the band's ringleader, but Michael was equally dead-set in spirit on the band's success, because he never intended to hold a job. In fact, in their leanest time, just after returning from Perth, Garry scored Michael a job at an electronics goods factory to keep Hutch above the poverty line. It didn't go well. "I got Michael out of bed and got us to work on time his first day," Garry says. "The next day I showed up at his place and woke him up, got him out, and got us there on time again. Then the third day, he just turned over in bed and I could see that he wasn't going anywhere. And that was it; he never went back. That was Michael Hutchence's one and only day job."

Michael found another extended family during the band's early days as they ascended to the top of the Australian pub circuit. Michael lived in a house with dear friends who took care of him and shared his soul with the one girl who knew him better than anyone else ever would.

Michael Hutchence had met Michele Bennett in her hometown, Melbourne, at a venue called Bombay Rock, around 1979, during a Models gig. "I was watching the show, very aware of someone's eyes on me," Michele says. "I turned around and saw Michael, a few rows back from me, just staring. I recognized him from the band, because I'd seen them before. And once I turned around, he came right over to talk to me." They didn't talk for long, because at the time, Michele was sixteen and had a curfew to deal with. The next time INXS played in Melbourne, Michele was there, and Michael watched her throughout their set. He dramatically hopped off the stage after the last song and strode directly to her table. "He was so charming and such a different person than who he was on stage," Michele says. "Even then, you could see that he had it, that he was going to be a rock star—it wasn't something that he'd have to grow into. But still, when he came over he was shy. He was so formal, he introduced himself by his full name, and asked me all about what I was studying in school. He was always so proper and English—pulling out the chair for me, everything. I remember he was so interested that I was studying Chinese."

Michael was smitten, and from the start, their relationship was sweet. They maintained contact by phone for a year until Michele finished high school and moved to Sydney to begin college. She also signed with one of Sydney's leading modeling agencies and moved in to a house in Paddington with a scenester named Nick Conroy and a singer named Jenny Morris—and before long, Michael moved in to live with Michele.

Conroy was a dapper style maven who worked for Joe Sillito, a leading fashion mogul. He'd seen INXS and approached Tim Farriss to tell him how great they were, in the men's room of the Macy's Hotel. "I was taking a piss, and there was Tim and, sure, I knew it was awkward, but I thought, Why not? and I just started telling him how great they were," Conroy says. "I ended up in some dingy hotel room of theirs, just preaching to them that they really had to understand how great a talent they were as a band. They just looked up at me a bit stunned, and completely unaware." Conroy used to take clothes from his workplace and loan them to the band for shows, and in the days before they got their image together, handed them over to his girlfriend at the time to be styled. "I was dating a shit-hot hairdresser then," he says. "And I'd have her come around and get them all into shape. They didn't even think about that then—they had no real concept of crafting an image. Well, how could they? They only had a few changes of clothes each. They were playing so much that you could smell it on them. They reeked of sweat, dirty clothes, beer—just rock and roll."

Their other housemate, Jenny Morris, became a celebrated singer-songwriter, one who toured and sang backup on several INXS albums (*The Swing, Listen Like Thieves*), and has collaborated regularly with Andrew Farriss over the years. Jenny remembers the day that Michele showed up in Sydney with Michael; he'd bought a beautiful blue and white sixties Citroën in Melbourne specifically to drive her back to Sydney. That car became their fifth housemate—it had, from the start, a mind of its own, just like its owner. "Michael never got the car registered or insured," Michele says. "I don't think he ever even bothered to get a license. Those details were never important to him. When you think about how he managed his finances later in life and set everything up so that he might live a certain way—it's interesting. He never really had a grasp of how to go about day-to-day living."

The pair returned in their French car (Melbourne to Sydney is approximately 439 miles, or 706 kilometers), with Michele's clothes and books in the trunk, and realized immediately that the motor was dangerously quirky—it behaved as if it were wired by a dyslexic. "Michael was the only one who learned how that car worked," Michele says. "He knew that you'd turn on the blinker to work the wipers. And the radio, all the rest of it—the wiring was all over the place." After six-odd hours of driving, their arrival in Sydney was anticlimatic. "That first night that we got into Sydney we literally circled the neighborhood he lived in for hours while Michael tried to remember where his house was," Michele says. "He was trying to be such a gentleman, picking me up in this beautiful car and chauffering me from Melbourne back to the house. But it didn't quite go as planned."

The Citroën became a fixture of the Paddington house; as it was Michael's pride and joy, he forbade his roommates to use it, but asked that they pamper it while he went on tour. They didn't, of course: as soon as he was gone, they drove it everywhere—and often returned home without it. "We always used to take the car somewhere and have to leave it there because it wouldn't start, or beg a mechanic come out and fix it, just to get it home," Nick Conroy says. "Michele and I took it to the beach one day, and as we returned across the Sydney Harbor Bridge, it suddenly filled with smoke. We were terrified, blindly rolling the windows down to see where we're going. Then the hood opened, covering the windshield, before it flew completely off. Somehow it didn't hurt anyone and we were able to pull over and go back and fetch it out of the middle of the road. We somehow latched it back on and made it home, and Michael never knew about any of this."

The night before Michael returned from that particular tour, however, a rambunctious driver plowed into the car, which, at the time, was parked directly in front of their house. Conroy heard it, and when he came outside, he found the Citroën smashed and the culprit's taillights fading in the distance. When Michael got home, Conroy did his best to block the sightline between Michael and his car, as he tried to explain what had happened. "Michael was heartbroken, but he didn't really care for long," Conroy says. "Material possessions were never anything special to Michael. They didn't matter to him when he had nothing, and they didn't matter to him when he had everything." The Citroën was repaired, but it finally got the best of Michael's patience: after one too many breakdowns, he abandoned it in a field, its trunk still full of his and Michele's belongings. "We got a call about three years later at the INXS office," Kirk says. "Some guy had found it on his property, with grass growing through the floorboards. It had never been registered, so there was no way to figure out whose it was, but there were books of lyrics in it to songs we'd recorded that tipped him off. He was very friendly about it, he just wanted to know if Michael had lost it and wanted it back."

Michael's roommates in Paddington went on to do great things: Michele Bennett became a top model in the eighties before establishing herself as a renowned film producer, Jenny Morris, as mentioned, is one of Australia's most respected singer-songwriters, and Nick Conroy is now based in Los Angeles and is a first assistant director in film and music video. But back then, times were lean and they did what they could to cheer one another up. When Michael got down about how far INXS was from their goals or Michele was depressed about the travel and sleaze that come with modeling, Conroy, the house jester, pooled their resources, bought a bottle of the cheapest champagne he could find, and toasted the beautiful future that awaited them.

Conroy insisted they drink out of his set of brightly colored metal cups—one of which, years later after they had made it, he sent to each of his former housemates as a memento. "I used to collect all kinds of things from the fifties, and I had these anodized metal cups, made for picnics, that to be honest had rusty bolts at the bottom of them," he says. "They were a bit off—but that's what we'd do: we'd drink cheap champagne—$3.99 a bottle. We had nothing, but it didn't matter. We were glamorous, and we knew it was coming."

Michael wasn't the best housemate: he cooked once (hash browns) in the four years they lived there, and he never, ever cleaned, though he was often asked to. He was charming enough, then and always, that he was looked after. "I remember touring north Australia and having a day off where we took boats out to a small island. We couldn't land them right on the beach, so we had to carry our picnic baskets through the water to get there," Jenny Morris says. "I have this picture of me, Michele, and the other girls all hauling these heavy loads, balancing them on our heads to keep them dry, and there in the foreground is Michael, carrying nothing. He was always such the little prince, but no one ever minded."

Beth Farriss, Tim's wife, remembers that "Michael was very shy—very, very shy. It took him a few years to flower, and to become liquid on stage. The band was always liquid on stage, but Michael had to catch up. And when he did, he became this wave, this presence that swung from side to side. Once that happened, something just took over in him: he became bigger and bigger as a performer, in every way. His clothes got bigger, his moves got bigger, and he came out of himself and became something else. It was amazing, to those who knew him, to watch the transformation, to see this lovely, gawky, skinny kid become a complete rock star."

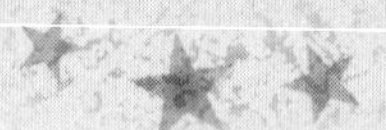

Michael Hutchence loved to read, he loved to write, and he loved to make love. He was shy, yes, but his sweet charm and inner charisma insured that he'd never slip through life unnoticed—at least, not by the female populus of planet Earth. "Michael could charm the pants off anyone—I mean it, everybody loved him," Garry Beers says. "I think he realized that he had this power over women when we were in high school, still playing together as Dr.

Dolphin—he, Andrew, and I. I remember going out with him one night and in the space of a few hours, we ran into two of his ex-girlfriends, both of whom were seeing other guys at the time, but got it on with Michael anyway. We were at a gig and he took one out to my van and I had to go get him out of there when, back in the bar, her boyfriend started wondering where she'd gone off to. We left her there, but the other ex-girlfriend and a bunch of people hopped into the van to go to a party. Michael just openly had his hand up her skirt in front of everyone in the back of the van, and she wasn't stopping him. And when we got to the party, he went off with *another* girl. All of them knew about the other ones and none of them cared: I couldn't believe it, I'm sitting there going, wow. Throughout his life, it was like that. Everyone loved him: men loved him, they wanted to be him; and women went crazy for him. I'm telling you, he was one of a kind."

Fame made Michael an icon, but there were always two Michaels: the boy who remained unsure of himself, the one who cared to make everyone else's life better before caring for his own, and the confident, indulgent rock star who epitomized bohemian utopia. The two sides were ideologically fused—both refused to come to terms with reality, and generally didn't have to.

"Michael was always a gentleman," Bono says. "If there was somebody in the room who needed to be made to feel at home, he'd do that. He always had the best lines. One of my favorites was, 'There's no one more obsessed with stars than other stars.' And you know, everything they say about him with girls is true. But in the sweetest way—there was nothing lascivious or coarse about him as a womanizer. He was just totally sweet and girls would fall for him. And yes, he would fall for them back occasionally. He had a tiny lisp, you see, that broke women's hearts—don't forget that lisp of his. They all wanted to mother him, all of them. It's hard to explain other than that he was flirtatious in a very becoming way. He made women feel *fantastic.*"

Michael always took notice of the quiet ones in his orbit, those unable to express themselves in a crowd. It was as if, once the former wallflower had evolved into a peacock, he identified with what he used to be, and strove to make others comfortable. But it was never contrived. Michael truly loved people; he loved hearing their stories, he loved, if he could, making their lives better, he loved humanity and all of its forms and flaws.

They were once much the same, but as they grew and as fame came upon them, Michael could not have been more unlike his musical collaborator Andrew Farriss. Yet they shared a creative bond borne of contrast and the desire to satisfy each other. "Michael was always asking me what he could do better musically," Andrew says. "He had such an ability to grab an audience or a listener's attention and never let go. You wouldn't expect that kind of person to be supportive, but he always was of my talent as a writer. The work of mine that I like most is what he and I wrote together."

Toward the end, Michael told friends that he couldn't stand writing with Andrew and couldn't bear recording with the band. But those feelings were fleeting, impulsive fits—hours or days later, Michael would be excited to reunite with his musical family once again. They were his true family—and family never breaks apart. "We disagreed a lot over the years, especially later on when he got completely complex," Andrew Farriss says. "But we never, ever argued, even in the worst of times, over the big issues in life."

"When I first met Michael he was kind of shy," Bono recalls. "But he grew into himself so gracefully. My idea of a rock star is Michael. I never felt like a rock star, I've always felt like I'm impersonating one. But Michael wasn't that at all—he was the real thing. We were very good friends, and good friends learn from each other, but to be honest I think I learned more from him than he did from me. What he had was *oxygen.* He was always so much better at walking through a room than I was, you know. When we met, I was just learning to loosen up in public, and here was this guy who blew in and out of any room like a breeze. He was just so *easy* that he relaxed everyone around him. It is a strange thing when your life is coming at you so fast that suddenly you have to walk into a room where everyone knows your name but they pretend that they don't. We went through that at the same time and it made me uptight, but not Michael—he negotiated it better than anyone I'd ever seen."

Michael's persona, once it took flight, was grand: his vocal gifts and sensual showmanship were topped only by his indulgent, poetic wanderlust. It was a chronic obligation of INXS's road manager to extricate their lead singer from local beds or beaches before hauling off to the next town. "We spent a lot of time finding Michael," former security chief Jeff Pope says. "We spent just as much time waking him up. He was able to remain asleep through almost anything. At the same time, he was a very self-reliant man. Even when he was wacked out of his head, his head was still on." In other words, wherever he wandered, Michael always found a safe place to sleep—and they realized that quite often he'd found one on the nearest beach. "We once lost Michael in Nice and proceeded to pilot our giant tour bus through these narrow French streets," Pope says. "And where did we find him? On a bench, next to the beach, looking like a beggar."

Michael had spent that night with Richard Lowenstein, who left him there and laughed, when, as Michael reached his hand out to wave good-bye, a passing man put money in his palm, taking him for a bum. It couldn't have been more ironic: Michael cared little for money, and had a lot of it. But he did put a high price on certain inexplicably indispensable possessions. One of them was a tank top he often wore on stage (seen on the cover of *Listen Like Thieves*), emblazoned with a phrase from "Dancing on the Jetty" (*The Swing*): "Watch the world argue." Somewhere in Ohio in the late eighties, Michael forgot to retrieve said article of clothing from the hotel laundry service before taking off, and then insisted that the bus turn around to fetch it. "It cost them about five hundred dollars to go back and get it, not including the laundry cost," Jeff Pope says. "He'd worn it so much by then that it was nearly a piece of string. I remember when he took it out of the laundry box, everyone on the bus just stared at this bit of cloth, like, '*That's* what we went back for?'"

"People assume that Michael was nothing but this big-headed rock star," Jenny Morris says, "but he never became that. He was always incredibly interested in other people, no matter how big a celebrity he was. There's a reason why men and women loved Michael—it was because he gave everyone the time of day. He'd look you in the eye and you knew that he was listening to you and that he was interested in what you were saying. He was one of the smartest, worldliest, wisest people that I've ever known. He had a gift, the same one that people like Bill Clinton have—he could make you feel special without even meaning to."

INXS fans remember Michael for many things, while the world at large remembers him more for his excesses than the one thing we should all miss most of all, the one thing Michael had that was never properly celebrated or justly recognized: Michael possessed a beautiful, nimble voice as rich as the greatest singers in rock and roll. He wasn't a natural; he worked hard to master his phrasing and improve his range, and spent hours on end in the studio until he was satisfied that he'd truly gotten inside a song. "I've never heard any critic declare that Michael Hutchence was a great singer, and it really pisses me off," Chris Murphy says. "I've read about all the drugs he took, all the girls he fucked, and how wild he was, but no one has ever said the truth: Michael had one of the sexiest, most fantastic voices I've ever heard. He's one of the greatest in rock history. Everyone should go back and listen to those songs right now—that guy had an incredible voice."

Bono knew he did. When the U2 front man first heard *Kick,* he was floored by the power of Michael's presence, and how the clean, unprocessed production captured his vocal gifts. "Michael's whisper on 'Need You Tonight' was so remarkable," Bono says. "We did *The Joshua Tree* that next year and I did a similar whisper on 'With or Without You.' He and I were kind of bumping into each other there."

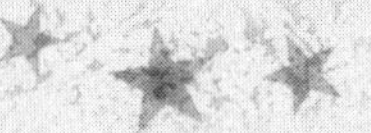

Michael was made to be a rock star: he sauntered like a cat, with brown eyes that burned of intellect and carnal knowledge. Women threw themselves at him, many in sight of their husbands and boyfriends—often with their consent. Michael loved sex and he got plenty of it, everywhere he went. And though some would say he only truly fell in love once, he spent his life in love with many.

"Michele was the female Michael," Joanne Petersen says. "They both had the long, curly hair, they looked great together, and you could see the very deep love between them. She was the love of his life, really." When INXS became the international band they'd always hoped to be on the back of *Kick* in 1987, Michael Hutchence embraced the rock star within, the role the world demanded of him. He'd been with his soul mate, Michele, for seven years, but their relationship could not survive what came next. "We broke up in 1987 and got back together on and off for a year," Michele says. "Then we really ended it and didn't speak for about a year. It was very painful."

"I think he felt that she was holding him back from really being a rock star," Kirk says. "She was grounding and he really wanted to *be* it, to live it and to do it. She was so down to earth that she made him feel like he was being held back."

Once Michael left Michele, he engaged in serious relationships with a pop star, the world's top supermodel, and a television personality. Kylie

Minogue was Michael's next girlfriend, and he transformed the Australian soap star from a good girl into a sex kitten within months. Years later, Kylie labeled Michael "the sweetest boy she'd ever met," and many close to Michael say that other than Michele, Kylie was the only woman who grounded Michael enough that he might still be here if their relationship hadn't faded.

Michael Hutchence met supermodel Helena Christensen while he was still with Kylie. Michael and Helena grew close from afar, through long phone calls, until they finally had dinner one night in New York. Kylie was flying in to meet Michael the next day, but he didn't want to see her. "I had dinner with Helena and Michael and a bunch of the band and our friends that night at the Plaza Hotel," Mark Opitz recalls. "Michael and Helena chatted away in a corner—nothing outrageous at all. You could tell that Michael was serious about her. She was great for him—she's a very non-model model."

It wasn't smooth and it wasn't easy, but Michael broke up with Kylie and took up with Helena. The couple stayed together for the next five years, spending most of them at the villa Michael bought in the South of France and in Helena's home in Copenhagen, where, in 1995, Michael suffered the accident that triggered the injury and depression that changed his life.

Michael's accident left him battered enough to require two weeks' recovery in a hospital. His injuries destroyed his sense of smell and marked the onset of a complex change in his brain chemistry. Anosmia—the loss of the sense of smell—is a common, permanent condition among the aged. It is often an early symptom of Parkinson's or Alzheimer's disease. Among younger people, it is most often those who smoke or indulge in stimulants who suffer a reduction in their ability to smell, as they grow closer to forty. Of the two hundred thousand or so cases of anosmia reported in America per year, 15 percent are caused by head trauma; most often, those cases are temporary, as the olfactory neurons are among the few in the human body capable of regeneration following injury.

Michael's sense of smell, however, did not return—a fact that bears mention. Humans can discern approximately ten thousand or so odors, and taste, as we know it, is more a result of the receptors in the nose than those in the tongue. Try tasting food while holding your nose; you'll not be able to taste much difference between an apple and a carrot. Losing the sense of smell is, essentially, losing the ability to taste, and Michael dearly loved both. Studies have shown that those who lose just one of their primary senses unequivocally suffer depression, and are three times more likely to commit suicide. "He and I spent a long night catching up just a year before he died, and he told me how much his loss of smell depressed him," producer Nick Launay (*The Swing*) says. "He said one of the most rock-star things I've ever heard. He said, 'Nick, do you know the worst part about it? Do you know what I can't stand? I can't taste my girlfriend's pussy.'"

His girlfriend at that time was Paula Yates, who left her husband, Bob Geldof, for Michael. When their affair went public, Michael lost Helena Christensen and began a tumultuous, complicated relationship that bore him a gorgeous daughter but tested the very limits of his soul.

Michael's accident signaled the onset of his troubles—he grew bitter and self-destructive in the years that followed, but even at his lowest, Michael cared to please others first. He gave his audience what they wanted onstage and off; and he showed his old friends how he used to be, as best he could, unto the end.

Michael's death in 1997 was a swift, surprising shock, an event that left behind questions with no answers. It was clear to everyone who cared that he'd been battling depression since the accident and had taken to more alcohol, prescription drugs, and then heroin to kill the pain. His relationship with Paula and the band's first-ever ebb in their commercial success did little to abate his darkness, and as it worsened, Michael cut off the friends who told him the truth: that he was less in control of his life than he thought. Instead, he spent his time with whoever told him what he wanted to hear: the party friends who swarm around those of Michael's caliber in VIP rooms everywhere. His true friends hoped that the birth of his daughter, Tiger Lily, would ground him. And she did: Michael loved his daughter with every bit of his being. He did everything he could to make a stable home for her, but in the end, the twists and turns in his relationship with Paula proved too insurmountable to do so.

In the months before his death, Michael made an effort to reconnect with his oldest friends; those he knew, despite the years, still knew him best. At his house in France, on a wall in the front hall, he made a collage of pictures of them, and of himself, in every stage from boy to man. It was a photographic map of his life, of where he'd begun and what he'd become, and the dearest souls he'd known along the way; it was an attempt to find his way back and make sense of it all. He spoke openly to Garry and Kirk about his relationship with Paula on that last tour, and they weren't the only ones who felt that Michael finally knew that he'd gotten involved in something too hard to handle. He had begun to realize that it couldn't be fixed and he wanted out for himself and his daughter.

Some close to Michael believe that he regarded death as his only escape. Tony Woodhall, Michael's personal security guard for the last six years of his life, saw Michael in the depths of despair more than a few times. At those moments, he saw a man that might view suicide as an option. "The night he died, I think Michael had an argument with Paula, then an argument with Bob, then he took a shower, and in there, under the water, he thought about it more, and felt even worse. And then he got out and he just did it," Woodhall says. "That's what I think happened. I've seen him get that depressed before."

During the recording of *Elegantly Wasted,* INXS's last album with Michael, Andrew Farriss was very aware that his writing partner was in a fragile frame of mind. Michael was writing lyrics that were more personal than ever—they explored his complex relationship with his family, his troubled personal life, and revealed more of his deep-seated feelings than any lyrics he had ever written. "He had a burning passion to say how he felt on that album," Andrew says. "It was overwhelming, because he was desperate to put it all down accurately. We'd worked together for so many years, and usually I'd question a lyric here or there, but on that album I didn't even go there. I just supported him because it was so clear to me how much he was trying to write passionate lyrics from his heart. I think, on that album, he said everything he'd always wanted to say."

Michael was very sensitive and compassionate, yet often anger got the best of him. Michele recalls one time that Michael was so upset that he nearly drove them both into a wall. "I don't even remember what he was angry about, but we were on his motorcycle and he took off, full speed, right at this corner," she says. "There was a wall straight ahead and we barely turned away in time. I never forgot it—it was the first time I saw that side of him."

After a soccer match between Ireland and Italy in the early nineties, Bono saw a similar wild abandon in his friend. Bono, his wife, Ali, Helena Christensen, and Michael had crossed from France to Italy to see the match and, afterward, went in search of a bar. "I remember him walking through the streets while these Italians screamed by in their cars," Bono says. "He went into the road, he was dancing with the oncoming traffic; they were bulls and he was a bullfighter. I remember saying, 'Hey, Mike, watch out, okay?' He just kept on. It was a little bit of 'that's who you are.' He wanted to get too close to what was coming around the corner."

As much as he tempted fate, Michael did not openly identify with suicide. He told Bono that if Kurt Cobain had been able to experience the life Michael had made for himself in France, one divorced from the pressures of being a rock star in America, Kurt would never have killed himself. Michael was convinced that, regardless of the physical pain (chronic stomach aches and back pain) and depressive angst that Cobain suffered, he'd still be alive if he'd been able to leave his home without suffering the insecurity brought on by the constant attention that came with his iconic success.

Michael Hutchence's death was ruled a suicide by the authorities. But the true authorities are those who knew him best, and their opinions are divided: some who saw him during the last year of his life saw a man in distress, on many drugs, and unwilling to truly be helped. Others claim that no depression or substance known to man could have driven Michael, a spirit stronger than any they'd known, to suicide. No one but Michael will ever know the truth, but if the research and soul-searching that informed this book is testimony as strong—if not stronger—than any coroner's report, Michael Hutchence's death was an accident, a mishap that occurred while following his bohemian soul to the edge of human experience.

"Australians just don't commit suicide," Nick Launay says. "They're far too happy to ever do that. And they're too strong. Michael loved life far too much to have ever done that. No, his death was an accident."

Considering Hutchence's boundless libido and sexual curiosity, factoring in the loss of sensation following his accident, it's altogether likely that Hutchence embraced autoeroticism in an effort to compensate. "Michael was always very kinky," Garry Beers says. "I slept in rooms next to his for years and let me tell you, the sounds I heard coming out of there, I still have no idea what he was doing to those girls."

It took Bono three years to write a song that made sense of Michael's passing. "Stuck in a Moment (You Can't Get Out Of)," from 2000's *All That You Can't Leave Behind,* became an American anthem for 9-11 healing, but it was written as the message to Michael that Bono never did deliver. "I didn't want to write a saccharine, sentimental song for him," Bono says. "I wanted it to be tough. It is the argument I should have had with him, put into a song. It's all the things I should have done if I were there. But I wasn't. It's just saying, 'Please, stop this. Please, please wake up.' You could have that kind of a conversation with Michael. He'd hear you. I just wish I had."

Michael Hutchence will forever be missed and he'll always be remembered for what he was—beautiful, generous, wise, and larger than life. "Michael spoke about life as a pendulum, in that the harder you pushed it, the harder it came back," Andrew Farriss says. "It's the basis of the song 'The Swing,' and I've always felt that if you believe in karma, or God, or anything spiritual, that analogy makes sense of this grand experience we call life."

Not Enough Time for All That I Want for You

MICHAEL HUTCHENCE DIED ON THE MORNING of November 22, 1997, in Room 524 of the Ritz-Carlton Hotel, Double Bay, in Sydney, where he was checked in under the name Murray River. That afternoon, housekeeping found his lifeless body. He was naked, on his knees, leaning face first against the back of the door. There was a belt fastened around his neck. The other end of it had been attached to the self-closing mechanism at the top of the door, but the weight of Michael's body had broken it free sometime between his passing and his discovery. In the room, police found photos of his daughter, as well as a book on autoerotica, the sexual act of strangulation during masturbation to achieve a heightened orgasm. There were no illicit substances on the scene, only a bottle of the antidepressant Prozac, prescribed to Hutchence. The coroner's autopsy revealed traces of cocaine, alcohol, Prozac, and what were officially reported as "other prescription drugs" in Michael Hutchence's bloodstream. His death was ruled a suicide by hanging. The estimated time of death was 10 a.m.

Hindsight is a curious condition: it allows us to cast the past in a context of our choosing. But tragedy casts the past in a stark light that renders hindsight insignificant. Tragedy is revelatory. Tragedy tears the moments that precede and follow it out of time. And those moments are what we remember most, because in those moments we learn the lesson tragedy teaches us—that life passes quickly, and that all that we hold dear can disappear in an instant.

Michael Hutchence spent November 21, his last day on earth, among loved ones: first his bandmates, then his father, Kell, and stepmother, Susie, with whom he'd grown very close. On the 21st, INXS had two days to go until they began a thirteen-date romp around Australia billed as a celebration of their twentieth anniversary. "It was a good time," Kirk recalls. "Everyone had things going on in their personal lives, but everyone was in high spirits and we were all in the same place again, back home in Australia, hanging out together in a way that we hadn't for a decade."

Michael joined INXS at ABC Studios during the afternoon and caught up with those of the band's crew that he hadn't seen. To all present, he appeared to be very happy. He'd asked a band associate to bring his Harley-Davidson to the studio, where he proceeded to ride it into the building, up in the elevator, and into the rehearsal room. He then burnt rubber until the place was filled with smoke. "Someone had a video camera there all that day and I have a copy of it," Michael's security guard, Tony Woodhall says. "Michael was being such a rock star. He was smiling, telling stories, and then he tore in on his bike. I remember after he died, his father called me to ask if he could see any videos I might have of Michael just before his death. He was looking for clues, for some understanding of how Michael was just before he died."

The band played well that day and the last time they saw him, Michael was laughing. "It felt like the tour was a bit of a midlife crisis for everyone because we were all dealing with things in our personal lives, as well as within the band," Garry says. "We'd been through management changes and even though we'd always played well, we'd finally returned to a place where we felt that we were working hard with a purpose. And Michael was the force behind that. He was really into all of us being together, hanging out together and making music together like we hadn't done in years." When rehearsal wound down that day, Michael made his exit by re-creating a Monty

Python sight gag the band had always adored: John Cleese's stiff-legged march of the Ministry of Silly Walks. "I feel most fortunate about the way we said good-bye," Andrew says. "My last memory of him is watching him turn around as he went out the door, smiling, laughing, and waving to us."

Tim Farriss does not share Andrew's sentiment: he and Hutchence did not part on the best of terms. Tim had expressed frank disapproval of Michael's affair on tour and how his friend was handling his complicated family life. Michael dismissed Tim's opinion and advice, insisting that he and Paula would be better parents to her daughters than Geldof could ever be. Michael thought he could do it all: be a rock star, be a dad, carry the band, and be the hero who rescued Paula and her girls. He told Tim that if he could find Paula a job in Australian television, all would be well; she'd have a reason to relocate. Furthermore, since Bob had agreed to share custody of their daughters (though, legally, the court had awarded custody to him), Michael believed that he could convince Bob to let Paula move all of the girls down under. And then, Michael assured him, they'd all live happily ever after.

Tim pointed out the obvious—that there was no way in hell that Geldof would willingly let his daughters go. He reminded Michael that he'd stolen Bob's wife, which was bad enough, so to expect that he might easily poach the man's children as well, was utter madness. They argued heatedly, and the last time they would ever speak, Tim stormed off. Michael died before they had a chance to reconcile, and to this day, Tim is haunted by the fact that the last words he shared with a man he so dearly loved were cross.

Tim's wife, Beth, has watched Tim struggle with his guilt since the day Michael died. It's been nearly a decade and Tim still can't discuss it without tears. "Tim has suffered so much regret over Michael's death," Beth Farriss says. "He blames himself, as everyone does when someone dies that way. But there's not the 'one thing' anyone could have done to save him. Michael was much more complicated than that. He had many, many layers and there was more going on than he was ever going to let anyone know. It's just so sad. Michael was such a lovely, gentle, soft, ethereal young man when we first met him. He was sensitive and deep, but very sociable. But in his older days he became so angry and aggressive. He'd pick fights; he'd say absolutely unnecessary things obviously meant to hurt people. It was partly ego, and partly chemical. It was hard to watch, because that other side of him was still there. That side of him would come out whenever he saw a child. He loved children so much and they loved him, too. It's still so hard for me to believe that his death was deliberate because he just adored his daughter and would have never purposefully abandoned her."

In the early evening of November 21, Michael left the studio to meet his father, Kell (who passed away in 2002, just two weeks after the fifth anniversary of his son's death), and stepmother, Susie, for dinner at the Flavour of India restaurant, walking distance from the Ritz-Carlton. He was there for two-and-a-half hours holding court, charming the staff; at one point, he leapt from the table to plant a kiss on the enthralled assistant-manager's lips. Those interviewed after the fact told reporters that Michael was in high spirits—laughing, joking, and doing imitations—and that he barely touched his food, opting for countless Marlboro Lights and bottles of Bengal beer instead. Kell told reporters that he was thankful to have dined with "vintage Michael" that night. Nevertheless, his father knew that the entanglements of his son's private life weighed heavily upon him. Paula and Tiger were in England and she wasn't sure that Bob would allow her to bring her daughters, and therefore Tiger, to Australia for the Christmas holidays.

When Susie excused herself to go to the ladies' room, Kell placed his hand atop his son's and leaned across the table. "Mike, tell me, is everything okay?" he asked.

"Daddy-O, what are you worrying about? There's no trouble. I'm fine. Really, I'm fine," Michael said, smiling. "I've never felt better."

After dinner Michael returned to his hotel, where he phoned friends, inviting them to an impromptu party in his suite. "That night, Louise, my girlfriend, and I, got smashed playing cards at our friends' house," Kirk says. "We ended up sleeping over there, which was unusual—one of us would always stay sober enough to drive home. I didn't hear Michael's message until the next morning when I stopped home on my way to rehearsals. He had called around midnight, after his dinner with Kell, and had said, 'Hi, Kirk, just having a few people over tonight. Come over if you guys want to for a few drinks.' He sounded fine; I never would have thought he was in trouble hearing that. I was so sad to hear that message the next day, because we absolutely would have gone. In those last months, I was so happy to have grown closer to him. He never used to invite me to any sort of social get-together. We'd hang out on tour, but outside of that we had different circles of friends."

Michael slid into the hotel bar around 11 p.m., where he chatted up his fellow patrons, flirted with a few lovely ladies, and lavishly applauded the young woman entertaining the room on piano. An hour later, he was joined by Kym Wilson, an Australian actress with whom he'd allegedly had occasional trysts, and her boyfriend, a barrister named Andrew Rayment. After a round of drinks, the trio relocated to Michael's room so that he wouldn't miss any calls from Paula, hopefully bearing news of her imminent arrival.

Wilson, who declined to be interviewed for this book, sold her story to *Woman's Day* magazine for a large sum of money, which she publicly pledged to donate to Tiger Lily and Paula Yates. According to the article, Wilson claimed that no narcotics were consumed in Michael's room that night; the three of them drank strawberry daiquiris and champagne as Michael talked about his future. She said that he didn't seem depressed; he was excited that he'd screen-tested for Quentin Tarantino's *From Dusk Till Dawn,* and that the feedback was very positive. He hoped to land a role in the feature, and intended, after completing INXS's tour, to return to Los Angeles to pursue further opportunities in film. He also spoke at length of the trouble between Paula and Bob, emphatically characterizing Geldof as a manipulative, evil man. Wilson's boyfriend fell asleep at the foot of the bed around 4 a.m., and about a quarter of an hour later, Hutchence insisted that the pair head home.

Between 5 and 10 a.m. on November 22, Michael placed about ten phone calls and received a few as well. He spoke to Paula sometime around 6 a.m. and heard that Bob had refused to allow her to bring her daughters to Australia for the tour and the holidays, although, just a few days earlier, he'd agreed to allow two of their three children—eight-year-old Peaches and seven-year-old Pixie—to accompany her there for a few weeks. Unfortunately he changed his mind—and legally had complete control. Without her daughters, Paula and baby Tiger would not be with Michael for the holidays. Nothing was going according to Michael's plan.

By Yates's account (initially published in the U.K. tabloid *Hello!* for a reported $1.1 million, then retold—and resold—to a bevy of news outlets for fees that ranged, allegedly, from twenty to thirty thousand), Michael couldn't bear the bad news. He was instantly desperate—he said he needed her and couldn't carry the tour without her and Tiger by his side. He insisted on phoning Bob to beg him to let Yates and the girls join him. Michael called Geldof at approximately 9 a.m. (7 p.m., London time). Geldof later characterized Hutchence's temperament as "hectoring, abusive, and threatening." When asked if they'd argued, Geldof replied that they did not—he said that it isn't an argument if only one person is shouting. It wasn't the first time Michael had phoned him to ask that he allow Paula greater custody of the girls. Geldof claims that Michael had done so for months, always angry, hysterical, and sounding "like he was off his face." His last call to Geldof was so emotional that Michael's shouting woke the woman sleeping in the room next to his at the Ritz-Carlton. According to her statement to the police, she heard Michael swearing profusely and distinctly heard him scream, "*She's not your wife anymore!*"

At about 9:30 a.m., Michael left a message on Michele Bennett's answering machine. Michele awoke shortly after the call, played the message, and heard Michael sounding very drunk, mildly incoherent, and seriously upset. She was alarmed, but not surprised. "I knew all wasn't well with him," she says. "I'd been getting strange calls from him at very irregular hours in the months before, as everything with Paula got worse. One time I could hear someone else in the room and he wasn't even sure where he was. The next time I spoke to him, a few days later, he told me that everything was fine. He didn't even remember having spoken to me at all. All of it was troubling. Every time he called in such a state, he sounded terrible, just distraught and full of vitriol. It didn't sound like Michael at all—he was irrational and lacked any kind of perspective. I didn't know what to do, and since I wasn't around him every day, I didn't want to jump to conclusions."

Michele had watched fame simultaneously deepen and assuage Michael's insecurities. His ego grew into a shell once the shy boy became a rock star, but within, Michael's insecurities remained: he doubted his looks, his talent, and the strength of his character. He might have sorted it all out as he grew into manhood, but the accident in 1992 that destroyed his sense of smell, set in motion a depression that supplanted the sweet side of him with bitterness, anger, and bile. His lifestyle and his relationship with Paula exacerbated everything, from the tabloid harassment to the drama with Bob. And on top of it all, the pressures of parenthood—something that came more quickly than Michael had anticipated—plus the band's first true career lull, towed him further down the spiral.

"He just didn't want to hear that the situation he was in with Paula might not work out the way he planned," Michele said. "He was very arrogant about it. He just said, 'Well, you know, I'd be a much better dad than Bob.' He really did want to be a father, I'm sure of that. But he was so influenced by Paula's version of who Bob was that he rejected any other point of view. In the last two years of his life, he surrounded himself with people who told him what he wanted to hear, though he'd call me and a few of his other old friends because he needed our perspective. But he didn't want to hear what we had to say. He was really in a terrible way. I only found out what the last two years of his life were really like after he died."

Michael felt best making others feel better and did not honestly reveal himself to many people. He did everything he could to live in the moment, to avoid stability in his personal life—as if stability might force him to confront some inner demon. He instinctually gravitated toward relationships that would upset the status quo and disallow him any sense of constancy. "He was the type of person who would choose to get out of a romantic relationship by entering a new one," Michele says. "It wasn't always the case, but it was often enough. Or else, when he wanted out, he made the situation unworkable for the other person rather than end it outright."

In the month or so before he died, Michele was happy that Michael had taken to calling her more often, and happy to hear that he intended to spend as much time as he could with his close friends in Australia. She hoped, now that he had Tiger, that he'd come to realize how much he needed constancy in his life, a foundation from which he could be a good father. "I know that he hated living in London by then and he was eager to enjoy the familiarity of those who knew him well here," Michele says. "That makes me think that he was fed up with what his life had become, and was ready to make some changes."

However he felt that morning, after leaving a message for Michele, at 9:40 a.m. Michael called Martha Troup, his personal manager and the band's U.S. representative. She was in New York (where it was 7:40 p.m.) and did not catch the call when it came in. A few minutes later, she checked her voicemail and heard Michael's message.

"Martha, Michael here," he whispered, his voice low and thick. "I've fucking had enough."

Troup phoned his room at the hotel and got no answer. She discovered that he'd left a message for her on another of her phone numbers, just minutes after his first call. Michael's voice was laconic and nearly inaudible on that one; he sounded like a man in a trance. Troup was terrified—she called INXS's tour manager John Martin in Sydney, and ordered him to go to Michael's hotel immediately.

At 9:54 a.m., Michael Hutchence made his last phone call, again to Michele Bennett. She answered this time, and was stunned by the inconsolable tone in Michael's voice.

"I need you," he said, his voice trembling.

"It's okay, Michael, I'm on my way," she said.

Thirty minutes later, Michael did not answer when Michele phoned him from the hotel lobby. She went to his room, where she found a handwritten note he'd slid under the door. It said that he intended to sleep in. She knocked for a few minutes anyway and heard nothing. She put her ear to the door and heard nothing. She waited. And she concluded that Michael must have passed out, overcome by sadness and substances. She wrote Michael a note saying that she'd phone later and would meet him for breakfast once he awoke. Michele slipped it under the door, unaware that it came to rest beside the lifeless body of the sweet man she'd once known so well.

That afternoon, Kirk Pengilly arrived at ABC Studios, as usual, well before anyone else in the band. He'd stayed the night at a friend's house and after a brief stop at home checked his messages and heard Michael's invitation to the party in his hotel room the night before. That morning, Kirk received a call from Karen, the mother of his child, who worked in a children's clothing shop adjacent to the driveway of the Ritz-Carlton. She told him that there were cop cars and an ambulance blocking the driveway and that clearly, something weird was going on over there.

In the studio, Kirk was joined by Garry and Tim, and Tim, an insanely zealous cricket fan, brought a television into the rehearsal room to stay abreast of the day's matches. Once the entire band arrived, David Edwards and Jeff Pope informed them that something had happened in Michael's hotel room, but they knew no more. It didn't seem too unusual—something *always* happened in Michael's room. Kirk figured that a guest of his had overindulged and required medical attention. He did not even consider—none of them did—the possibility that harm had come to Michael. His bandmates were aware that Michael had been dabbling with heroin for the past few years, but they never once worried that he'd overdose; his will and constitution were stronger than that of anyone they'd ever known.

David and Jeff left the studio to find out what exactly had happened, leaving the others to take in cricket. "After two hours we started to really wonder what was going on," Kirk says. "Then, all of a sudden the cricket match was interrupted, and a newscaster reported that Michael Hutchence had been found dead in his hotel room. We were in shock. Truthfully, we didn't believe it at first." Minutes later a reporter and a cameraman from ABC News, whose headquarters were located in the same building, burst in to the rehearsal room to interview them. They kicked them out, and panic set in; Tim ran to the bathroom and threw up. "We immediately locked every door and wouldn't let anyone in," Kirk says. "And we began to realize that this was very, very real."

Soon after, David and Jeff returned and confirmed the terrible truth. Tony Woodhall and the band's tour manager arrived moments later, with several cars to shuttle them out of the studio and away from the media storm that had already gathered. Andrew was taken to a friend's house and eventually returned home to his wife and children. Kirk owns a farm a few hours from Sydney, and after meeting his girlfriend, Louise, who had fetched Kirk's daughter, April, from school to protect her from the press, they made their way there.

Kirk's farm is located in Kangaroo Valley, which at the time, was alight with brush fires. They drove through the smoke, an apocalyptic orange glow on the horizon. "The whole valley was the color of an intense sunset, overhung with ominous black clouds," he says. "When I got there, I got smashed, just completely smashed drunk. Eventually I crawled into bed, and during the night I had this dream. Michael visited me in the dream. He was an owl and I was standing in a field and he spoke to me, and he said, 'Don't worry, I'm finally free. It's better this way. I'm really, *really* at peace now, so don't be upset. I'm finally free.' I woke up after that, looked at the clock, saw that it was three a.m., and then I walked outside into the field behind my house and bawled my eyes out. There was moonlight coming through the smoke and I could see the mountains and I cried until the sun came up."

Michael's death sent Garry Beers into a trance. He'd lost himself in the past few months, and watched his life change drastically. In a short space of time, he had lost his self-respect, his marriage, and now his friend Michael. Michael's death also brought up feelings of loss that Garry had yet to come to terms with. Garry's father, Bill, had succumbed to lung cancer in 1991, and though the two men spent enough time together toward the end that they were able to say their proper farewells, Bill's passing still weighed heavily upon his soul.

Garry had always been a stable, reliable, no-frills man; musically he was the regulator in the band, the member who signaled the chord changes when the others might forget them. Whether the band was playing to twelve people in a pub or twenty thousand in an arena, Garry was the kind of guy who had a bass tech, but took pride in setting up his own gear, and still does. Garry was always consistent of character, but in 1997, he strayed—drastically. His affair with one of the backup singers on the *Elegantly Wasted* tour was a mistake that he regrets to this day. When he came to his senses, he ended the affair and asked that she leave the tour when the band returned to Australia. Garry confessed his infidelity to his wife, Jodie, as soon as he got home, which set a chain of events in motion that led to their separation and eventual divorce.

It took every fiber of Garry's strength to keep himself together and continue the tour. And then Michael died. "We'd had such good chats about life in those last months, what he was going through and what I was going through," Garry says. "All I kept thinking about the day he died was that we'd never properly finished those talks. He and I were in the midst of very difficult problems, each of us facing things within ourselves that we were desperate to work out. And now we would never do that together."

Garry drove to Wamberal Beach, less than a mile from his home in Ourimbah, parked his car, stripped to his shorts, and dove in to the deep blue waters of the Pacific Ocean. He floated under the sun, trying to make sense of everything, and thought of Michael. "I kept thinking of how it had been clear that depression set in for Michael after his accident and only got worse through his relationship with Paula," Garry says. "He was always interested in everybody else's problems and what he could do for other people; he never put his problems on anyone. It wasn't that he couldn't articulate how he felt—it was that he believed that no one else could help him." After what seemed like a moment, but was more like an hour, Garry swam ashore, as renewed as he could be. "While I'd been in the water, our tour manager had left a few messages on my cell phone, each one sounding a bit more panicked," Garry says. "I called him back and he asked what I was doing, and I said, 'I jumped in the ocean.' Total silence. 'No, no. Not like that. I went for a swim. I'm all right, mate, no worries.' "

Tim Farriss spent the days following Michael's death in utter shock. INXS security chauffeured him home from ABC Studios, where he got into his pickup truck and without telling anyone, drove to his cattle farm in Kangaroo Valley. He doesn't remember the drive or arriving there or his wife and children joining him later or much of anything else but hours of sobbing and confusion. He's thought about it all for nearly a decade, and it still makes no sense to Tim. "Michael wasn't the kind of man to quit. He wasn't the kind of man cowardly enough to commit suicide," Tim says. "I was a grounded man, with a family and a wife, for so many years. And he'd seen that, he'd been close with us and he knew how much work it was. But he wanted it, he *really* wanted it."

Tim wasn't sure that Michael realized what starting a family meant, and how deep of a commitment it is. He worried that Michael regarded a family and children as just another acquisition. "Those last two weeks, we argued about it intensely because we didn't agree at all. And I'm so sorry about it. Fucking bastard," he says, his eyes filling with tears. "I'm the one who is left behind, still going on. There's nothing I can do about that, but I'm sorry for what we thought was in his head and what he knew he had, what he could have had and what he didn't allow himself to have. It takes a lot of guts sometimes to go for something that isn't easy. I still search my soul for how it could have been and how I could have stopped it."

Jon Farriss arrived at ABC studios that day and noticed several camera crews outside. At first he took it as a good sign, an indication that anticipation was building for the start of the band's comeback tour. The radio had not been on in his car, and he had no idea that Michael's death had been announced. Gary Grant intercepted Jon on his way to the rehearsal room and was visibly distressed. Upstairs, Jon realized that something was very wrong: the crew was sitting around in silence with their heads bowed and his bandmates were nowhere in sight. Jon took in the scene: he heard the hiss of the monitor system, saw Michael's stool, the glass of water beside it, and his lyric pad. He found his bandmates in a separate room and saw the horror in their eyes. Gary Grant closed the door.

"Michael's dead," he said. "They found him in his hotel room."

Jon's heart started pounding hard in his chest then sank into his stomach. He fell to pieces and remembers little else. He'd known Michael had been dabbling in heroin and hated him for it, and assumed that his friend had overdosed. Nothing had been confirmed, but he did not believe the initial reports that Michael had hanged himself. He refused to entertain the idea that he might have committed suicide.

"Are you sure he's dead?" he kept asking everyone. "I mean, has anyone seen him? Are you sure he's really dead?"

It was too much for him to bear. He and Michael were inseparable friends. They'd lived together in Hong Kong and been debauched bachelors together long after their compatriots had settled down. Andrew was Michael's muse, but Jon was Michael's wingman.

Jon went home after a few hours, listening to the reports on the radio the entire way. Memories flashed through his mind, images he couldn't control or comprehend. He thought of Tiger. He thought of the fact that Michael's hotel was just down the road from Jon's house—virtually around the corner. "Why didn't he call me?" Jon asked himself over and over. Jon got home and stayed inside for days. He hired security to guard the gates of his property and keep the media away. He drank for days on end and for the first time he went through all of the video he'd amassed over the years. He watched their music videos, interviews, assorted film clips, personal movies of them—all of it. He'd never taken stock of the scope of what they'd done since 1977. The clips flashed before him like a dreams as he prayed and cried.

Andrew Farriss went to a friend's house the day that Michael died, then returned to his family's home in Wahroonga. Andrew dealt with the loss very slowly, intensely, and methodically. "I was horrified that someone who had been such a good guy at heart and had gone so far and been so true to himself had suddenly decided to disappear. I was a zombie for a year afterward. It made me reevaluate my values and belief system." Andrew is a very meticulous, deliberate, and analytical man, though he has no doubts about whether Michael's death was deliberate or an accident that occurred during an autoerotic act (when pressed, he says that Michael's death, as per the coroner's report, was deemed a suicide and will say no more). He has, however, spent years hypothesizing on the combination of factors that drove him to it. "Those self-reflective moments where you wonder if you could have done more to help him in some way are hard, because you can't undo anything," Andrew says. "I wanted to, but I couldn't control his life when he was at the top and feeling low. He wasn't a teenager with an attitude—he was a grown man with a very strong will. I miss him and I think the world misses him, too. There isn't anyone like him around anymore."

In the year following Michael's death, Andrew experienced writer's block for the first time in his life. A prolific composer within and without INXS, Andrew had never gone long without writing music. But in a moment, his creative voice was silenced. Michael's death tapped a sense of loss Andrew had yet to reconcile, that of his mother, Jill, in 1995. And Michael's passing was the end of Andrew's other half—the creative catalyst that brought out the best in him. "I'd always heard stories of songwriters who broke up with their wives or suffered a loss and were inspired to write an album about it," Andrew says. "Not me. For a full year, I couldn't write any songs. I was so distraught and disconnected over losing my mother, then Michael, that I couldn't do anything. I was completely numb." Eventually, Andrew expressed his feelings in music long before he could in words. "After a few months, I sat down and wrote two ambient, classical piano pieces," Andrew says. "They're very dark and very, very cold. They're like a requiem. After I finished them I didn't write or even play for some time. But those pieces were a turning point. Looking back, I think that I was bidding my mother and Michael farewell. If I hadn't written them, I don't think I would have ever written again."

Michael Hutchence's funeral took place on November 26, 1997, and it was a resplendent spectacle worthy of Michael's complex life. His friend and idol, Nick Cave, sang a gorgeous valediction, his haunting ode "Into My Arms." Over one thousand guests filled St. Andrew's, the Anglican cathedral in Sydney, among them, all of Michael's girlfriends—Helena Christensen, Kylie Minogue, Michele Bennett, and Paula Yates—as well as Tom Jones, and Bono's wife, Ali. U2 sent a tremendous floral arrangement but the band could not attend—they were half a world away in the midst of their Pop-Mart tour. "We'd boarded the plane that carried us around for that tour and had just got off the ground in Phoenix when someone came up and told us that Michael had died," Bono says. "Everything just went off for me. It was weird; I thought immediately of Michael's dad, who was the most wonderful man. To me, his father was a clue as to who Michael would have been if he'd been able to grow old in peace in the South of France. I still have a vision of Michael that way: as an old man, gray-haired, debonair, and generous, watching the girls go by on the promenade."

Michael's mother, Patricia Glassop, made strides to have the funeral be televised—which surprised no one who knew the family. In the years following her divorce from Michael's father, Kell, and as Michael's star shined brighter, she'd begun to do interviews, for which she received payment. Once, when Paula and Michael joined her for what was promised to be a quiet dinner following the christening of a family friend's baby, they arrived to discover a table of journalists, photographers, and acquaintances who lined up for snapshots and autographs from the couple. At the time of his passing, Michael and his mother were estranged.

Celebrity manager Harry M. Miller approached Glassop when he heard of Michael's death, offering to "handle" her son's funeral, free of charge. Miller struck an exclusive deal with the Seven Network in Australia, granting them permission to film inside the cathedral during the ceremony and the sole rights to peddle the footage for international broadcast. When the members of INXS, Paula Yates, and Michael's father, Kell, learned of the arrangement—in the press no less—they were mortified and insisted that cameras be banned from the church. The Reverend Boak Jobbins of St. Andrews denied their request; he felt that the cathedral doors should not be shut to anyone, regardless of the obvious commercial motives involved.

The invited packed St. Andrews that afternoon, while thousands more filled the neighboring streets to listen to the service over loudspeakers positioned outside. It was a funeral and an opera, a spectacle and a ceremony; it was a pageant as grandiose and transcendent as Michael himself. Nick Cave enforced due reverence by refusing to sing in the presence of television cameras. Once they were shut off, Mr. Cave put his soul into a performance befitting his biggest fan, Michael Hutchence.

There might have been another performance, one that would have drastically shifted the mood. Paula Yates had asked Tom Jones to sing Michael's favorite song, "What's New, Pussycat?" Tom wasn't going to refuse a woman in mourning, but Michael's family was; they understandably deemed it inappropriate and vetoed the idea.

Just a few days before, in a lofty room at ABC Studios, INXS had rehearsed together for the last time. The morning of the funeral, they gathered there again, joined by Michael's younger brother, Rhett Hutchence, to rehearse something else: how they would carry Michael's coffin out of the cathedral at the end of the ceremony. Hours later they did, proceeding slowly up the aisle, as the lovelorn majesty of "Never Tear Us Apart" radiated through the high arches, and Michael's sonorous, luxurious tenor announced his final exit.

"The funeral was just extraordinary, it was the most beautiful ceremony I've ever seen," recalls Joanne Petersen, INXS friend and longtime representative at Warner Bros. Australia. "All of his women were there—Kylie, Helena, Paula, and Michele—and everywhere you looked, there were gorgeous people. It was so overwhelming, as a spectacle and as a farewell to such an amazing person. And it was followed by the best party in the world. Everyone who knew him and loved him was there reminiscing and having a good time, as much as they were sad. I remember saying to Helena, 'Michael would have loved this.' She smiled and said, 'Well, it's not the first time we've had to carry Michael out of a party.'"

Chris Murphy had seen little of Michael or INXS since he abandoned his post as manager two years before. At the funeral, he broke down, cried uncontrollably, and was nearly inconsolable. He felt, and still does, that Michael's death was an unnecessary, avoidable tragedy. Murphy had, in the years since he'd left the band, returned to Australia to develop his record label and publishing company. He'd bought a farm a few hours from Sydney, remarried for the third time, and focused more on raising his children than working within the music industry. He'd kept his nose out of INXS's business, but often spoke to Andrew Farriss and offered his guidance when it was sought. Earlier that year, however, he'd been moved to interject. He'd seen an ad in the paper advertising INXS's upcoming tour and the fact that tickets were still available. He controlled himself then. Not much later, while driving in Sydney, he spotted theater marquees advertising INXS's upcoming tour, and the fact that tickets were still available. Again, he bit his tongue, but weeks later, when he came across more ads in the paper, confirming that tickets were still available at even the smallest theaters on the tour, he could take it no more.

After the Concert for Life debacle in 1992, Chris had strongly advised the band against touring Australia until the year 2000. He felt that a minimum of eight years away was required to put the controversy to rest; they'd then return triumphantly to their homeland, to crowds that had genuinely missed them. His worst fear had come true; here they were, five years later, fronting a tour that wasn't sold-out. Murphy was certain that it would ruin them.

It was late August, still well in advance of the tour, when Chris phoned Tim Farriss, to wish him a happy birthday (Tim was born August 16, 1957) and to speak his mind.

"Tim, you know I've not interfered in anything you've done since I left, have I?" Chris asked. "I've never said a word, and I think you know there are some things I could have said. I've minded my own business, but there is something I've got to say now and please listen: cancel the tour. Just fucking cancel it. *Do not do this tour.*"

"Mate, you know, we're going to do this tour," Tim said. "It's too late, everything's booked, we're doing it."

Chris kept on anyway, insisting that no matter what the band's manager, Paul Craig, or their booking agent claimed, it wasn't too late to call it off. "I said, 'Tim, this is scary, you *need* to cancel the tour. If you have to, make something up. Someone can have an overdose, it doesn't matter, just cancel it.'" A week later, Murphy received a call from Martha Troup, who informed him that the band had fired Paul Craig and that she was now the band's full-time manager. The tour went on as planned.

The next time Murphy heard from the INXS camp, he was informed of Michael's death. "I was on my farm and I walked outside and thought, 'Michael, you dumb fuck.' Then I thought, 'Fucking damn that goddamn fucking tour!—I still believe in my heart that the tour was the final straw. The Geldof thing, Paula, cocaine, antidepressants, prescription drugs, alcohol—sure, that was all part of it. But he'd been doing those chemicals in one form or another for years and always handled himself. Why was it suddenly this time that his body and his mind couldn't take it?"

Murphy believes that Michael's return to Australia, combined with the band's shaky circumstances career-wise, pitched an already depressed, beleaguered man over the edge. "Look, I'd been their manager for fifteen years, and I'd like to think I got it right at least seventy or eighty percent of the time. For me to know, in my heart, with no shred of doubt, that they should cancel that tour, is significant," he says. "I honestly believe that Michael arrived in Australia, exhausted by all of the shit going on in his life, to rehearse for a tour of two-thousand-seat theaters that weren't even sold out, and that did it. There was a lack of dignity to it that he couldn't bear. I remember that when I spoke to Andrew the day after Michael died, I told him that he should call a band meeting, because they were going to be bombarded with press, and I gave him just one bit of advice: *keep your dignity.* Don't do anything that will lower it, because your dignity is all that you have left."

"It was wonderful watching the circus that erupted after his death," Garry Beers says. "Suddenly so many wonderful, special friends of Michael's crawled out of the woodwork to sell their stories. They'd say that Michael told them how unhappy he was in the band, and that he wanted to leave, but couldn't bear to tell us—so instead, he hung himself. It was ridiculous and disgusting."

The band did one official interview, with George Negus, a journalist they approached, and nothing else. They did retain their dignity, never making a publicity event of their mourning. They turned down countless interview requests, movie deals and offers from promoters eager to book tribute concerts in the singer's honor. They only gathered publicly for a memorial to Michael when U2 played Sydney later that year. U2 had put together a film montage of their friend, which they played during "I Still Haven't Found What I'm Looking For," throughout their tour. That night in Sydney, Bono gave a heartfelt dedication to his friend, expressing, as best he could, how truly special Hutchence was. Andrew Farriss, who'd been in such a state of shock since Michael's death that he had not yet cried over the loss, broke down uncontrollably backstage as he tried to thank Bono for his moving speech.

The band members miss Michael, each of them in their own way, every single day of their lives. It took nearly ten years of healing before the writing of this book was even possible, nearly ten years before they were at all able to share the Michael they knew with the world.

After Michael died, Paula Yates came completely undone. She arrived in Australia with Tiger Lily for the funeral and was so distraught that twenty-four-hour security was hired by INXS to protect her from the paparazzi—as well as from herself. She demanded to visit Michael's body in the morgue and from the moment she laid eyes on him, it was clear that Paula might try to follow him to the grave in time for the funeral. She was drinking heavily, taking drugs, and utterly desolated by his death. During the funeral, Tony Woodhall, Michael's former security guard, sat beside Paula to assure that, if she lost control, no harm would come to her sixteen-month-old daughter. "Throughout the service I had one hand holding her dress in case she moved suddenly," he recalls. "Honestly, I was worried that she was going to dive in to the coffin with him. It was very difficult. Michael's mother didn't want her seated anywhere near her because she and Paula did not get along. But when we walked in, Paula went straight to the front and sat where she wanted. It seemed to me that the situation might erupt at any moment."

After the funeral, Yates spent the next few days in a Sydney hotel. Her minders forbade her from taking drugs and alcohol—she was, after all, breast-feeding her infant daughter. Somehow, Paula managed to acquire substances anyway: she would surreptitiously phone local doctors she knew to attain prescriptions for sleeping pills and whatever else might numb her pain. She was caught, more than once, trying to ingest lethal doses of them.

She was inconsolable and manic; uncontrollable tears turned to unhinged happiness in an instant.

A full-time nanny looked after Tiger, but her mother begged to have the child with her at all times. Tiger's minder took her away on several occasions when Paula's behavior suggested that her mother's milk might be laced with substances that could kill a baby.

Drama ensued in the wake of Michael's death as it had in the years that preceded it: in many ways, the events that followed were as mysterious as the circumstances of his death. His family argued over his will, as the world argued over whether he died deliberately or accidentally, during a kinky act of autoeroticism. And of course, every one of Michael's least intimate acquaintances weighed in on the subject via one media outlet or another while those who knew him best watched the world argue, respecting his memory with silence.

Michael's finances and the dispersion of his estate became fodder for sensational headlines. In his will, Michael left half of his estate to Tiger Lily and divided the other half between Yates, his father, brother, sister, and his mother Patricia Glassop—even though he was estranged from her at the time of his death. He also left his two favorite advocacy organizations, Amnesty International and Greenpeace, four hundred thousand dollars each. Colin Diamond was the director of most of the companies that held Michael's money in trust. Technically, by enlisting his property and assets to those companies in trust, Michael had relinquished ownership. As director of those companies, Colin Diamond did not directly own Michael's assets, but he certainly did control them. In addition, Michael appointed Diamond coexecutor of his will.

In the end, Michael Hutchence's holdings, from his collection of luxury cars to his French estate to the London mansion he shared with Yates, were sold off. Yates received the London home but sold it in 1999 allegedly because she was almost bankrupt. She downsized considerably to a half-million dollar townhouse in Notting Hill.

Michael's mother and sister refused a settlement of $1 million from the estate, claiming that they were due at least $4 million. Exasperated and misdirected, they chose to levy a suit against the remaining members of INXS, claiming that they were due money from the royalties earned by Michael's music as well as the monies the band received from two life insurance policies in Michael's name. In 2001, Glassop and Tina Hutchence published their tell-all, each narrating consecutive chapters, where they shed what light they could on Michael's early years, and spent most of it attacking everyone—band members, managers, girlfriends—for destroying their relationship with Michael, and in the end, Michael himself. The last quarter of the book is exclusively devoted to detailing the legal entanglements of Michael's estate and their struggle to procure money, for Tiger Lily's sake they claimed. "The feud between Michael's family and Paula was such a mess," Kirk says. "We in the band stayed well away from it. It wasn't any of our business, really. Michael's financial situation was his deal, and as long as Tiger was looked after by the executor, which we've always been led to believe she was and will be, we just left it well enough alone."

Michael had asked Bono to be Tiger Lily's godfather but to his great dismay, Bono had refused. It was too complex of a situation: Bono was dear friends with Bob Geldof; they'd grown up in the same Irish new wave scene in the seventies. He was also very close with Helena Christensen. He'd done his best to be Switzerland, keeping the peace and remaining neutral during Michael and Paula's affair and subsequent relationship. He loved Michael, but he could not be Tiger's godfather—he'd be choosing sides, and hurting too many of his close friends by doing so. "We drifted apart after that," Bono says. "Michael was very upset with me, and as the situation grew messy between him and Bob and Paula, I had to step even further away. Bob would tell me his side, and then Michael would call me and scream about what Bob was doing. It was very difficult. I just wish I had known how far gone he was in. I was worried that he was hanging around with the wrong kind of people—I'd heard rumors that I didn't want to believe. I was busy and lost in my own business, but I missed him and I wish I'd known how bad of a state he was in. I would have gone after him, I would have forced him to face up to a few things he was ignoring. He wasn't the type of man to tell you, 'I'm in trouble.' I wish I could have had the chance to tell him the truth he didn't want to hear: that he *was* in trouble."

Michael would not accept or understand Bono's reasons for declining the honor of being Tiger's godfather, and he did not approach any of the other men who knew him equally well—his bandmates—to fill the role. Instead, he chose his investment advisor, Colin Diamond, to be the one who, in the eyes of the church, would look after and protect the child, as if she were his own.

Michael Hutchence was cremated, to his mother's dismay, and a battle over his ashes ensued. To keep the peace, they were divided between Paula Yates and his parents, Patricia Glassop and Kell Hutchence. Kell, Patricia, the members of INXS, and Michael's brother, Rhett, and sister, Tina, charted a yacht to take them into Sydney Harbor, where, at sunset, they set Michael free. The sun had shone all day in a cloudless sky, but as they prepared to tip Michael's ashes into the water, the sky went black and a solitary clap of thunder boomed in the distance. On the horizon, a single vein of lightning cracked the air. And as quickly as darkness had fallen, the skies cleared again and the swift breeze that played over the bay, in the minds, and hearts of those present, carried Michael's soul away from them forever.

Paula Yates never really recovered from Michael's death. She moved into her Notting Hill home and each night slept on a mattress, on the floor, with the urn full of his remains by her side. She took antidepressants, was attended by friends who feared for her well-being, and left her bed as little as possible. In the last years of her life, Paula struggled with substance abuse and tremendous depression and was checked in to a psychiatric clinic after an attempted suicide by hanging. Upon her release, Paula embarked on a public campaign against the perception that Michael's death had been a suicide. She insisted that it was accidental—an autoerotic act that had gone too far. In interviews, she related sordid stories of her sexcapades with Hutchence, regaling the eager tabloid media with tales of S&M

and orgies. Paula refused to believe that Michael would deliberately desert her, and his newborn daughter, and was intent on convincing the world of the same. She disclosed in interviews and a documentary film that the police had released in the years following Michael's death, further details of what was found in his hotel room, including a ring-bolt (a device commonly utilized in autoerotic acts) that undeniably spoke to her point.

Yates did all she could to have the coroner's verdict overturned. She'd do anything, she said, to keep Tiger from believing, when she was old enough to understand, the media's perception that her father had committed suicide. Her campaign did not go over well with Michael's father, Kell. He said that Paula's zeal for painting such a picture was motivated by remorse for her actions—actions that played a huge part in driving Michael to kill himself. Kell publicly referred to Paula as a woman with a guilty conscience.

Kell and his second wife, Susie, petitioned to gain custody of Tiger Lily, claiming that Paula was an unfit mother. During the same period, Michael's mother, Patricia Glassop, and his sister, Tina Hutchence, also filed a petition to gain custody of the child, while their legal quest to recover Michael's missing fortune continued. By June 1999, Michael's estate was valued at a mere $160,000, but was owed over $3 million in unpaid loans doled out to three different offshore holding companies. Michael's home in France was being rented for five thousand dollars a week, none of which made its way back to the estate. (Years later, after the legal entanglements were finally sorted, the French property was sold to Adam Clayton of U2.) Michael's legacy, in the two short years following his death, had been reduced to mysterious deeds, lawyers' fees, broken hearts, and loose ends.

Paula Yates descended further into desperate straits, marked by several attempts to reinvent herself and relaunch her career. She endeavored to convince the public that she'd left drugs and drink behind, but a string of inebriated appearances at significant public events proved that rumors of Yates's sobriety were greatly exaggerated. Paula spent the fall of 2000 holed up in her Notting Hill town house with four-year-old Tiger Lily, consumed by lawsuits and loss.

On September 16, 2000, at about 10 p.m., Yates showed up at her neighborhood liquor store disheveled, barefoot, and drunk. And at 11:15 a.m. the next morning, Yates was discovered dead, in her bed, surrounded by the remains of a binge: vodka bottles, a half-empty bottle of barbiturates, and heroin. The coroner's toxicology report found that the heroin Yates had consumed contained a significant amount of morphine, which was ruled the cause of her death by overdose. (Yates had taken a dose that the authorities said might cause an inexperienced heroin user to overdose, but would not be lethal to an experienced abuser.) She was found by her daughter. A journalist friend of hers was worried about Paula and had repeatedly called the house that morning until, eventually, Tiger answered the phone. The little girl walked into the bedroom, told the woman on the phone that mommy was sleeping and that mommy would not wake up.

Heavenly Hiraani Tiger Lily Hutchence is a gorgeous child, full of Michael's wide-eyed compassion and Paula's sharp intelligence. After the death of her mother, the English courts granted custody of her to Bob Geldof over the members of Michael's family. Bob, who has spent the last few years campaigning for father's rights in domestic litigation, fought so that Tiger might be raised in a family environment, amid her three half-sisters, all of whom had been very involved in her life since her birth.

Tiger's parents loved her dearly. They shared an intense love that bore a beautiful girl, a love so intense that it tore them asunder yet demanded that they be brought together. "All of it is just so incredibly tragic," Kirk says. "That poor, beautiful girl. I think the best thing that could have happened was for Tiger to be raised up by Bob. She should grow up among her sisters, because they were already in her life. I hope one day Tiger will realize that she can come to any of us in the band and talk to us at any time, whenever she's ready, about her dad. We grew up with him and we would love to share all that we knew of him with her. I dearly hope that at some point she will because we'll be here, waiting."

CONCLUSION

Execution of Bitterness

IT TOOK A GREAT DEAL OF SOUL-SEARCHING for INXS to decide if they should go on. They have been invited to play at many one-off special events in the last eight years and when they have chosen to do so, have found that it was a more healing experience than they expected it to be. The first occasion was a performance at Mushroom Records 25th Anniversary Concert in Melbourne with Jimmy Barnes on vocals. Mushroom demanded their presence: the label had released the Jimmy Barnes/INXS collaboration "Good Times" and according to the label's founder, Michael Gudinski, it put Mushroom on the map: it was their first single to debut in Australia at Number 1.

INXS has tried out various replacement singers—among them Terence Trent D'Arby, who sang with them beautifully at the opening of the Sydney Olympic Stadium. They've also toured infrequently over the last couple of years with Jon Stevens of the Australian band NoiseWorks on vocals. They chose to be careful, realizing that INXS without Michael was an entity that must be properly redesigned. They reconfigured their management team, and wondered how, with one of the band's two primary songwriters gone, they should recast the creative process. INXS had too long a legacy to desecrate it with hasty decisions, and it took nearly a decade to suss it all out. But while they've laid low, they've not been forgotten: in 2001, the band commanded two top slots on the British charts. One was a reinterpolation of one of their earliest songs, 1980's "Just Keep Walking," sampled by Par-T-One in the song "I'm So Crazy," and the other was "Precious Heart," a remix of "Never Tear Us Apart" by Tall Paul. In Australia, "One of My Kind," the Rough Traders' remix of "Need You Tonight," charted as well.

"The most intriguing thing for us today is wondering whether we should rehash a modern version of what we've done, or do our best to stay true to what we used to do—make something apart from everyone else," Andrew Farriss says. "We want to make something that truly matters, but we often wonder that if we release an album that bears no relevance to any of the work we've done before, will it just be seen as weird and odd? We've no intention of becoming a jukebox of ourselves—that's not healthy. We'll see what happens. I'm just happy that we're entering times where bands and live music and good playing are important again. As a fan of music, in my opinion, it hasn't been that way for some time."

Andrew is right—rock music is more fertile now than it has been for what feels like ages. The grunge fervor of the mid-nineties, which drove record companies searching for the next Nirvana to sign too many less-than-able bands, set off an onslaught of crap. A downturn in the global economy, plus the corporate consolidation of the music (and all other media) industries has devoured what little soul was left in the music business. At the dawn of the millennium, rock, traditionally an album-oriented genre, took a backseat to teen pop and hip-hop, two styles defined by singles. It makes sense that as the industry had less to spend, they eschewed rock bands who might not come into their own until their third album in favor of prepackaged bootylicious Britneys and rap superstars who might justify their investment with but one Top 40. The only rock music that thrived in this climate was the pop-punk of bands like Blink 182 (and their endless imitators), who combine a suburban American hand-me-down carbon copy of the Sex Pistols, with production as slick as 'N Sync and content as sophisticated as Avril Lavigne. It is a sign of the times in America that such punk pop is as digestible and acceptably rebellious as Jessica Simpson.

But that isn't all there is. The last two years have proved that rock is not dead, it's evolved, returning to the danceable rock hybrid that INXS invented. Bands like Scotland's Franz Ferdinand and Las Vegas's the Killers have justifiably gone from underground darlings to platinum-selling crossover pop acts.

Both take their cues from the marriage of dance, funk, and rock that INXS and a handful of their peers, such as New Order and The Cure, put together. The huge pile of "The" bands, i.e., The Strokes, The White Stripes, The Hives, The Stills, The Rapture, The Futureheads, The Arcade Fire, The Libertines (and plenty more) owe their careers to INXS, New Order, The Cure, R.E.M., The Smiths, Echo and the Bunnymen, Depeche Mode, and U2. Those eighties heavyweights were the trailblazers who created what is labeled "alternative" or "modern" rock today. They made music innovative and cutting edge enough for the fringes yet catchy enough to win in the mainstream. They truly achieved the highest honor: they were both cool *and* successful. They invented a sound without definition, one popular enough that stations nationwide changed their formats overnight.

"There has been a reemergence of rock bands lately, which is great," Andrew Farriss says. "I've watched it grow in Australia and it's happening everywhere. The best part about it is that it gets people out of their houses, and allows them to come together and talk and meet and dance and party. And that is what makes culture evolve." It is true: not only has the sexy rock-funk beat of the past come back into vogue, so too has a demand for able players—true musicians bonded by collective creative chemistry.

In twenty years, INXS did all that a band could hope to do. They sold millions of records, traveled the world, played music to crowds of thousands, and made their mark in rock history. They brought pop music to countries like Argentina, Mexico, and Guam—terrain that hadn't been entertained since the Nixon administration—and to populations that had never seen an international band live in the flesh. INXS defined the sound of their times. They have so much to be proud of, and thankfully, they're not done.

"I think that if Michael were here today we'd be approaching our music the same way," Andrew says. "If he were with us, we'd be making the same album we're going to make this year. We'd have taken some time apart and we'd have come back together a very united, very focused group of people. We probably would have pursued projects outside the band for a while, but that wouldn't have mattered. We're a family, and families need to fight and cry and stay away from each other for periods of time. The best families do that—and then they come back together. That's what we would have done if Michael hadn't died, and that's what we're doing even though he did. We'll miss him for the rest of our lives. But we're going to go out there and honor him by doing what he was always the first to push us to do: we're going to put our necks on the chopping block. That is what we've done since the start, and have never, ever been afraid to do."

It's been eight years since Michael Hutchence died, and as much as time has marched on and the world has changed, his absence has proven that his death marked the end of an era.

Michael was the last rock star of our times: he was as slinky as Mick Jagger, as commanding as Jim Morrison, and as fractured as Kurt Cobain. Michael truly was a postmodern rock icon, his lyrics were Romantic poetry and Utopian idealism delivered by a Shamanistic Valentino.

Michael was a man whose insecurities ran ever deeper as his public image grew larger, and in the end he lost himself in the long shadows they cast over him. But even when his ego was swollen and his weaknesses were at their most overpowering, something in Michael never forgot that he was nothing without his family—his dearest friends and the members of INXS. It has taken his bandmates this long to mourn Michael and to understand that as a band, their work is not done. "After thinking about it all over the years, eventually you have to realize that there's nothing at all you can do about it," Kirk says. "He's gone. And you have to thank God that there's a great legacy in all the music we made together. At the end of the day, that's what life is about; it's about being remembered for what you've done when you die. If you leave nothing behind, there's no point to your life. Michael always talked about that. All that he really wanted in the end was to know that we *mattered.* He wanted to know that we'd served a purpose. He wanted to know that we'd given people memories."

ACKNOWLEDGMENTS

Andrew Farriss

I would like to thank Shelley, Grace, Josephine, and Matthew for their love and support; Jill and Dennis Farriss; Tim, Jon, and Alison; and all of my family and friends.

There are so many people to thank but too many to list here.

Special thanks to Chris Murphy, Martha Troup, Bill Leibowitz and David Edwards.

I dedicate this book to the memory of my friend Michael Hutchence.

Garry Beers

I would like to thank Jodie, Lucy-Mae, and Matilda Beers. Bill and Lola Beers, Kerry and Ray Williams, Scott and Jenny White, David Jackson, Fiona MacPherson, Chris Murphy, Gary Grant, Martha Troup, Bill Liebowitz, John Gray, Ben Pettit, Albert Molinaro, Ted Kornblum, David and Cosima Edwards, Jo Whitehead, Nathan Hull, Michael Murchison, Sam Evans, Chris Thomas, David Nicholas, Richard Clapton, Mark Opitz, Blair Simmons, all the amazing young musicians I work with who inspire me to still stretch myself.

All the talented and devoted people who have played such an important part in our recording and touring career, you know who you are, thank you.

To all my family, my friends, and our fans who have helped along the way, thank you, we wouldn't have made it without you.

And of course, my beloved bandmates, what a trip!! Love always and forever.

Tim Farriss

Thanks to Buffy, Jake, and James Farriss; Jill and Dennis Farriss; Alison Farriss; Jon and Andrew; Bill Leibowitz, Richard Lowenstein, Chris Thomas, Chris Murphy, Gary Grant, Sam Evans, David Edwards, Martha Troup, Niki Turner, Bruce Patron, Max and Pam Reefman, Martin Reefman, Mathew Barry, Harold and Pam Sharman, George Williams, Shea Caplice, David Hancock, Bryan and Sally Lynch, Amanda and Peter Bazarow, the Pengilly family, Lynne Bugai, Danny Jones, David (Chipper) Nicholas, Mark Opitz, Nile Rodgers, Nick Launay, Richard Clapton, Andy Wooloscroft, Tim Parsons, Bill Silver, Niven Garland, Ben Pettit, Angus Vail; Queen, the Go-Gos, the Stray Cats, Hall and Oates, and Cold Chisel.

Thanks to all my friends and family—-you know who you are—-and to the fans who have supported INXS along the way!

Jon Farriss

There are so many people I would like to thank personally. It started when I was a young boy—to all my musical influences, to my neighbors for putting up with me learning how to play drums, to all the bands and musicians I have played with.

Thanks to my beloved partner, Kerry Norris, for showing me who I am again and believing in me, Jill and Dennis Farriss; Tim, Andrew, and Alison; Kerry's family; Chris Murphy, Bill Leibowitz, Martha Troup. All of our crew over the years, all of the people who have worked with us through our career. My dear friends—you know who you are! Rob Kern (how 'bout 'ya, you're the goods); Colin Diamond, all my techs; everybody who has stuck by me through the highs and lows; thank you to my bandmates, INXS; and the universe for blessing me with many opportunities.

A heartfelt thanks to all the fans and supporters of the band throughout our incredible journey.

Kirk Pengilly

There have been countless people over the years who dedicated long hours and relentless hard work for the betterment of the band's career. From our first ever tour manager, Neil Wright, to the many dedicated staff and assistants that worked with Chris Murphy over the years like Giselle McHugh, Kim Frankiewicz, Sam Evans, and Paul Craig, who all worked up to eighteen-hour-days when needed under Chris's whip. We always had an amazing, focused team keeping it together for us, so we could do what we were supposed to do—make and perform music. Martha Troup has been with us longer than anyone (other than Chris Murphy) on and off, and closely worked countless hours with Chris in the U.S. (and abroad) through those critical years leading up to and including *Kick*. After a couple of years apart, she then came back and worked with us until a short time after Michael's death and is a great friend to all of us. Her advice, guidance, and caring have been invaluable to us all. Bill Leibowitz, who has been our legal man in the U.S. and elsewhere for most of our career, cut groundbreaking deals with Chris on our behalf, and is also a great friend. Others like Michael Long, John Martyn, Mark Pope and, of course, all the "road crew" that put in more inhumane hours than anyone over the years and rarely complained. Also, in Australia John Gray, Sandy Arnold, Mathew Alderton, and Ben Pettit dotted and crossed the i's and t's and made sure things added up. To all the supportive people at our record companies, publishing, public relations, video makers, promoters, booking agents, and journalists who have been so important to INXS's success, I thank you and ask you to forgive me for not singling you out for fear of forgetting someone.

In addition to the above, for their specific role in this book and/or my life, I would personally like to give thanks to Layne Beachley, the Beers, Peter Borland, Anthony Bozza, Richard Clapton, David Edwards, Dennis and Jill Farriss, Gary Grant, Nathan Hull, Karen Hutchinson, the Hutchences, Nick Launay, Richard Lowenstein, Duncan McGuire, Michael Murchison, Chris Murphy, Mark Opitz, Bruce Patron, Jack Pengilly, Pat Pengilly, Mark Pengilly, Drew Pengilly, April Pengilly, Jeff Pope, Rick Sales, Chris Thomas, Jo Whitehead, Tony Woodhall, and to all the other many friends, relatives, and professionals who have supported and put up with all of us over the years through thick and thin. Thank you all from the bottom of my heart.

Anthony Bozza

I'd like to thank everyone in the INXS extended family—and after nearly thirty years it is quite extended—for opening their hearts and memories to me. Without them this book would not have been possible. A special thank you goes out to Michele Bennett, who spoke on record about her relationship with Michael for the first time. So too, thank you to everyone who helped me paint a portrait of him in his absence. I'd seen Michael on stage plenty of times, but I'd never met him—thanks to all of you, I now feel like I have.

Thank you David Edwards. And thanks to Jo Whitehead, Paul Horton, and everyone in the INXS management office who well looked after me during my stay in Australia—your efforts were very much appreciated. Thank you, too, Michael Murchison. Thank you so very much to Kirk, Garry, Andrew, Jon, and Tim for granting me complete access to your stories, your diaries (Kirk and Garry), and every bit of yourselves that went into the writing of this book. And above all, I thank all of you, and Michael, too, for the music.

I'd also like to thank Richard Abate, my intrepid super-agent at ICM, without whom I'd be nowhere. My editor, Peter Borland; production editor, Tricia Wygal; and everyone at Atria Books deserves a hearty back slap for putting this book together so well and keeping everything on track. Thank you to my parents for their support, and thanks most of all to Hilary Broderick for putting up with me, reassuring me, feeding me, and taking me on walks when my deadline loomed gloomily overhead. Hil, I love you very much, I'm blessed to know you, and I couldn't have done it without you.

INXS

INXS would like to thank David Edwards. They would also like to thank Martha Troup, Bill Leibowitz, Jaimie Roberts, Peter Rosenthal, Ben Pettit, Jo Whitehead, Nathan Hull, Paul Horton, Tony Woodhall, Jeff Pope, Cosima Edwards, Richard Lowenstein, Mark Opitz, Chris Murphy, Gary Grant, Lynne Bugai, Dan Jones, Matt Marsland, everyone at www.inxs.com and the INXS street team, Keith Naisbitt, Brian Blumer, ICM, and their families for their love and patience, everyone who was interviewed and contributed to this book, and to all of the INXS fans around the world—THANK YOU!

VISIT THE ONLINE WORLD OF INXS AT INXS.COM

Enter the band's virtual world at INXS.com and discover:

- daily newsfeeds
- band blogs
- audio and video exclusives
- CD, DVD, book, and merchandise store
- discographies, gigographies, biographies, and lyrics
- games, chat rooms, legitimate downloads, and much more!

Plus a secret slide show of extra-exclusive photographs to accompany this book. Go to this hidden URL: http://www.inxs.com/slideshow

Join INXS's online fan club and receive:

- advance notice of show announcements
- priority ticketing
- unique fan-club-only releases
- exclusive merchandise offers
- VIP content online and direct access to the band on the road

To obtain a one-month trial membership, visit INXS.com/join, choose Basic Membership and enter this promo code: story05

FARRIS
Dirty Honeymoon
Australian Tour '93-'94
XS
LIVE
BABY
LIVE
PASS
PERFORMER
ALL ACCESS
KICK '88
MEMORIAL DRIVE
21 OCT. 7.45 p.m
FRIDAY 21st
at